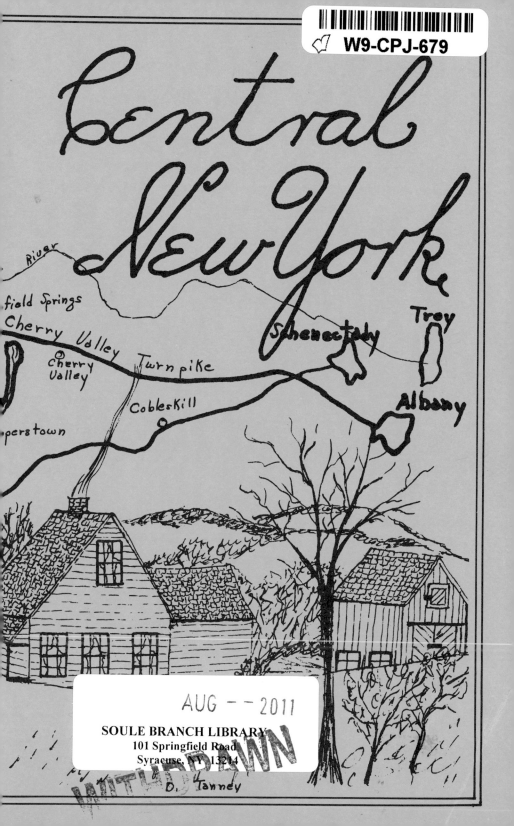

Central New York

River

field Springs

Cherry Valley

Cherry Valley Turnpike

Schenectady

Troy

Cherry
Valley

Cobleskill

Albany

perstown

D. Tanney

THE ETERNAL HILLS

The Eternal Hills

by

DONNA SPOONER TANNEY

The true story, of a section of rural
NEW YORK STATE,
and
of some of its offspring who lived through
its most glorious period

1973

HOMESTEAD BOOKS
BROOKFIELD, NEW YORK

February 11, 1989 at
Gates Hill Homestead
Donna Spooner Tanney

ISBN 914821-50-4

First Printing 1973
Second Printing 1975
Third Printing 1988

Printed in the United States of America
by Worden Press, Brookfield, N.Y.

to my husband, without whose
encouragement, help, and enduring patience
this book might never have been written . . .

Preface

The story you are about to read is typical of many an area. I have endeavored to place the tale upon a human plane, by using the actual life happenings of its cast of characters. As the story progresses, perchance many a doubting eyebrow will be raised. I list below my sources of reference material, to verify the authenticity of the tale.

I might also add that in the recording of events, I did encounter a few seemingly blank areas. These I filled in after careful research, thought concentration, and prayer. In at least seven instances, my assumption and writing of the episode later proved to be correct. The strangest part of all this was that at no time was I seeking verification of what I had written, but rather the evidence turned to light of its own accord, and in the most unexpected places.

In conclusion, I ask that the reader bear in mind that this is not the story as the author sees it, but rather the story as the participants lived it. I regard it as a tribute to our forefathers, to their thoughts, dreams, and lives. If in the re-creation of the tale I can help someone to see beyond the confines of this life, I shall be well satisfied.

Reference material:
History of Madison and Chenango Co.—Smith
History of Madison Co.—Hammond Co. 1872
History of the Village of Brookfield—G. Watson 1941
Madison Co. Directory—H. Child Co. 1868-9
Madison Co. Biographical Review—1894
The Young America—1875
Field & Stream—1890
Brookfield Couriers
Brown Genealogy—Co. 1906
Records of William Spooner—Co. 1883
History of Seventh Day Baptists in Europe and America

vii

Veterans of Oneida Co. (Civil War)
Census of 1790 & 1850
Map of 1853—township of Brookfield
Diaries of Frances Hills Spooner—1862, Devillo Fitch—1870
Obituaries: Frances Hills Spooner, Henry Spooner, Frank Spooner, Eudocia Hills Hickox, Fordyce Hickox, George K. Knapp, Lucy Hills White, James M. Hills, Chloe Clarke Hills, Capt. Samuel Clarke, Hosea B. Clarke, Judge Joseph Clarke.
Scrap-book and small flowered book belonging to Eudocia Hills Hickox

Thanks also:
Elva Spooner
Betty Spooner
Laurence Spooner
Donald Keith   Caroline Keith
Sherrill Palmer
Joseph Dansevitch
Frances L. Palmer
Violet Worden   Dean Worden
Rev. Stephen Reese
Viola and Arthur Whitford
Esther Woodworth Geary
Susan Beebe Stevens
Alice Ramsdell
Geneva Watson
Lewis Harris
Dr. Robert Whitford
Gertrude Smith
Cora Fisher
Charles Spooner
Mrs. A. K. Benedict
Onondaga County Historical Society,
Oneida County Historical Society
Elizabeth Avery

Donna Spooner Tanney
Historian,
Township of Brookfield

Introduction

I knew, without asking, where she would be. Seated, as always, in the high-backed wheel chair, by which she was imprisoned; a wisp of hair about her gaunt, wan face, her fragile, blue-ish hands crossed resignedly upon her lap; she appeared to exist only through her still perceptive blue eyes.

I was but five then, and I had repeatedly shouted my questions above the chug and roar of our old Model T. Ford, all the way from New Hartford to Brookfield. Either my parents couldn't hear me, or chose to ignore my persistent queries concerning the May Day customs.

At last we arrived at Grandpa's, whereupon I decided to take my problem to a more captive audience; one who might appreciate a small girl's company. I trudged straight into the front bedroom; where stood the inevitable wheel chair, drawn up alongside the two huge windows.

"Aunt Dosh," I begged, without further introduction, "Will *you* tell me about May baskets, and flowers?" May was soon approaching, and I wished to be certain I had my instructions in proper order, for hanging of the traditional baskets.

I guess all she heard was "May" and "flowers", for, to my utter dismay, she launched into a lengthy discussion of the Pilgrims and their treacherous Mayflower journey. And nothing I could say would deviate her from that story, to the one I wished to hear.

When I was six, she passed away. But in the attic were trunksful of her treasured letters, pictures, diaries, and beautiful clothes, fragments of her life.

I suppose it was only natural for her to plunge into the tale of the Pilgrim fathers, for she was rightfully proud of her ancestry. Her mother, Chloe Clarke Hills, traced her lineage from an Englishman, Joseph Clarke, who had landed in Boston in 1637, and eventually settled in Newport, Rhode Island. In 1801, one of his descendants, Captain Samuel Clarke, left his home in Westerly, Rhode Island; to settle in Beaver Creek, Madison County, New

Eighteenth Century Pioneer Route

Connecticut Rhode Island

Willimantic

To New York

State

Norwich

Old Mystic

Mystic

Stonington

Westerly

New London

Thames River

Narragansett

Narragansett Bay

Newport

Rhode Island Sound

Block Island Sound

D. Tanney

York State; an ox-team journey of about twenty days. With him came five of his sons and three daughters.

Chloe was his grand-daughter; and in 1832, at eighteen, she married James Hills, a relative newcomer to the town. Born in Rutland County, Vermont, in 1806, he had come to New Berlin, in the fertile Unadilla Valley, with his parents, Daniel and Sally Hutchings Hills. At twenty-three he had continued on to Bailey's Corners, where he "experienced forgiveness of his sins," under the ministry of Dr. Eli S. Bailey. Dr. Bailey was most influential and indispensible about town; being a combination preacher, physician and cabinet maker. When he built his home on the first four corners of the village in 1812,° it just naturally followed that "Beaver Creek" be re-named "Bailey's Corners."

The name "Hills" seemed peculiarly appropriate to James and Chloe, for they raised their home under the shadow of Beaver Hill, in the narrow Beaver Creek Valley, surrounded by hills. It was a little Cape Cod cottage, (it still stands); † in which Uncle Jimmy, as he came to be known, hoped to raise several sons to prolong the family name. But alas! Such was not to be; his sons were all daughters, five of them!

Upon arrival of his first daughter, they happily called her "Lucy"; after both aunt and great-aunt. Four years later another girl appeared, named "Frances". Jimmy bore it with fortitude. In 1840 disappointment was severe when "Sarah Ann" came into the world, but Jimmy said, "Better luck next time." By 1845 when "Phebe Eudocia" (Dosh, pronounced Dough, as in bread, Dough-ssh), made her undeniably feminine appearance, Jimmy had resigned himself to his fate. The grand finale in 1850 produced one last maiden, Amelia; and Father Jimmy then bragged that it wasn't every man who could have five darn good looking girls; and that he sure was looking toward the day when he would have all those son-in-laws helping in the fork factory!

And now that you have been formally introduced, I will turn this tale over to Dosh, for this is *her* story.

° Presently home of Sherrill Palmer, Main St.

† Presently home of Mrs. Fern Parks, Academy St.

Chapter One

In 1834, eleven years before I was born, the thriving little village of Bailey's Corners was incorporated and re-named Clarkville; in honor of my mother's uncle, Judge Joseph Clarke. He was the first postmaster of the settlement; and also served as township supervisor, and clerk, justice of the peace, New York State assemblyman, and senator, at various intervals during his career.

Clarkville was situated near the center of Brookfield Township, in the southeast corner of Madison County; where stretched a vast belt of virgin timber, adorning the hills on every side. Beaver Creek, with numerous springs from the hillside keeping it in constant water supply, and boasting of a fall of seven-hundred twenty-five feet along its twelve mile course, was the home of some of the largest lumber and grist mills around; as well as of many other industries, which took their source of power from its currents. The farms about the township ranked among the highest in the county in number of milk cows, sheep, and horses; as well as in production of hops and potatoes. There were factories in the village; among them the fork factory which my father owned with his brother-in-law, Welcome Dennison, a cabinet factory, cheese factory, cutter factory, a tannery and three blacksmith shops.

My great-Uncle Hosea, brother to Judge Joseph, and also to my grand-father David Clarke, owned the meadow north of my parents' house, as well as the one directly across from it, which extended to the creek. On the north meadow was his so-called "black shop", and here he was engaged in the cultivation, trimming, and packing of teasels; which were used to raise the nap of woolen broadcloth. Teasels were of great importance in Clarkville; since when they were ripe, at least fifty-percent of the boys and girls in the village, including myself, were employed by him.

Our cottage stood between these meadows, on a ten-acre plot of ground which extended up the hillside and into the woods; a little farm on which Papa raised our garden, some chickens, pigs, and kept a couple of cows. Papa was a good man; quiet, easy going, and

1

usually dominated by Mama, who ruled the roost with an iron hand.

I idolized my two eldest sisters, Lucy and Frances. Lute, (Papa's nickname for Lucy) was the one we took our troubles to, when Mama wasn't handy. She conscientiously performed all of her given duties, and often some of ours. Lute was never pretty, though she did wear clothes well. The only fellow who ever paid her any mind was George White, son of Capt. Daniel White, who owned White's Mills, south of town. Mama and Papa never took much to George; for I saw Mama raise her eyebrows in that certain way, and whisper to Papa, "He's got too good an eye for the ladies," and Papa nodded, "Don't think he cottons much to workin', either." But Lute had attained the age of twenty, and according to Mama, was "Like as not to be an old maid;" so they kept their comments to themselves.

Francie, on the other hand, had received more than her share of good looks. Though many young blades cast glances after her, she had just one fellow, her steady—Frank Leonard. Everyone assumed that sometime they'd wed, until that fateful April day when Uncle Hosea's horse was stung by a bee.

That same day Francie, after a bit of begging, had promised to take me upstreet, just to window shop. Such wonderful things went on in the village! Even the clip-clop of our wooden heels upon the board sidewalks entranced me. There was the milliner, through whose window was displayed the latest in milady's headdress; the tinsmith, always cleverly cutting and soldering his material into some useful article; the cabinet maker, whose door might be ajar enough to view the huge lathe, turned by a couple of husky lads; the dry-goods store, with the bolts of lovely yard goods, ribbons and laces, the penny candy-sticks, horehounds and licorice; the jewelryshop, with it's beautiful rings, bracelets, watches and pins, which I so longed to own; and last but not at all least were the three blacksmith shops. Surely in one of them would be a horse, in process of being shod! Horses and I had a natural affinity, but since we lived within walking distance of the village, Papa felt a horse was something we could do without.

Francie and I, dressed in our street clothes, stepped briskly along our drive. It was a lovely spring afternoon, and in the meadow north of our cottage was Uncle Hosea, his horse and walking plow, taking advantage of the weather. The soil was moist and the earth turned well for the middle-aged man stepping agiley along

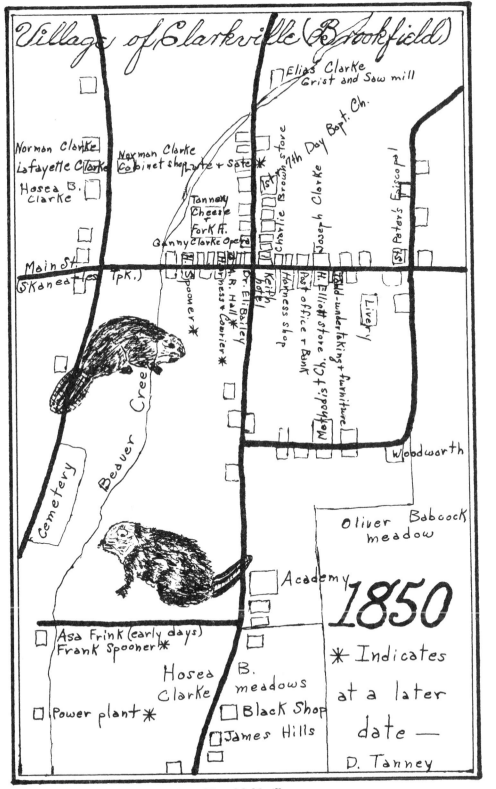

Map of Brookfield village

in the furrow. Suddenly and without warning his horse leapt through the air. Uncle braced himself between the plow handles and the reins which girded his back; commanded a sharp "Whoa!" meanwhile drawing the horse in a large left hand circle onto the unbroken sod. It was a good try and Uncle might have made it without casualty except that the remains of two old stumps were directly in his path. They missed the first but the animal hung the plow on the second one, snapped the harness in the process, and leaving Uncle by the stump, dashed crazily about the field.

Francie and I ran up on the sod side. "What can we do to help, Uncle?" inquired Francie. "You alright?"

"Whew!" said Uncle, wiping the beads of perspiration from his forehead, "Ain't had such a tussle in quite a while! Must be a dang bees nest back there a ways, and one of 'em lit on the horse. Looks like he's calmin' down now—must have run himself out—lookit that mess—snapped half the straps on it! Say, you two girls headin' up-street? I'd be much obliged if you'd stop by one of the harness shops and see if they've got a fellow they'll send down to give me a hand. I'll have to catch that critter and stay by him, but I'd sure like to get going and finish this chunk up today.—Looks like rain—"

"We'd be glad to, Uncle, and we'll hustle right along," answered Francie, gathering her skirts about her, in order to save them from the road dust. My nine year old steps were no match for her hurried ones, and I ran most of the way to the harness shop. Their main entrance was opened wide, and the mid-afternoon sun, high in the April sky, illuminated the interior. A lone figure, seated on a short three legged stool, labored to pull taut his stitching on a heavy leather strap. A shock of thick brown hair slid over his forehead, and he tossed his head to throw the offending lock from his line of vision. He glanced up in obvious surprise then, to behold a girl, the loveliest one, he felt immediately certain, he'd ever feasted his eyes upon. His just under six-foot frame unfolded, and rose to its feet, his gaze meantime sweeping the diminutive seventeen year old.

A single auburn tress trailed from beneath her sunbonnet, and dangled tantalizingly about her cheek, still flushed from the pace of our walk. Her wide blue eyes met his, questioningly. Almost automatically his eyes dropped to her ungloved hands. No ring! He returned his gaze, regained his senses with an ill-concealed sigh of relief, and managed at last to inquire, "Yes, Miss, what may we do for you?"

Francie, too, had lowered her eyes, embarrassed by the young stranger's apparent appraisal, but raised them shyly then, to meet his serious brown ones. Something about his manner, and accompanying look, had caused the heart beneath her breast to suddenly leap and thump in a wild stacatto beat. Trance-like, she replied, "Uh-Uncle Hosea's horse just ran away and riddled her harness. He asked us to stop by and see if you could send someone right down to give him a hand."

"Golly, I'm the only one on duty here this afternoon," frowned the young man, "but I *guess* I could lock up for a while. How far is it, to the place?"

"Just down past the Academy, but we are going right back; so if you want, we can go along and show you."

"I'd be much obliged if you would," smiled the young man, already tossing a harness on the shop's horse.

I opened my mouth to protest that we hadn't been window shopping yet; but then I realized that we were about to be treated to a buggy ride, so I closed it in a hurry. The buggy was a one-seated business model, with a narrow seat. It was a tight squeeze, with me in the middle. Little conversation ensued along the drive, but shy glances passed between the pair.

A short distance from our house, Uncle squatted on the still cool ground, sorting strips of broken leather; while a strong south wind swayed the branches of the horse-chestnut under which he labored. Francie pointed. "There—there's Uncle Hosea, under the tree. And this is our house—across the drive."

"Much obliged for showing me the way," said the young fellow again. "By the way, I didn't get *your* names."

"Oh," laughed Francie nervously, "this is my little sister, Dosh, and I'm Francie, Francie Hills."

"Francie—mmmmm—it's a nice name," he savored it as one would a piece of maple sugar candy. "Guess I'd better introduce *myself*." He had tied the shop horse to our front yard hitching post, and hustled around to assist Francie down the high buggy step. "I'm Henry Spooner, most folks call me Hank. We've lived up Gorton Hill way a few years; but I started work in the shop just a few weeks ago. Gosh, I'm real glad to make your acquaintance, Francie, and, uh,——you, too, Dosh. Hope to meet you again?" It was clearly a question.

"Oh—yes, um—I hope so." replied Francie, never before at a loss for words, but who acted as if the cat had got her tongue for sure.

He glanced nervously in Uncle's direction. "Well, I'd best be going, thanks again." He tipped his hat, and strode away.

We strolled toward the house. "Francie," I tugged at her sleeve. "We haven't done our window shopping!"

She purported to ignore my statement; and I repeated myself, in more urgent tones.

"Hush! Hush! He'll hear you!" she remonstrated. "We'll have to wait until he's gone. Do you suppose I want him to think we made a special trip back home, just to show him the way?"

"Well, we did, didn't we?"

"Yes, but we can't be so obvious!" she whispered.

Now this sounded like a lot of Greek to a nine-year old girl; and I returned nastily, "What's the matter, Francie, you stuck on him? Oh, Oh, Francie!"

"Phebe Eudocia Hills!" You be quiet this very minute!" she ordered, in a tone I knew I'd better respect; and with that she climbed the stairs, where she remained sprawled across her bed for so long that I thought she must be coming down with some terrible illness.

» » » » » » « « « « « «

The following Saturday, a knock sounded on our front door. Mama answered, to encounter a strange young man.

"Mrs. Hills? Is Francie at home?" inquired an easy voice we both recognized. We jumped simultaneously; Francie almost knocking me over in her haste.

"Why, hello," she cooed, just as if she'd expected him, all along. "Mama, this is Hank Spooner, his folks live up Gorton Hill way. I—we—Dosh and I, met him uptown the other day. He works in the harness shop," she hastened to explain.

"Pleased to make your acquaintance, I'm sure. Won't you come in and set a spell?" invited Mama, leading the way to the parlor. "Aren't you folks the ones who moved here from Cedarville?" Not waiting for an answer, she continued, "Land sakes! How did you happen to do that? I always heard that was right good farmin' country! Limestone soil, and all that. ——James, wake up! We have company!"

Introductions went around the family circle, and polite conversation followed, during which we discovered the Spooners had five sons, but no daughters. Mama marvelled at this turn of coincidence.

Hank explained that his parents had leased the farm in Cedar-

6

ville, but it had been sold, and they had heard of this one, to lease, near Clarkville. He continued that they were dissatisfied with the crop yield the previous season here; so that they were now giving serious consideration to heading "West."

"Well, now, I'm just a little farmer," put in Papa, "Got ten acres here. We make forks and implements in the factory, and do some blacksmith work besides. But if I didn't have that, I'd think twice about the west myself, I hear it's great country! 'Course I 'spose I'd have to go alone," he grinned at Mama.

"Now James, you know right where I stand on that!" snapped Mama. "Some of my kin have been in this valley, right over across that creek, for nigh on to sixty years. I figure, if it's good enough for them for sixty years, it ought to satisfy us for another thirty. Begging your pardon, boy, but I don't put much stock in rollin' stones. But we won't bore you with our family bickering." With that she bustled out into the kitchen, to return in a short time with the tea-table.

After a bit, the conversation lagged, Hank said he must be leaving, and Francie showed him to the door. I watched them pretty close, and I saw that same look again, in both pairs of eyes.

"Do you 'spose your folks would mind if I took you to the dance next Saturday night?" he ventured.

"I'll ask."

"I'll stop by during the week, to receive the verdict." he grinned.

Came Saturday evening, and a radiant Francie attended the dance, with Hank. They were together from this time forward.

Then came the crushing news that Hank's people had decided to move westward in a caravan; as soon as their fall crops were sold, and try to stake a claim before winter set in. A claim was of one-hundred sixty acres; and following a fourteen months residence on the same, it could be purchased from the government in advance of public sale for $1.25 an acre.

Among those traveling with the wagon train were Thomas and Ann Dennison York, whose daughter Antionette had married William Spooner, Hank's eldest brother, on Christmas day of 1853. Deloss, Antionette's brother, and William planned on staking a claim together; while Antionette, a teacher, was in hopes to establish a select school in the new country.

Hank was faced with the hardest decision of his nineteen years; and he discussed the issue with Francie. "Honey, if I had

Chloe & James Hills (Papa & Mama)

anything at all to offer you, besides my love, we'd go with the folks, and get married, before we left. Law says a male of fourteen, and female of twelve is legal, you know. Pa needs all of us. William will be making his own way now; Beaman is sixteen and Leonard fourteen, they'll do men's work; but Albert and Ma will have to shoulder the responsibility. Pa's not young, Francie. He was thirty-seven when he and Ma were married. You see, Grandfather Spooner, back in Vermont, raised nine children, and Pa was the only son to live. Gramp was poorer than a church mouse; if it wasn't for the pension he collected, being a veteran of the Revolution, they'd have starved to death. 'Course Pa was a grown man before Gramp got that, so the worst was over then; but Pa stayed on and farmed it with him, to help bring up the younger girls.

He mastered the trade of house joiner from Gramp—you ought to see the job Pa can do on a house! Those logs fit together like they grew that way! He'd help us build a right nice one, if we'd go west.—But see where Pa is today! Never's owned an inch of land, and he's past sixty.

Francie, I'd kind of like to get started, something for *us*. I've mastered the harness trade now, and I know I can make good at it. There's a great opportunity in the harness business here, and maybe soon, I can ask your Pa for your hand. Am I right, Francie, or just selfish?"

"It's what your heart tells you, Hank. I'd die to see you go, knowing you might never return, but I can't tell you not to."

"I'd come back to you, honey; if I had to crawl! But I guess I just had to feel out your reaction, 'cause I've already inquired about room and board uptown."

» » » » » « « « « « «

Hank appeared content until the holidays. He spent them, and the Sabbaths with us, but we all sensed his growing uneasiness. One Sabbath in January he read Francie this letter from his Mother:

Dodgeville, Wisconsin
January 7th 1855

Dear Henry,

We live in Dodgeville now, and Albert works in the blacksmith shop for fifteen dollars a month and boards. Leonard works in the harness shop. I don't know but he will work a year for twenty-five dollars. We have taken a farm about two and one-half miles from here. We are agoing to sow and plant seventy-five acres. The man puts on one span of horses and finds all the tools and half the seed, and lends us our seed to sow and we pay him in the fall.

They raise fifty or sixty bushels of oats to the acre and thirty or forty of wheat. The land is very good and rich here. I don't think we shall buy any land until fall.

William and Deloss have lost their land. Deloss is to work in the tavern for twelve dollars a month.

It is very pleasant here now. The ground is as bare as it is in July. We have not had but one little snow this winter. It has been warm most of the time. It is as good land here as anybody can ask for and very cheap. You can buy good land from five to ten dollars an acre. I think we shall buy second handed land instead of going further to get government land. There is enough land that can be bought for six shillings an acre about one-hundred miles from here. Some folks make a great deal here digging mineral.

We are agoing to buy us a cow and some hens before long. You wrote about Jim in your letter. Our poor dog is dead. Somebody shot him when we had been here about three weeks, and so we have lost Jim. Leonard was mad enough about it. Leonard has got a fiddle and he plays on the bones, and they call him bone now.

We had an oyster supper New Years night and eat four cans of oysters.

The boys don't go ahunting much. They have to work.

Give my love to Mr. Murphy's folks, and tell Deett they have a great school out here. They have two-hundred and fifty scholars. It is going to be a great place here. Tell Miss Elliott I will write to her soon. Tell them this is the place for them and anybody else that wants to get a good living.

I don't know as I can write much more now. Ask Ambrose Gorton about my newspapers and please to send them.

Give my love to all the good folks in Brookfield town; this from your

Mother, Hannah Spooner

Hank hesitated, then blurted, "You know, Francie, I've been thinking I ought to go west to see for myself what it's like, before we decide to settle down here. I could make it during slack season for the shop, if I started now. But—if I should take to it, do you 'spose you'd like to move out west? Oh, I know, I shouldn't ask. This little valley, amongst these hills, is really all you know. I don't imagine either of us should give voice to an opinion; until we are qualified to compare the two territories."

"Hank, I've seen this coming for some time; and I'm afraid it's something you will have to do before you will ever be satisfied. I'd say the sooner you go, the better it will probably be for both of us; besides, I know you're aching to see your folks again." answered Francie, hurt to think he intended to leave without her.

"You really think I should?" He was excited. "I've saved enough to take me both ways, and I figure I'll be back, come the first of March. You won't worry, will you?" She nodded almost imperceptibly. "You know there's no one else, nor ever will be, don't you, honey? Then I guess—if you're sure it's alright with you—I'll be off come Monday morning, the sooner I get going, the sooner I'll be back."

Francie saw the stage off on Monday, and coming straight home to the seclusion of her room, she sobbed her heart out. The fact that Hank had promised to return was of little comfort.

Later that week I ran into Frank Leonard, outside the Academy. "Say, Dosh, how is Francie?" he inquired. "I haven't seen her around lately."

"She's a pretty unhappy girl, Frank," I responded, glad for the opportunity to visit with my old friend. (He had been like a big brother to me, ever since he and Francie had first gone steady.) "All she does is cry. You know," I added slyly, "Hank left the other day, for the west."

"I heard that," he frowned. "Do you suppose she'd mind if I come down to visit for a while?"

"Why don't you walk on home with me? We'll soon find out!" Once inside our kitchen, I shouted gaily, "Francie, surprise, surprise! See who's come to visit us!"

After a couple of minutes in which I suspected she arranged her hair, and attempted to camouflage her tear-stained face; she appeared, apparently more than glad to meet her old friend. Shortly she bundled warmly, and the two of them ambled over to join the gang skating on the creek that afternoon. Upon their return, she was more like the Francie of old, than she had been for some time.

Chapter Two

Sarah Ann, generally known as Sate, was the middle girl in our family, which warranted her little distinction; though she sought to distinguish her family positon in many other ways. Five years my senior, we found little in common, beyond our inevitable squabbles.

Amelia, (Meal), was our baby; five years younger than I. She was my life-size-doll; and I doted on buttoning her in her second best, brushing her dark curls, and strolling her upstreet; for the townswomen to admire.

Papa's fork-factory was not in the best of circumstances; due partially to the depression of 1837, which hit the country shortly after he began his enterprise. He carried a side line of black-smithing, which included many related jobs, such as fixing wagons, ironing sleds, hooping barrels, mending whiffletrees, and even re-pairing fryingpans. Bills were seldom paid with money, as the banks would not redeem the paper currency for "hard money", so cash was near impossible to come by. Papa's account book con-tained credit by cider, apples, butter, loads of manure, shingles, bricks, hay, pears, mutton, wood, lumber, and even work by school-boys at four dollars per month. Papa, as well as the entire country, had over-extended his credit; which no doubt accounted for the eventual fold-up of the fork factory.

Since the expenditure of money in those times for children's toys was known as the height of folly, we girls devised our own means of entertainment. There were corn-husk dolls, and clothes-pin dolls, dressed in elaborate costumes fashioned from bits of left-over materials. Had we been especially helpful that day, and Mama in one of her better moods; she might permit us the luxury of play-ing "lady" in some of the store-room clothes, (items stowed away until such time as they could be grown into, or remodeled.) This furnished Mama with a few precious moments, apart from the prying eyes of her daughters; and at such times she could usually be found in the out-house; which until her dying day she trusted, had never divulged her deep, dark, secret. For Mama had one back-door sin; she smoked a clay pipe; but little did she realize that through the years her trusted building had emitted telltale wisps, signaling a familiar scent. But Mama was not one to josh with; and we girls never let on that we even suspected her transgression, except in whispers, between ourselves.

Chief among our summer pleasures was a jaunt across Uncle's flat to the creek, where we foraged endlessly for turtles, pieces of quartz, flint or arrowheads. At one time a battle must have raged on that land; or else the arrowheads were washed downstream from the Stillwater area, near the head of Beaver Creek, where the Oneida Indians had encamped along their trail many years before. Each spring the normally babbling stream became a tumultuous watercourse, swollen by seasonal rains and spring thaws. Enormous sheets of ice would come crashing downstream on its torrents, piling up as minature icebergs against the tree trunks and bridge abutments, and smashing everything in their wake. The rising waters would flood across Uncle's flat land, almost inundate his black shop, and extend nearly to our door. Throughout the nights we would toss, sleeplessly attuned to the mounting roar, until nature had abated her fury, and the waters subsided.

Church attendance and preparation for the day comprised our Saturday forenoons. Although the beliefs of our New England ancestors were not as strictly enforced as in Pilgrim times, their influence was still felt on our everyday life, and especially so on the Sabbath Day. We had inherited our observance of the Seventh Day through the Clarke family, and our ancestors, (seven generations removed,) Samuel and Tacy Hubbard, who were the first to embrace the Seventh Day in America, in 1665, at Newport, Rhode Island. Lute, Francie and Sate sang in the choir galley, while Meal and I perched beside Mama on the hard wooden benches. Though Papa usually attended, he refused to join the institution; for he could not bring himself to agree with their doctrine of communion restricted to church members only. Papa felt that if a man believed in the Lord, he should be allowed communion on that basis alone; and this was one matter in which he stubbornly held his ground.

As soon as we were able, we girls acquired work away from home. Lute was a proficient seamstress; and often left home for a spell, to board with such families as required her services.

Francie found employment with Uncle Hosea in the black shop, working on the teasels. Teasels were a fall crop, which grew upon a stalk, three to five feet in height. When matured, they were cut, dried, combed, sorted, and packed in large, thin boxes for ship-

First & Seventh-Day Baptist Church, built in 1837

Main Street, Brookfield, looking west, as it looked mid-nineteenth century

14

ment to woolen factories with which Uncle contracted, in New England. In usage, the teasels were fastened in a row to an iron strip or clamp, so that the sharp little hooks which surrounded the "blossom end" were turned backwards; while the woolen broadcloth turned in an opposite direction on a cylinder, thus raising the nap of the yardgoods, by the scratching of the hooks. The finished teasels were sorted into three sizes, each used for a different grade of broadcloth.

About all that could be said for the black shop was that it offered a shelter; and the work was performed on the second story, away from the dampness and din of the ground floor, where a horse-shoeing was often in progress. As the cool, dark days of fall inevitably descended, the workers would shiver, and bundle all the warmer; while on especially frosty mornings, weather became the main topic of conversation.

Uncle, however, was equal to the occasion. Entering the black shop, he would remove his stovepipe hat, which all the men about town wore; and carrying it carefully in his hand, he would climb the stairs, pushing up the trapdoor with his shoulders. After replacing the door, he would ceremoniously shake out his bandana, fold it, and tuck it inside his hat. Not until then would he loudly remark "Brr—did you know it?", but never once mention the weather.

It was family tradition to pass Thanksgiving with Grandma and Grandpa Clarke. They farmed it on the Skaneatles Turnpike, about a mile west of the village. All of their children who lived within horse and buggy distance were present, with their offspring; and each family contributed toward the dinner. When all had squeezed around the bountiful meal, the women praying silently that their improvised table would withstand the strain, Grandpa invariably cleared his throat, and in his most sonorous tones, began his annual Thanksgiving Day grace: "Oh, Lord, we thank Thee most heartily for this gathering here today; we thank Thee for the providence which Thou hast provided in the bygone years. Though when our parents entered these hills they had little but faith in Thee, Thou didst keep them in the wilderness, even as Thou didst the children of Israel. We thank Thee, Lord, that Thou didst instill in our hearts the same faith which our parents and grandparents, and those who came before, knew. Although of our eleven children brought into this world, we survive with only seven on this earth, we thank Thee for each of them, and for the joy they have brought into our lives. Lord, we thank Thee also, for our daughter who has seen fit to devote her life unto Thy service, and though she be on the other side of the world from us gathered here, we know that Thou wilt be with her, to protect her and her beloved." He paused, cleared his throat, and resumed. "And now we do sincerely pray that each one of our other children will feel a burden upon his heart, to keep his own little ones in a constant and close walk with Thee. And finally, Lord, we thank Thee for the plenty we have spread before us here today; we ask that Thou wilt bless it as we partake of it, and if it be Thy will, to bless and keep each one gathered here, until we meet again. We ask it all in Jesus name, Amen."

We children looked forward to these gatherings, and perhaps the opportunity to hear Grandma Clarke again· relate the story of her three weeks as a young girl, enroute with the wagon train. No village was in existence upon their arrival. Her parents, Asa and Thede Frink, were among the first of the valley settlers, and chose for themselves, some of the choicest land, through which the Beaver Creek ran. But what they lacked in store goods, was recompensed many times over in neighborliness between the scattered cabins, as each lent a hand to the other, in work, and the loan of such tools and goods as they had.

Great-Grandma Thede Frink, despite the death of her first husband at an early age, had not only salvaged her own staunch Christian faith, but had instilled this same faith in her children. And without a doubt their faith was strengthened by the sufferings of Lucy, one of Grandma's younger sisters. She had married one Martin Jerry Murphy, whom Grandma simply stated "had slipped away from the fold." Grandma (Lydia Frink Clarke) had arrived at this conclusion shortly after Lucy's marriage; when Martin entered upon the sinful (according to Grandma) business of establishing distilleries, in several states, which were sold at a profit, when once in successful operation. As proof of his downfall, she cited his untimely demise, in 1825, while on the western side of the Ohio River. Due to the absence of cemeteries in the wilderness, his body was transported across the river, into Virginia, for burial. Lucy's daughter, Martha, followed her father in death by two days; while their youngest son, eighteen months of age, was scalded to death the following week.

In due time, the news of Lucy's tragedy reached the Beaver Creek settlement. (then Bailey's Corners.)° Deeply concerned over their widowed daughter and sister, her parents Asa and Thede

° Later Clarkville, finally Brookfield.

Frink, and brothers, sisters and in-laws hit upon a plan. Lucy's pride, they well knew, would not lead her to accept charity; for she had married Martin against her parent's wishes; who, with the judgement of years foresaw in him a character unlike that to which Lucy had been accustomed. Aside from the love they bore for her, it was their bounden duty to care for their own, and amongst themselves they took up a collection, with mind to put through a bold plan.

A young man, whom Lucy had never seen, but who was of both a gallant and adventurous spirit was engaged. At his disposal were placed horse, wagon, and outfit of tin utensils, with instructions to seek out Lucy and bring her home. Eventually he found his way to her Ohio doorstep, where he inquired as to whether she'd be interested in his wares. She replied briefly that she was widowed and could scarcely feed and clothe her children, let alone buy anything unnecessary. He continued the conversation, during which he casually mentioned that he had come a long way, all the way from Bailey's Corners, N.Y. With this disclosure she became excited and inquired eagerly for family and friends, whereupon he divulged the real purpose of his errand. Lucy and her four surviving children forthwith returned with him, to Bailey's Corners, where her parents and family had made ready a tiny home, for her arrival. Here she remained for the rest of her days; with Grandma insisting forever after that the Devil had got ahold of that Murphy man for sure; and that 'twas only by the prayers of her believing family, and the Grace of God, that Lucy and her remaining children escaped his firey clutches.

Grandma's girlhood was one of pure drudgery, with but few simple pleasures, and she was inclined to "pooh-pooh" her granddaughters' desire for life's little extravagances. She was loath to bestow a compliment; certain it would pave the path to the unforgivable sin of vanity.

It was Thanksgiving, 1854; and I was the proud possessor of a new dress, apron and bonnet which Lute had renovated for me. The dress was of dark blue broadcloth; the apron and bonnet a sky blue calico print, which matched my blue eyes perfectly. (Francie and I bore the same auburn coloring, though she had inherited Papa's features, and I Mama's.) I tip-toed slyly into Grandma's bedroom to admire myself in her small dresser looking glass. Grandma soon happened upon me. "How do you like my new outfit, Grandma?" I queried, innocently, hastily replacing the glass.

"It's just lovely, Dosh," she replied, with just the hint of a smile playing at the corners of her eyes.

"But do you think *I* look pretty in it?" I persisted. "I mean, doesn't it go just right with my eyes?"

"Humph," returned Grandma, scanning me up and down, "I guess if you act as well as you look, you'll be alright!"——And this was as much of a compliment as I could wheedle her into giving me.

Chapter Three

Christmas holidays were spent at home; with all of us exchanging our handmade gifts. That year (1854) Sate knit new scarves for all, Mama fashioned us mittens; while Papa went all out for Lute, Francie and Sate, building each of them a cedar hope chest. Meal and I received a cradle, crafted by Papa, and sizeable enough to accomodate our entire family of clothespin and stocking dolls. Lute stitched new aprons for everyone, Francie crocheted tidies and embroidered hankies. I did a charcoal sketch for each family member, complete with hand made paper frame. Mama stated it had best be a special Christmas, since she "had a premonition it might be the last one we'd have as a family."

Mama's intuition was next to infallible. On Valentine's Day Francie received a card from Hank, stating that he missed her more than he could have imagined, and bemoaning that he hadn't taken her, as his wife, with him. Did she still feel the same? And if, as he was praying, she still did, to let him know; he would come straight back and they would set the date. Francie's reply was dispatched on the next stage, saying that she hadn't changed her mind.

"Oh, Frank," Francie hesitated, encountering him in the store next day. "Will you walk me home? There's something—important —I should tell you."

"Anytime, dear lady. Must you ask?"

It was unseasonably warm; a late February thaw was in progress; and everyone was revelling over the prospect of an early spring. The couple picked their way down the hill, avoiding the slushiest spots, while he waited, patiently, for her disclosure. "Gosh, it's nice out today," he finally volunteered. "Hear that creek talk! She'll really be aroaring about tonight!"

"Yes," she agreed, absentmindedly, then blurted, "Frank, I had a letter from Hank a couple of days ago."

"Hank?" He stopped dead in his tracks; and turned to face her. "Well, what did *he* have to say?"

"Oh, Frank, I just don't know how to begin," she faltered miserably, twining the ends of her scarf together. "You remember that I told you Hank and I wanted to be married before his folks went off to Wisconsin, but Hank figured he didn't have enough to offer me?"

He nodded silently, too sick at heart to reply.

"Well, he will soon be on his way back east; and, she grabbed a breath, then plunged ahead, "He has asked me to set the date for our wedding."

He stared above her flushed cheeks, searching her eyes, hoping to read there a denial of the words her lips were forming. But there was none. "So—" he finally managed, propping himself against a giant elm tree, "this time old Frank will be out of the picture for good. Yep, I guess I should have known it was too good to be true. I had hoped, when Hank left—"

"I know," Francie filled in swiftly, "I know what you had hoped, and once I thought perhaps it might turn out that way. But you know now that it couldn't possibly be, don't you? I—loved Hank from the first moment I saw him. I'm sorry, Frank, but I have to be truthful—I want you to know you are one of the greatest fellows I've ever known; and that you've been the best friend a girl could ever hope to have, all these years."

"Good old Frank," he smiled wryly, endeavoring to cover his hurt.

"I mean that, Frank," she repeated. "I mean that—about the best friend."

"For sure, Francie?" he replied soberly, pausing in the slow gait they had resumed, to look full into her face.

"Real sure." She returned his even gaze.

"Then, Francie, promise me just one thing, if things ever go wrong for you, if you're ever in trouble, you'll call on me; for I will *always* be waiting to help you."

"I *do* promise; and we will always be friends, remember that."

"Friends," he repeated, "forever, as true as the Bible." He took her mittened hand in his and gripped it tightly, impetuously kissed her on the cheek, (for they were outside our front door); turned, and was gone. It would not do for her to see the tears he could no longer check.

» »» »» »» »» «« «« «« «« «« «

Hank returned on March 5th, due to the early spring. He was immediately re-employed in the harness shop; and they set the date for the tenth of that month.

As it happened, March 5th was my birthday; and Mama was baking bread. Bread-making was a once a week project; since it was quite an undertaking to heat the bee-hive oven. Even the kneading of the dough was half a day's chore, usually dispensed to one of us girls. Half a bushel of flour was dumped into the wooden trough, and mixed with nearly a pail full of warm water, a cup of salt, and one and one-half quarts of good hop yeast. The mixture was allowed to raise twice, and during the second rising, a fire was placed in the oven. By the time the dough was sufficiently high, the oven was in readiness. While Mama shaped the five-pound loaves, someone hurriedly swept out the oven. The loaves were then placed into the oven, the door tightly latched, and left to bake for two and one-half hours.

Mama swiftly "threw together" an extra large cake, which she placed in the oven, alongside the bread. It was a gold cake, so called because only the yolks of the eggs were used; the whites were reserved for the boiled frosting. Sugar was expensive, so this cake was a real treat. As a rule, our desserts consisted of such staples as molasses or ginger cake, or cookies, since these were made with the cheaper blackstrap molasses. During the week, when cake or gingerbread were desired, they were baked in a large kettle, hung upon the fireplace crane, over the coals.

We invited both Hank and George down that evening. It was an engagement, welcome home, and birthday party combined! That occasion was my last birthday spanking, received from the boys, but not until I gave them a run for their money!

The next five days were a mad, happy scramble. They hadn't planned a large wedding, for not only were funds limited, but time as well. Nevertheless, since Francie's letter of acceptance had been posted, sister Lute had volunteered her services, and together she and Francie had fashioned a gorgeous gown of deep blue sateen, with headpiece to match.

It was a mad whirl—for scarcely had the excitement of the

wedding subsided when Mama hostessed a family quilting bee. Several adept needles labored over two lovely quilts which were tied off and presented to the bride. Once this ceremony had been accomplished, some of the cousins struck up a lively number on the fiddle and bones, another begun the familiar "calling off" chant, and a square dance was soon in progress.

Apparently the performance was so promising that Lute and George were inspired to repeat it, for exactly one month later, Lute became Mrs. George L. White, with Hank and Francie as the attending couple. Shortly thereafter Hank bargained for a harness shop of his own, and hired George as his helper.

» » » » » » « « « « « «

SPRING—1855

School recessed in April. I was delighted to find new playmates in the neighborhood. They had come to board the summer with their aunt, Mrs. Morgan, who lived across the creek. The boy was a couple of months older than I; his sister, Mae, a year younger. His real name was James Fordyce Hickox, though he was known as "Fordy." Fordy was the life of our gang, and we girls looked to him for ideas as well as protection. No day was ever dull with him in our group.

As our initial project, we decided to paste together May baskets, to hang onto the doors of the newly marrieds. We constructed our little baskets from brown paper, coloring them with inked on designs. But what to do for flowers! The garden myrtle and daffodils had not bloomed as early as usual!

"What say," piped up Fordy, his freckles alive with enthusiasm, "we climb up the ravine in back of your house! I bet we find some spring beauties!"

No sooner said than we were off, in our excitement neglecting to ask Mama's permission.

Climbing the ravine was an adventure in itself. Sections of it were extremely narrow, and here the spring fed stream, swollen by seasonal rains, raced and pounded tumultously over the shale rock shelves in breathtaking cascades. Cautiously we crept around them, hauling ourselves up the slippery, treacherous sides of the gorge by whatever tree or bush we deemed secure enough to support us. Once above these perilous spots, the gully widened, and we were on safe footing. We paused, panting, and dropped our bodies into the moist, spongy carpet, the accumulation of years decay. Above us

21

the giant hardwoods towered, interspersed with sweet smelling hemlocks, which dangled precariously over the edge of the ravine; while all about us was the majestic stillness, broken only by the occasional baying of a village dog, echoing back and forth among the precipices.

"Let's have a contest!" shouted Fordy, interrupting the magic moment. "Bet I'll be first to find a spring beauty!"

Taking up the challenge we scrambled off, each in a different direction. In a few minutes I shrieked, "I've found some!", while the Hickoxes came racing over to determine the wealth of my find. (Several years later Fordy disclosed that he'd known they were there all along, but not wishing to spoil our fun, he hadn't revealed his secret.) There were plenty to fill the baskets of the two brides, as well as those of Mama and Mrs. Morgan.

Fordy arose then, with inspiration number two. "How about climbing up on the ledges?" The ledges ran horizontally along the slopes of Beaver Hill, and one of the best examples of them protruded directly in back of our house. There were three of them there, each a little higher than the other, and came as close to resembling a mountainside as anything we had in Clarkville. In the spring of the year, they were clearly visible, and presented quite a temptation to the wandering youngster, as, with effort, one could climb to the topmost one. The landscape from this point was something to behold; for the entire village, as well as the settlements toward Gorton Hill, South Brookfield, and DeLancy could be seen.

We clambered up over them; then, played "King On the Mountain" on the highest one, with Fordy as king, myself as Queen, and Mae as our Princess daughter. (Queen Doshie, Fordy called me.)

Suddenly I realized we hadn't advised Mama as to where we were headed, and we immediately hurried homeward. Half-way down the bottom ledge, I lost my footing, and slid heavily down its face, a rubble of stone rolling beneath me. Upon this intrusion, a startled skunk poked his nose out of his front door under the ledge.

"Stand still!" commanded Fordy.

Mae ran; I froze, terrorized. "Run!" screamed Mae.

"I can't," I sobbed. "My ankle!"

The skunk whirled and poised. Just as he let loose his spray, directed toward me, Fordy dashed between us. The force of it caught him full in the face. The skunk disappeared and so did Fordy, straight down over the bank into the ravine, where he plunged his face again and again into the frothing torrent. In a few moments he returned, his cheeks nearly as red as his shocks of tousled hair, and his eyes a mere two slits. "Come on Doshie, I'll take care of you now," he spoke manfully. Gallantly offering me his arm, and swooping up the forgotten spring beauties in his spare hand; he directed Mae to assist me on the other side.

My ankle had swollen to a painful double size. Tediously we made our way home. Mama was beside herself with worry; but when she noted the shape we were in, she decided to forego the customary trip to the woodshed that such an episode should have produced. Dr. Bailey examined my ankle; pronouncing it nothing more than a bad bruise and sprain.

Fordy bore the brunt of our misdeed. He stoutly asserted that it was all his fault, begging, "*Please*, don't punish her, Mrs. Hills. She hurts bad enough already!" Mrs. Morgan sent him directly to the creek, cold water or no, with a bar of home-made soap; admonishing him that no supper would be forthcoming, until all that vile perfume had wafted far downstream.

Chapter Four

From the day of the Henry Spooner's marriage, a series of glowing letters streamed into their household, detailing the golden opportunities on the booming western frontier. One of the first read in part as follows:

"Dodgeville, Wis.

Dear Sister;

I had a letter from Hank. He wrote that you folks thought you should not come out here this summer on account of the cholera on the Mississippi River. I have not heard of any cholera on the river lately, but if he should not come here this summer or fall, I shall come there, although I hope that he will come here.

The folks in Dodgeville are agoing to have some great times, celebrating the Fourth of July, and I should be glad if you were here to see the performance. There was a circus at Mineral Point last Friday, it was the best one, the folks say, that was ever in Wisconsin, but I think that there is some in York State that would beat it quick enough. Albert thinks of starting for Iowa or Minnesota in about a week from now, to look him up a place to build a shop. I am sorry that you can not come out here now, because you would get such a beautiful place. I cannot think of anymore to write now, so goodbye. Write soon. This from your brother, Le Spooner"

In the autumn Leonard wrote again:

Dear Brother:

I think if you only knew how nice our sixty acres of grain looked and all of these nice plums and huckleberries and a great many more nice things, you would pack up your harness shop and come out here in less than a week.

At first I thought of writing to have you send Dr. Bailey out here, but the second time athinking I concluded that it would be a very foolish plan unless he learned how to doctor horses and cows for there is no kind of human beings out this way that knows who sickness is. This from Leonard Spooner

A note from his cousin, Amos Brown, was penciled on the same large sheet:

"Come before it be everlastingly too late. Bill, me and Put are going to see if we can find a place as soon as harvest is over to set us up a shop for manufacturing Saks wagons. Your business is first rate out here. Come and you will know all. I have seen that young chap that used to come down to spark Sis from Waterville. That is all, so goodbye, Amos"

Still the paper had not been filled—as needs it must be, considering the cost of imported stationery—to say nothing of postage; so Hannah Spooner completed the messages.

"I must write you a few lines about the west. I want you should come out here to live with us. I am sure you and Frances would like it better than where you now live. If you was only out here you won't think how fast folks make money. You would not have to work half the time to get a living here. You may work all the time there and not but just live.—I know all about that place, and you will have hard work to live, to do your best, for you have everything to buy, and things are high.—Now is your time to come, while you are young, and settle here, and some day perhaps you may be rich, for all the folks are getting rich around here and they come with nothing. I can't bare to have you stay there and spend your days, and only make a living and not hardly that, when I know you could do so well here, and you won't find a healthier place in the world than it is here. Hannah Spooner

Next spring the Spooners relocated, in Loganville, Wisconsin. On May 11, 1856, they posted the following: bound for Brookfield, Clarkville Postoffice, New York State.

Dear Brother:

Our folks have bought them an acre of land in Loganville. They are going to commence to build them a house in about two weeks. They will build it large enough so that you can live in it till you can build you a house. There is two wagon shops going up, the owners are building them now, and all it lacks of making a city is a harness shop.

Bill has got his old engine going. He expects to do good business but whether he does or not, remains to be seen. They are going to have a gristmill there this summer anyway, and a woolen factory if they get around to it. One of the wagon shops is going to make carriages and buggies. You can get a first rate job if you will come out. I think the best thing you can do is to sell your shop if you can. You can make money as fast again out here as you can there, so march right along, we are ready for you, so goodbye, old Hank. Give my love to everyone that lives in York State. Le Spooner"

Albert had concluded the letter with:

Dear Brother:

There is the greatest number of immigrants coming into this Western country that ever was known any year before, and I hope that you will be amongst that crowd. Come, come, before it be everlastingly too late. Remember the day is coming when if a man has not got a well filled

Map of Wisconsin

purse he may as well be in the Eastern Country as out here. It beats all how things are coming up round about this place. They are looking as well as could be expected for the rain. But never mind the rain, it rains in other places, too.

Now to business. We want you to come out here, if you please. Mr. Gibson has built a large house by the lot we bought for you, and it makes a great difference. Mr. Pollock has built him a house further up towards the bluft. There is houses going up in all parts of this town as fast as they can get lumber from the mill. There is a large frame wagon shop agoing now, it will be in operation the first of July. Well, I guess I had better not fool my time away with these things any longer, because if you come out you will see them and if you don't come, you don't care anything about them, so goodbye, Albert

Letter piled upon letter, as "western fever" ran ever higher at the Hank Spooner residence; and when George and Lute White paid their frequent visits, the tempo was accentuated.

At last plans were laid for a tentative move; and at Papa's, following the family Christmas dinner, the conversation turned, inevitably, to the west.

"So—" began Grandpa Clarke, "When be ye leavin' for the west, boys?"

"Before I answer that," parried Hank, "I'd like you folks to hear Mother's last letter. You brought it, didn't you, Francie? I believe it will answer most of your questions."

Francie nodded, delved deep into her bag, and came up with the following:

December 14, 1856

Dear Children:

I received your letter, and was glad to hear from you and that you was well, and had sold your shop, and was coming west. We should be very glad to have you out here. I think you can get a living here if you can anywhere. It is a first rate farming country and you will find plenty of land. We have got one-hundred and twenty acres, and if you will help pay for it, you can have a share of it, and there is plenty of other land around here.

27

I think you can do first rate making harnesses. There is a number of folks that want some nice ones made, and horses are pretty here now.——

There is a house between here and the village that we think you can hire or buy, and some land with it.

You had better get you some leather and harness trimmings and fetch with you. They will be cheaper there than they are here. Fetch me some dried apples, if you please.

We have moved onto our land and built us a log cabin and you can come in with us till you get a house.

We have had a letter from Albert. He is well and is to work a mite from Warren. He was driving team when he wrote. I have written to him to come home and work in the blacksmith shop in the village here, I expect him or a letter this week.

Frances can do first rate at her trade here, and I guess she won't get homesick. You will come to Milwaukee and then to Madison, and from there to Lone Rock on the cars, and that is this side of the Wisconsin River. You will have to come twenty miles when you leave the cars, and there will be a stage by the time you come that will take you to Loganville. It has got to be quite a place. There has been seventeen more framed buildings since last year. There is three stores, one tavern, and two wagon shops, two blacksmith shops, and William's shop. They are agoing to build a gristmill next spring. I think you could get a lot in the village pretty cheap, if you would set up a shop there.

William is building him a new house in the village, and has got him a good yoke of oxen, and is going to drawing furniture to sell.——

Don't fetch a great many things with you, it won't pay. You better fetch some butter with you, for there ain't much here, and it is two shillings a pound. Flour is cheaper and other things that you will want.——

We have got plenty snow here. I want you to write and let us know when you are coming, so we may be ready for you. I will bid you goodbye, till I see you. From your Mother, Hannah Spooner"

"Mother Spooner doesn't know it, but we don't propose to leave till spring," continued Francie, carefully refolding the letter. "Did you notice what she said about plenty of snow? Hank is afraid we might get snow bound on the rails, so he's concluded he'd best pick up some piece work, for the winter, here. The trip will be prettier and more comfortable in the spring; besides, I hate to leave Mama, Papa and the girls—any sooner than we have to—"

"Well, ain't Lute and George agoin' with ye?" burst out Grandma, snorting. "Land sakes, I never heard the likes of such girls. Why, when *my* Pa and Ma come here all they had was a covered wagon, seven younguns, a pair of wore out oxen and a few hand tools. Had to shack up in the wagon half the summer, till we could build us a log cabin. *Nowadays*, they travel on the cars, in style! Got a house, and relation, all ready and waitin for ye out there, a village, with stores, and everythin. YOU YOUNGUNS CAN'T HOLD A CANDLE TO THE OLDFOLKS! Ye ain't no grandchildren o mine! I'm plum ashamed of ye!" Such an outburst from Grandma was not uncommon, and of late she had been more outspoken than usual, for she had been "ailing" for some time.

"Now, Lyddy, it's the way of the world, and its dang new-fangled ways. Might jest as well face it, they jest don't grow like thet anymore," spoke up Grandpa, who was resting in the Boston rocker, his beard so apparently supporting the weight of his head that we all figured he had snoozed off during the reading. "You know, durned if I wouldn't like to go myself, if I be jest a mite younger. Always wanted to see the west—" His voice trailed off, as he settled back into his routine noon-day nap.

" 'Twouldn't take much coaxing for me to go," put in Papa, taking us all by surprise.

"Well, now, I tell ye, James Hills, ye ain't agoing to do no such thing," Mama snapped. "I was born here and I aim to die here! Even if business ain't good, we've got us a right nice little place here, s'all paid for, spot for a garden and berry bushes, 'sides our two Ayrshires for my butter and cheese money! What we've got in this house ain't much like some folks have, I reckon, but it shields us from the winter winds, and keeps the rain out! And one things for sure—I ain't aimin' to part with it for what I can stash away in a lumber wagon, with a piece of cloth stretched over the top! 'Sides that, all our friends and kinfolk are here, and I ain't aimin' to part with them, either!"

"Thought I'd get your goat with that one," chuckled Papa. "Simmer down, old girl, just wanted to see if I could still get a rise out of ye! By the way, Ma," he gave Grandma a sly wink, "have ye heard from my old gal *Lucy* lately?"

Lucy was Mama's next older sister; namesake of Grandma's sister, Lucy Frink Murphy, who had so narrowly escaped the devil's clutches, down in Ohio. Not until five years after Mama's and Papa's marriage did Aunt Lucy marry Solomon Carpenter, D. D., from Stephentown, N. Y., and during this period of Lucy's maidenhood, Papa joshed Mama plenty about her pretty school-teacher sister. Aunt Lucy and Uncle Solomon left for Shanghai, China, (being the first Seventh-Day Baptist missionaries to serve among the heathen there,) when I was only three. I thought their travels the ultimate in adventure; and news from Aunt Lucy was treasured, to be savored again and again.

"It so happens, James, that I have, and was jest about to say so, before everybody got all riled up over the west. Lucy asked me to read it at the Christmas gathering, so here 'tis," Grandma replied, squinting through her tiny spectacles, and beginning: "Dear Folks, Solomon and I wish with all our hearts we could be with you on this wonderful day. We remember each of you in daily prayer, and send love and regards to all. Christmas over here will never be quite the same as in the States, nor can it ever compare to those we passed as children.

Though we are well, happy and contented in our calling here, the thoughts I penned upon our leavetaking nine years ago, remain as true for us today as they were then."

I knew the "thoughts" to which Aunt Lucy referred by heart. They had been published, in verse form, in the Sabbath Recorder of August 26th, 1847; and a copy of her poem, entitled "The Missionary's Farewell," had received an honored place in Mama's scrapbook.

"Home of my happy childhood, one last, one sad adieu,
Too long, too fondly cherished, I go, sweet home, from you.
There is a clime more lovely, it's glory, who can tell?—
It is for that I bid thee, my much loved home, farewell.

Mother, dear Mother, say not this heart can love you less,
'Een though my vagrant footsteps a distant soil should press;
Can love like ours be broken, though seas between us swell?
In tears, alone, is spoken for you the last farewell.

Father, no earthly treasure could ever make me go—
Nor fading crown could win me, from thy embrace below;
But thy dear voice has bid me, obey my Father's will,
And is not God my Father? Guide of my youth, farewell.

Sisters, my gentle partners in life's young playfulness,
Go, and in your gladness one bounding heart you'll miss;
Then what shall cheer the wanderer, when life's rough surges
    swell?
The hope to meet beyond them, sweet sisters, all, farewell.

Brothers, the hour is coming, when we shall meet no more;
The tears for you shall henceforth fall on a foreign shore;
But oh! To part forever—the anguish, who can tell?
Start it, blessed Savior—we could not say, farewell.

Friends, when the pangs of parting shall all have passed away,
Before life's star knows no setting—the spoiler finds no prey—
Till each dear voice the anthem of sweet deliverance swell;
And I in peace can bid you, my friends, a short farewell.

Church, where my vows were plighted, be every blessing thine,
May many a fair plant brighten thy undecaying vine;
In heaven's sweet dew upon thee, and love thy temple fill,
And every blessing crown thee-Church, Kindred, Home, farewell."

Grandma's voice droned on, breaking into my reverie, "I al-
ways did say," she concluded, "that Lucy took after me in her likin
to travel."

I listened intently to the rest of the conversation; the yearning
in my heart growing with every word. No one yet knew that I, too,
had inherited this same love of travel.

» » » » » » « « « « « «

All too soon it was spring, and on April Fools Day the two cou-
ples departed; bound for the west, loaded with trunks of goods they
considered indispensible. And a tearful goodbye it was, for all ex-
cept Grandma; who stoutly shed not a tear, as she bade Lute and
Francie a fond goodbye, reminding them that, God willing, she
would see them again, in "the sweet bye and bye."

» » » » » » « « « « « «

"Mama," cried Sate, dashing into our kitchen, "A letter from the girls!" She was drenched from a sudden spring shower, and stood, dripping pools of water on the worn plank floor. Meal and I dropped our dish wipers and waited, eyes glued on Mama; while she tore the edge from the envelope, with maddening care, before she proceeded as follows:

Loganville, Wisconsin
April 28, 1857

Dear Mama, Papa, and girls:

We arrived here on schedule with no mishaps. It was a wonderful trip on the rails, despite the smoke and soot, for over 1000 miles. We passed much great farm country; though I don't know as I should care to live there. It is most all level; and without the hills it just isn't as pretty as back east. But as we got farther up into Wisconsin, the land grew progressively rolling. Of course the last twenty miles was on board stage, which proved to be a good uphill climb for the horses. I remarked to Mother Spooner that I bet they felt at home amongst the hills here; but Father Spooner said pshaw—these were nothing but mole hills, compared to Vermont's Green Mountains, where they hailed from.

The village of Loganville is set into a hillside, and a fairly steep one. Their church stands halfway up the hill; where it overlooks the village like a shepherd, keeping watch over its flock. Narrows Creek lies at the foot of the hill; and the slender valley it creates contains excellent farm land. Along the creek are located the gristmill, sawmill, and other industries; while just over the hills on either side are great sprawling valleys, similar to the Unadilla.

This village is nowhere near as big as Clarkville, but it is growing by leaps and bounds. Many of the settlers live in log cabins, tiny things chinked up with mortar; some built of all hand hewn logs. Those buildings made of sawed lumber are mostly unpainted, for the folks are just too busy to tend to such things for a while.

We four let the cabin that Mother Spooner wrote to us about, just a step from the village. It is a one-room affair; kitchen on one end, bedrooms on the other. Our

32

Joshua & Hannah Spooner

A log cabin in Loganville, Wisconsin

"bedrooms" are divided by a curtain; and we don't have much for furniture! So you tell Grandma that we are getting "broke in" to frontier life after all!

We have a big garden plot all ploughed and fitted, and have already put in our potatoes and peas. Mother Spooner has two hens setting, and when the chicks hatch, she is planning to share them with us.

Hank has gone into the wagon shop for the time being, making harnesses. The proprietor offered to let him use a corner of it, until he can get his own shop built. He figures on raising it before fall, if we can get the lumber. George is helping him; so we are pretty well set.

The climate here is much like home, maybe a mite warmer. Mother Spooner set out daffodil bulbs last year; they are in bloom now; and I don't think they are that early back home.

I hope this letter finds you all well. Give my love to Grandma, Grandpa and all my friends. Lute, George and Hank all send their love. Write soon.

Francie

"OOOOOOH, what a lark!" said I, then wailed plaintively, "Don't you wish we could go!"

"I'll be blamed if it doesn't *almost* make me want to," replied Mama, adding thoughtfully, "But we couldn't go, even for a visit; with Grandma so ailin'. Even if we could afford it——Guess we'd best get busy at *our* garden. Can't have those westerners beatin' us like that! Come on, girls! Jump into those dishes! I'm steppin' outside to ask Uncle Hosea if he'll favor us by plowin' and draggin' our chunk of ground soon's he finishes his. And tomorrow, be the Good Lord willin', we'll start plantin'!"

Chapter Five

Although Uncle Hosea was a prosperous business man, he was one of the working variety; having pursued the precise occupation of a wheel-wright in his youth, and usually dressed accordingly. At exactly seven, on a hazy summer morning, I heard his familiar "Whoa!" to Maggie, his sprightly black road mare, ring out. I raced to the front door, (still in my nightie), to see him hitch her to the post in our front yard. Uncle was all spruced up in his town clothes; and as I was idly wondering why, he spied me.

"What's the trouble, you're not up and about *yet?* I've come down apurpose to see if you'd go ridin' with me today."

"Where? Where? I danced excitedly. Uncle's rides were memorable.

"Oh, got to do a little buyin' today." He closed the door behind him and trailed me into the kitchen. "Thought mebbe we'd hit Sherburne afore the day's over. How's about borrowin' your youngun for the day, Chloe?" At Mama's assent, he continued, "Hustle into your bib and tucker now, time's awastin'. Can't afford to fool it away!"

I doubled up the stairs, and in ten minutes flat I was ready, togged in my second best. I clambered up into the high buggy seat beside Uncle, and waved a gay goodbye to little Meal, who watched pathetically from the front door.

Maggie pranced off, tossing her head and chewing the bit; with Uncle Hosea holding up on the lines. "She ain't been gettin' much exercise; but she'll feel different before the day's over. 'Course she's nothin' more'n a colt," he explained. She soon settled into a smooth and even gait, trotting over the level lands and tugging up the hills. The sweetish fragrance of clover in full bloom and new mown hay hung in the air; while the field corn was most knee high, as the old timers stated it should be on the Fourth of July. It was the third; and despite the early hour the day promised to be a sizzler. She'll be a hay-day!" Uncle observed.

We followed the Skaneatles Turnpike to De Lancy, a hamlet consisting of a few houses, a store and a postoffice. Here Uncle left the pike, and heading south we proceeded for about a mile, stopping frequently at such farmsteads as might have wool to sell. We then bore to the left, traveled east for a spell, and climbed through an obviously poorer section, which Uncle called Moscow. Reaching the summit of the steep ascent, and turning right once more, we found the hilltop road ahead and behind us as straight as an arrow, flanked on either side by large, rolling meadows. Directly to our right lay the remains of an abandoned church and graveyard, which, Uncle said, had been a Quaker meeting house; this area having been settled by Quakers some fifty years before. The land in this area looked fully as productive as that upon Beaver Hill; where we often visited; but the buildings in general were in a much poorer state of repair. I inquired of Uncle as to why this should be so.

"Well," he replied, stroking his chin with his free hand, "This is pretty deep for you; but most of these farms were leased from the time of first settlement until a couple of years ago; and some of them are still under lease."

"What is lease? And why does that make any difference?"

Uncle sighed. "I expect I might just as well go back to the beginnin; nothin else to pass away the time anyhow."

I fixed my eyes on Uncle; for I knew he was about to tell a tale. I guess that's why we hit it off so well; he loved to tell them, and I loved to listen.

"Now you know all about the Pilgrims, and how they came to New England."

I nodded eagerly.

"No need to go into that then. So, after the first few white men came to the New World, and found out things was good, the word got around, and they commenced followin' the leader, just like a bunch o' birds. Did you ever sight, in the fall o' the year, a couple o' dozen birds headin' south, all callin' their consarned fool heads off? Mebbe fifty, sixty more atrailin' behind; until finally, there just might be two-three-hundred, even a thousand, all together, afollowin' the leader. Now just what would you call that?"

"A flock of birds, migrating for the winter!" I piped up eagerly.

"Right you are!" he commended me, "and ever since man's beginning there have been times when he has migrated, too, for one reason or another. So, after the Pilgrims once settled down at Plymouth Rock they began to multiply, and soon had to start spreadin out, in search of enough land to take care of themselves. Of course, other settlers were comin'; in ever increasing numbers each year, on the boats from England, mostly. Some remained in Massachusetts, some made their way down the coast, to Connecticut and Rhode Island. But always they hung rather close to the shore, for several reasons. One, to venture farther inland was to run the risk of Indian attack, for the land there was in the hands of the red men. Two, near the shore line and harbors they kept in close touch with the Mother country, and in this manner they could procure the supplies they deemed necessary to their way of life, as long as they had the currency to pay for them, or something to exchange. The

36

third reason, of course, was the abundant supply of food available from the ocean."

"But after these people had been in this region about one-hundred and fifty years, they realized that some of them must leave, to seek out new territory. The majority were farmers, and stories reached their ears regarding land—plentiful land, much more productive and less stony than that on which they labored to eek out a livin! Now, previous to the Revolution, their ties would have been much more difficult to break; for at that time their villages were neat, compact, and their homes comfortable, much like those in the Mother country. But durin' the war everythin' changed; there was no more trade with England, and the colonists had to learn to shift for themselves."

Uncle closed his eyes, and rubbed his head with his free hand, obviously thinking deeply; then continued, "Close upon the heels of the peace treaties with England were several new treaties between the Indian nations and our newly formed government, which opened up vast new tracts of land, available for pioneerin'." One was the treaty of 1784, by which the Iroquois Nation ceded to the Federal government the lands west of Canada Creek and the Una-dilla River. Prior to this date these streams, which formed a boundary known as the "Line Of Property", divided white and red men's territories, all the way south to the Pennsylvania border. In 1791, having completed the surveyal and division of certain of these lands west of the Line Of Property, the State of New York decided to sell these holdings to individuals for homesteading. Accordingly, they set a minimum price of three shillings per acre, which amounted to about seventy-two cents. A notice of the forthcoming sale of such lands was posted in the Albany and New York newspapers."

We stopped by a stream and Maggie sniffed the bubbling water carefullly, then tasted, and drank. "Takes a mighty warm day for her to do that," observed Uncle. "A horse is mighty particular about his drink, even when it's pure mountain water."

"So then what happened?" I prodded, anxious that he should finish his discourse, before he began one on horses, and their habits.

"Now, where was I? Oh, yes, about the sale of lands. Well, even with all this, it still took something to drive them from their homes, sort of the straw that broke the camel's back, you might say. It came in the form of a tropical hurricane, one of the kind generally known in the south seas, but this one blew far north and was exceedingly destructive. At this time there were established forts at

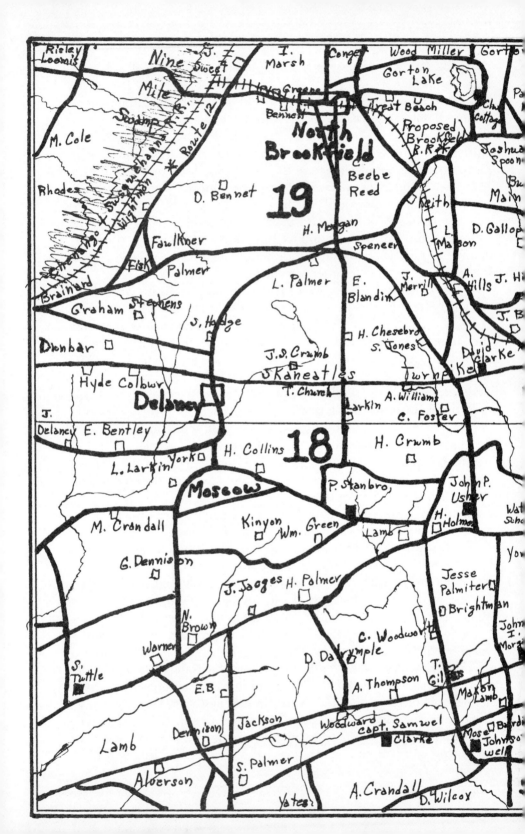

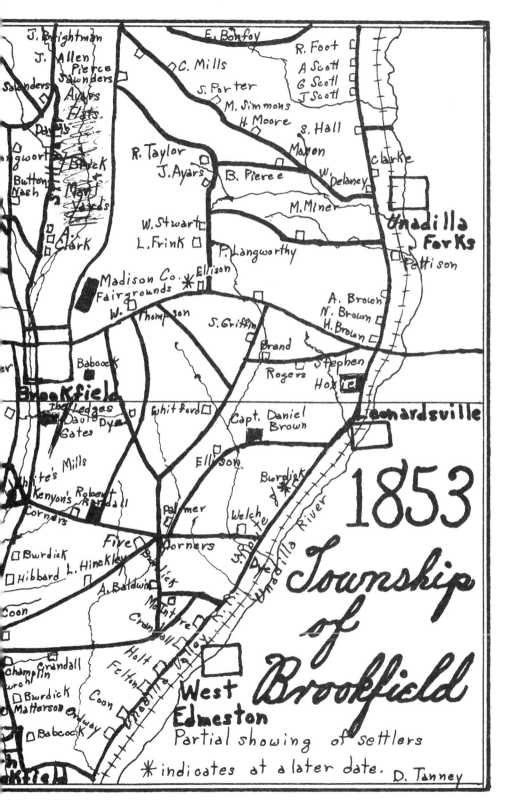

Map of Brookfield Township

Herkimer, Cherry Valley, Stanwix and Schuyler, but none in this locality."

"One lone white man had settled in this region, Percifer Carr, who, with his wife, had been overseer of the Colonel Edmeston estates, located on the east bank of the Unadilla River, for some twenty years. The Carrs, of necessity, remained loyal to the Crown of England, and therefore were classified as "Tories." Durin' the War of Independence a couple of skirmishes took place upon their estate. Three colonial milita scouts were killed in the first battle; and in the one which followed, a band of Oneida Indians, loyal to the colonists, killed Carr's two servants, and carried Mr. and Mrs. Carr off to Canada, as prisoners. It was not until 1783 that they were released, and returned to start completely anew. Despite the destruction of most of their previous efforts upon the estate, the Carrs were hospitable folk, and newcomers to the region were often directed to the Carr's doorstep."

"In 1791 a traveler through the area and his accompanying party visited at the Carr's, with the intentions of journeyin' much farther on, to the Genesee River Valley. Carr informed them that there was plenty of virgin land available, just across the river; land on which, with the exception of the surveyors, white men had never set foot. The party's leader was Capt. Daniel Brown, a clothier from Stonington, and he was no less than sixty-six years young. I say young, for the love of adventure was still in his heart, as he sought to establish his sons in the new and promising land. This he accomplished, for he lived upon the homestead they established another twenty-five years. But I'm getting ahead of my story. The Captain, his family, and the friends in his company crossed the river, where each selected a spot of ground upon which he busied himself."

"Captain Brown's site was about a mile or so due west of what is now Leonardsville, and included a mill site, upon which he erected the first saw mill, in 1792. Here the family erected a cabin and made ready to pass the winter of '91; but with the advent of the brisk autumn winds, the others in his party remigrated to their homes in Stonington. Browsing their cattle in the woods, and cuttin' such brush hay as they could scrape up for fodder, while grubbin' their livelihood off the deer and wild life, the Brown family put in a real tough winter; but they and their stock survived; and Captain Brown has gone down in history as our township's first actual settler."

"But, Uncle, someone said that a man called Hoxie was the first settler here!"

"To tell the truth," smiled Uncle, "they were right. Stephen Hoxie was a land agent, and he and Phineas Babcock purchased thirteen lots in the southeast corner of the nineteenth township, early in the spring of '91, before Brown arrived. Now their land was purchased for about fifty cents an acre, apparently in advance of the new state law. But the owners of these lots, though clearing them in '91, did not settle here until '92—which explains why Capt. Brown captured the honors."

"But let me get back to the point of my story. As it turned out, the buyers of these lots, all purchased in 1791, in advance of the advertised sale of lands, were the lucky ones. As we say, referring again to our feathered friends, it's the early bird that catches the worm. The land sale was poorly attended, owing to a brief notice, and lack of communication; with the result that those in closest touch with Albany and New York through governmental or business connections, were in the best position to buy. Wealthy capitalists, always on the alert for a lucrative investment, snapped up the remaining unsold lands in the nineteenth township, for seventy-three cents an acre, and the entire eighteenth for seventy-eight cents per acre. Although in reality there were three buyers of this property, Michael Myers, Jedediah Sanger, and John I. Morgan, most of the land in the township of Brookfield eventually came under the jurisdiction of Mr. Morgan, who had surveyed a large percentage of the territory."

"Gracious, Uncle, you know lots of history!"

"I make it my business, Doshie. A good Democrat knows his politics; and a good politician knows his history."

"And is a storyteller, too?"

Uncle chuckled. "It's true. Every mite of it. Well, for the next four or five years the traffic on the trails leadin' west became heavier, as family after family followed the lead of their friends and relatives. But these unfortunate immigrants were faced with a difficult choice; either they might lease their land from the landowners, under the Perpetual lease system, for perhaps as long a period as one-hundred years, or they could purchase it, at a price, which in some cases was advanced to as much as fourteen dollars an acre. Now, the State had not intended this deplorable situation, and had even originally planned to reserve two separate lots of two-hundred and fifty acres each, in the center of the township, to be used for purposes of religion and education. But these plans had been lost in the shuffle, and the incoming settlers found their situation considerably less than anticipated. If they chose to lease their land, which,

Stones of Capt. Daniel Brown & wife Abagail, on their original farm, overlooking Unadilla Valley

Hotel, Main St., Brookfield. Built in 1815 by Ethan Babcock, who in 1793 erected the first cabin in Beaver Valley. Photo about 1900.

for lack of capital, most of them were forced to do, their rent was payable in Albany, on a yearly basis, in products of the soil. This meant wagon loads of wheat, and long so-called trains of cattle, sheep, hogs, geese and what-have-you, were continually being drived eastward."

"Thereupon began the rise of the turnpike era. Turnpikes were well constructed, built upon a stone base of as much as ten inches, but they were a trifle expensive for travel. The cost of moving freight on them averaged about ten dollars a ton, per one-hundred miles. Within a short time there were in New York State alone, one hundred and thirty-five turnpike companies, comprised of wealthy stockholders."

"Again the poor settlers had little choice. Their contract called for goods delivered to Albany, and if they chose to travel an unimproved road, they ran the risk of broken wheels, axles, less mileage per day, and so on. The speculators made money hand over fist from the little fellows, both on the land and the pikes. Added to this was the fact that if the settlers *should* be fortunate enough to improve their holdings, the improvements would be added to the eventual purchase price of the farm. Not much of an incentive, was it?"

"Now maybe you've heard of Locust Lodge, below the village? Well, that place is the old John Morgan homestead°—the center of a huge estate, and 't'was his summer home for years. John had an only child—a daughter, Catherine. She married a prominent man— John Dix; and the entire Morgan estate was in their custody, 'til about three years ago; when Wait Clarke concluded to take the bull by the horns, and discuss the hopeless situation of the lessees with John Dix.† Worked out right well for everybody. Wait persuaded Dix to sell their holdings, at humane prices; and Wait came out with the job of handlin' the real estate! 'Sa mighty big job—the Morgan estate included holdings in Oneida, Herkimer, Chenango, and Madison Counties."

"A while back I mentioned the eighteenth and nineteenth districts. The southern half of the township is the eighteenth, northern is the nineteenth. Dividin' line runs east and west, just below your house. Therefore we are now passin' through the eighteenth dis-

° Present home of Paul Paulson.
† John Dix—later became Civil War General & Elected N.Y. State Governor in 1872.

trict, and it don't take a real smart feller to see that most of these places look kind of backward, as compared to those over the hill, toward Leonardsville, where the early birds nabbed their land just in time."

"You know, a lot of these folks amovin' west now, might have stayed here, if only they could have *owned* this land a little sooner. You take Josh Spooner, for example. Just about forty years old, he was, 'fore he got enough goods together to dare to make his move. Over the Green Mountains he rolls, two great ridges of 'em. Winds up in Cedarville, hopin' to make a better livin', but the farm's bought out from under him. He tries it in Brookfield for a spell; can't make it here, 'cause he can't buy, and the rent is sky-high. He moves again. Same thing all his life. Sixty-three years old now, and just bought his first parcel of ground. Time he gets it half worked up, he'll be alayin' in his grave. The world just ain't right for the little guy. But Josh's just one of them—Yorks, Browns, Collins, Burdicks, I don't know how many have left already. Another migration, aheadin' to the west."

"Come to think about it, I guess you might liken those speculators to the blue jay. Such a big, splendid, and showy bird, but the jays go around arobbin' the little bird's nests, eatin' the eggs and such. Now mind, I ain't sayin' that these fellows *robbed* the poor folks, just that they were kind of hoggish, like the jay. Yep, there's a time when the big fellows can really do a service to the little ones in a community, and a time when they can't." Uncle never did elaborate on this last statement, for we had pulled up in the yard of another sheep farmer.

The transaction over, Uncle returned, took up the lines, and we were off again. "Uncle," I coaxed, "when did you come to Brookfield?"

"1801, and our village wasn't Clarkville then, 'twas Beaver Creek. I was four years old, just about knee high to a grasshopper."

"You remember it?"

"Yeeup! Just about the first thing I do remember. The old oxteam, ploddin' ahead of the covered wagon, with Pa, Ma, and us nine kids. Ma rode a good share of the way on horseback, to save the oxen. Took us most three weeks to get here. Pa settled over here in the eighteenth district, 'bout down on the Columbus town line. When we boys got old enough to work, we came over to the village. Pa followed us in 1818, after he got his pension. Your Grandfather, David, settled west of the village, where he lives now. Joseph joined the Navy, and became Colonel of his regiment, in the War of 1812. Then he started smithing, and entered politics on the side."

"Then my Grandma Clarke was here before Grandpa?"

"Yep, her folks was Asa and Thede Frink, some of the first to settle the valley."

"Grandma came in '96, when she was eight years old," I broke in eagerly. "Five families came together, and located along the creek. Great-Grandpa Frink lived across the flat,° next to the cemetery. Cemetery land came off his lot, so Grandma says."

"Now let me tell you something," continued Uncle, obviously caught up in the past, "my Pa was *pretty* well off at one time. He made out right good in the Army, became a Captain, and after the War he saw fittin' to re-enlist in the reserves. 'Course we lived near to the coast, in Westerly, where shippin' and fishin' was the major industry. By investin' his money, he saved enough to buy his own sloop. 'Twas makin' him a tidy profit 'till sloop, cargo, and all was captured by a band of marauders."

"Pirates?"

"Guess that's what you'd call 'em. Pa figured the army'd help him recover it; but they didn't aim to get involved in such trifles. Naturally Pa was pretty sore about it; and when his term was up, he left the service. Havin' no livelihood, and little to invest, he figured we'd strike out for new ground, along with the rest of the flock. Whooaa, Maggie!"

We rolled into the drive of another farmstead; and I held the reins while Uncle Hosea stepped aside to bargain for the wool he hoped to buy.

A couple of barefooted girls approached me timidly. "Oh, he's beautiful!" exclaimed the first. "Does he bite?"

"*Her* name is Maggie," I replied, "and Uncle wouldn't own a horse unless it *was* beautiful! Go ahead and pet her—she's safe."

"Oooh! Do see the buggy trappings, Sally!" cried the other.

"It's *custom made* for Uncle. His son, La Fayette Clarke, manufactures buggies and carriages in Clarkeville."

"I ain't never been to Clarkville." remarked the first wistfully. "Is it a nice, big place?"

"Not as big as Sherburne, where we're going; but it's a right nice place. It's named after Uncle's brother, Judge Joseph Clarke. He was in the assembly, down in Albany, and he was a *Senator*, too. Fact is, the Clarkes have had a finger in most of the pies around," I answered, with a twinge of hauteur.

° Home of the late Jean F. Spooner.

Uncle's droning voice came to a sudden halt. He returned to the buggy; slapped Maggie lightly, and was unusually quiet 'till our arrival in Sherburne village.

The day was getting on, and the town was alive with well-dressed citizens.

"Doshie," Uncle stared at my polished but obviously too short shoes, "I declare you need new footwear!" and straight into the cobblers he strode. The shoe-store was lined with shelves of lovely, ready-made styles. At home the cobbler made our slippers to order, though mine were generally hand-me-downs, from my sisters re-heeled and re-tapped for me. The choice was agonizing; but I at last made my selection; Uncle paid the clerk, and we stepped outside.

"Wheeew! Must be just about noon!" observed Uncle, squinting toward the sun, and checking his big gold pocket watch for confirmation. " 'Pears to me the corner hotel might have a good bite to eat; maybe even a little cooler in there."

Keeping up with Uncle's strides was always a bit complicated, as Uncle was a big man; and was all the more complicated now, since attired in my second best, and with *brand new* slippers on my feet, I felt I should mince along in the manner properly befitting a lady.

The hotel, to my mind, was a palace. Far away ceilings and monstrous windows dwarfed the tables; while magnificent hanging chandeliers dominated the room. Nothing I had seen in my twelve years could equal them; and I vowed silently that if ever I owned a house, I would have chandeliers just like those.

Uncle ordered the daily special, plus strawberry shortcake for dessert.

"Strawberry shortcake! We don't have berries around home much before August!" I whispered, as I magnanimously ordered the same.

Our shortcake was delicious, and topped with heaps of whipped cream. Uncle was still silent, as if something were on his mind. At last he dipped his fork into the cream, held it aloft, and scrutinized it thoughtfully. "See this whipped cream, Doshie? Looks pretty good, doesn't it? Have *you* ever whipped any?"

I nodded, wondering what was coming next.

"What puffs the cream up?" he continued. "What changes it from a liquid to a semi-solid? The air—it's the air that's beat into it. Now the reason that it looks and tastes so good is that *just the right amount of air* is beat into it. But have you ever beat any too long—

got *too much air* into it? Then what happened? Made butter—that's what—it was spoiled as far as whipped cream goes! You know, Doshie, people are just like that cream, they all need a *little air* whipped into them, to give them confidence, so's they can do their best. But not *too much air*, Doshie, not too much!"

I gulped, and digested the moral of his illustration along with the shortcake. It was a lesson I never forgot.

Having stressed his point, Uncle never mentioned the incident again, and on our return trip he was particularly gay. Maggie had been fed, watered, and rested in a livery stable; and appeared as fresh as ever. As she jogged along at an easy pace, we overtook a slowly traveling buggy. Apparently he had been waiting for someone to do just that, for as we started to pass, he immediately let out his horse. Maggie began to snort and prance, since it was seldom she was outdone on the road.

"Let her out! Let her out! I begged, tugging at Uncle's shirt sleeve. "I know Maggie can beat him any old day! I bet a penny she can!"

With a grin and a jerk of his head, Uncle Hosea loosed the lines; I clutched the dashboard, and Maggie lurched forward, bent on passing the other rig. She was beside it in a second, and for about a quarter of a mile we raced neck and neck; until Uncle gave Maggie her head, at which point we lost the other horse in our dust! Guffawing, he brought the snorting mare back under control, pulled up under a shade tree, and fished into his pocket for my penny.

It was along towards evening when we reached Grandpa Clarke's, about a mile west of Clarkville, where Uncle paused to rest Maggie and say Hello. There sad news awaited us, for we found that Grandma had suffered a paralyzing stroke that very day. Three days later, on the sixth of July, she passed from this world into the better one she was always certain had existed.

Chapter Six

It was a humid July evening in Loganville, Wisconsin. Hank stretched his lanky frame across the homespun bedsheet, and spoke thoughtfully. "Honey, there's been something on my mind all day, in fact, for a week now. I guess now's as good a time to get it off my chest as any. You know, Francie, I believe the folks are right. Now *is* the time for us to get ahead, and we *are* fools if we don't take advantage of it! Here we have the most beautiful land that lays outdoors all around us; and what are we doing about it? Absolutely nothing! Francie, have you noticed the way the crops take hold 'round here? You've never seen anything that can match them, nor I either! 'Course I know this's virgin soil, but there is just too much bed rock and shale back home. There's stone around here, lots of it, but it's small stuff; stuff a man can handle easy. It's about the same clay sub-soil that we have at home, but this earth here is different —it's loamy—beautiful loam. The growing season must be well nigh a month longer than it is back east. Francie, I *know* we can make a go of it at farming, maybe someday we'll raise a flock of younguns, and they'll need something to keep them out of mischief!" He grinned. "What say we try our hand at it? The farm, I mean," he added hastily.

Francie paused in the methodical brushing of her hair. It was nearly waist length, and every evening, following it's one-hundred strokes, she braided the auburn tresses. She was glad he had approached her at such a moment, for perhaps with the brushing he might not so easily perceive her mind. "Why Hank, I really don't know what to say. You took me by surprise. I thought you were happy with the harness shop. I know you're doing a good business now, and there's not any other around to run you competition."

"Gosh, I still like the harness work, Francie, don't take me wrong. The business gives me opportunities to meet a lot of people. I like people. Get to see a lot of country, too, but I guess probably that's my downfall. I meet these fellows; they all want to show me what a great spread they own. Proud as punch, they are! And what do *I* have? A handful of tools, some leather and trimmings! A harness I can brag about—on some *other* man's horse. Honey, they show me their grain fields, their barns, their stock, and they're *proud*. Means the whole world to them, next to their families. And when they grow old, they'll have something to fall back on; but we ain't going to have anything! You know, Pa says I can have a quarter of his land, just by paying for it. With Albert gone, it's too much for him, Beaman and Leonard to handle. Then there is the Bliven forty I can get, 'sides a ten-acre chunk Bliven's begging me to take. All told, that would make us ninety acres; and I *know* we can make a darn good living on that! I've got it all figured out, just how I could do it. We could stay right on in town for the time being, and I could work on the harnesses long's I have orders. And when orders were slow, I could be out breaking sod; maybe commence building us a little house between times. T'won't need to be very big, leastways, not 'till we get those kids!"

"Why don't we think about it a little longer," replied Francie. Her hands quivered in spite of herself. The very thought of being trapped in this unfamiliar land, for the rest of her life, frightened her. She knew she was wrong; all the instructions she had ever received shouted that her responsibility was to submit herself to her husband, and his will—but—never to see Mama, Papa, her sisters, and friends! "You've done so well at business for yourself that it's hard to picture you as a farmer," she parried. Then, to avoid further deliberation, she blew out the candle, snuggled down close beside her husband, and kissed him softly. Now she could forget the troubling issue at hand, in the comfort of his unflinching love.

Morning followed, projecting their problem in the brighter light of day. Up to this point, living here hadn't bothered this much, since it had always seemed a temporary measure; certain to be followed by a return to York State sometime. But to own land meant forever, to live, die, and be buried here!

"You know, Lute, I'm no farmer," she fretted, "and I don't know as I can make myself out to be one. You know how hard Hannah works, she's every bit as good a farmer as Josh."

"Oh, Francie, you're being silly. Hank doesn't expect you to go out and break the land! All he expects, or hopes for, is a little understanding and faith in what his heart is set on doing. You know, you have one of the best husbands in the world, he's loving, kind, and true. I only wish I could say the same for George—what if you had one like him, who turns his head at every new skirt he sees! I wish George would buy *us* a farm, *way* back in the hills; maybe I'd have him to myself for awhile, instead of only when he's tired, or has to come home for some clean clothes and something to eat! You're going to have to make a *few* sacrifices; everything can't be soft and easy; Hank's willing to work night and day for you, if necessary!"

"Lute, you sound more like Grandma every day; but I s'pose you are right. I *do* have a lot to be thankful for; he *is* the greatest fellow in the world, and tonight I'm going to tell him so; and also to go ahead with his plans for that farm!"

Within a short time Hank began breaking a couple of steers for

49

a yoke of oxen. The dumb beasts consumed most of his leisure for two months, and called for more patience than talent; though usually a tremendous whack on their heads succeeded in driving the lesson home, when all other means had failed. As their knowledge increased, they performed simple tasks, such as drawing in fence rails; and their master commenced a rail fence around the plot where he intended to sow his wheat.

Francie joined him often; holding the oxen when needed, and lending a hand when possible. Together they found a new closeness, in working toward a common goal. And when the fall rains had loosened the earth sufficiently, he hooked the steers ahead of the walking plow, and set about breaking up the sod. The harness orders piled upon each other; and Hank was indeed busy day and night.

In the meantime, George exhibited discernible symptoms of his chronic disease, the wanderlust. To break the land involved more effort than he cared to invest; and the available women in town were few; since most, like their mates, seemed absorbed only with the success or failure of their individual enterprise. Quite a number of Clarkeville's women were undoubtedly grieving his prolonged absence. But lady luck was with George, for a message arrived at this very time, detailing the prolonged illness of his Mother. This was all the excuse George needed. Reluctantly, Lute packed their belongings, bid a wistful goodbye to Hank and Francie, and they were gone.

The last tie with home was severed now. Francie's gaze focused on the departing stage until it vanished in its dust. A reluctant tear coursed down her cheek; and she dabbed it hastily with her glove.

"You all right, honey?" queried Hank anxiously.

"It's just a speck of dust that blew in my eye. It'll go away."

"You know, you look mighty pretty today, Mrs. Spooner. In fact, I'd say you are without doubt the prettiest girl in all of Sauk County! And twice as sweet! It's a darn shame to spoil such a pretty portrait by a speck of dust." He leaned forward, kissed the tear stained streak, and assisted her into his Father's borrowed buggy. "That a new bonnet?"

"Lute helped me with it yesterday. Something to remember her by, she said." Her lips trembled perceptibly, and she rushed on, "She's pretty clever with millinery, you know. I've been telling her she should go into business. Don't you agree?"

"She might be forced to, before it's done. It's a hell of a shame that a nice girl like Lute got stuck with him, but we'll keep hoping for the best. 'S'pose it would take a miracle to change him. Wonder what they'll do when they get back home.—Say, would you like to go up to Ma's for a while, honey? We're almost there, and I can just as well close up shop for a while longer."

"If *you* want to."

"Francie—Oh, honey! I know what you're going through, believe me, and I know it's going to be doggone lonesome around here for some time. Let's hope Ma will ask us to dinner; it'll help you over the hump. Ma's been through this, too, you know, when they left Vermont. She knows how it is. You know, Ma thinks the world of you and Nett. I've heard her say you're like her own daughters—the ones she wanted, but never had. I know Ma helped Nett a lot, before Nett started Delten Academy. Try her, Francie. You need someone for woman talk; and maybe Ma does, too. Whoa —boy.—Ma? Brought company for you!" The gaiety of his greeting belied the fear that gnawed at his being, and the doubts which knotted his abdomen.

» » » » » « « « « «

As the season progressed Francie appeared to enjoy her new environment, but when the cold winter skies descended, a cloud of gloom settled over her being. She endeavored to dispel it by inking Christmas greetings to the family back in Clarkville, and with the construction of little gifts for the Spooner household. A family holiday spent with Mother and Father Spooner, their sons, William's family, Antionette, and little daughter, Etta, could not assuage the longing in her heart, on her first Christmas apart from home. Her feelings were intensified when she received a letter from Sarah Ann:

Clarkville, N. Y.
December 10, 1857

Dear Francie and Hank,

I'd like you two to be among the first to hear my news. George Woodworth and I are being married in January. You remember George, don't you? We'll be living here in town, with his Mother.

Mama, the girls, Aunts Thede and Gracia are holding a quilting bee for me after Christmas. Lute and George are living at Fly Creek now. Lute was over to give me a hand with my outfit, and also one for Dosh, who is standing up with me. Surprised? We get along famously now, maybe because she knows she's getting rid of me, at last! She's really not such a bad sister—we just couldn't see eye to eye before. Little Meal is all agog; she is surely growing up fast!

We have invited only his immediate family, and mine. I wish you and Hank could be here. Love from your sister, Sate"

"George Woodworth?" puzzled Hank. "Who is he?"

"Son of Samuel and Polly Babcock Woodworth. Polly's father was Ethan Babcock, first settler in the Beaver Valley. And you probably never heard of Sam, 'cause he's been gone quite a while."

"Dead?"

"I doubt it. Sam and Polly never got along very well. One day, after their children had grown, he shaved, changed his clothes, placed a small mirror in the upper window ° where he could see it, on his way out of town, and just vanished. Poor Polly left the mirror in that window foreverafter; hoping, I guess, that if Sam happened back he'd take it for a welcome sign. A mirror was used for that purpose in those days, after a quarrel. At any rate, if Sam was around to see the mirror, he ignored it. Maybe he enjoyed his freedom, or maybe it was his way of torturing her. I surely hope Sate's marriage turns out better than that!"

"I imagine Sate knows what she's doing," returned Hank, studying his wife intently. In unguarded moments he detected the intense longing for home, which she tried vainly to conceal. "Would you like to go back east for the wedding, honey?"

"Oh, Hank, that's so sweet of you, but I wish you wouldn't ask me. You know we can't afford it. You can't spare the time to go, and I certainly wouldn't go without you. I'll think of something nice I can make to send them, and that will be almost as good as being there myself."

» » » » » » « « « « « «

Francie deluded herself into believing her depression was known only to herself, but even Josh and Hannah noticed. Throughout the long winter, while Hank busied himself cutting

° Present home of James Jennings, Church St.

wood, splitting rails, delivering logs at the saw-mill, and making harnesses, Francie occupied herself with baking, sewing, and helping Hannah. Even so, the days loomed ahead; endless, dark and lonely.

But at last it was spring, the birds returned to the valley, the willows along the banks of Narrows Creek budded, and the brown sodden remnants of last year's grasses sent forth their beauteous emerald green shoots. Then with the spring came her reprieve, it was easier for her to smile, the constant lump in her throat subsided for a time; and she praised the Lord for her deliverance.

The oxen, according to Hank, were "going to pan out to be the pullingest yoke in all of Sauk County"; and the field of early planted wheat surpassed any he'd ever seen in Clarkville, or surrounding territory. Another garden was planted; and Francie and Hank knew happiness.

» » » » » « « « « « «

Chapter Seven

Back in Clarkville, the summer was rather uneventful. Fordy and Mae were in town again. Fordy, of working age now, was employed in the fields by local farmers. When the teasels or hops were ready for harvest, all three of us were engaged by Uncle Hosea; and since Fordy picked somewhat faster than we girls, he assisted us in filling our boxes. Prior to picking time, we also worked in the hops; grubbing, trimming, and tying the best vines up onto the tall cedar poles. The hops were fast growing; and their vines wound the poles in no time.

Now and then Uncle would stop by to check up on our progress. We soon learned to gauge his mood; if it were unhurried, we sought to engage him in conversation. This was not a difficult chore; for it was Uncle's favorite pastime; especially when the subject evolved around horses, history, politics, or his family. Uncle was a singer, the possessor of a booming bass voice; and he had worked out a musical rhythm, to which he recited the names of his grown children, in order. "It went like this: "Rudolphus Leroy, John Delancy, Marquis LaFayette, Albert Montmorenci, Barbara Marie,

Antionette Electa, Hosea Moreau, and Norman Leslie," and during this simple sing-song we three would clap our hands and jog to the beat. If we could really wind him up, thereby gaining a welcome reprieve from the day's labors; he would recite poetry—of the somewhat less than classical variety. These three ditties were his favorites—which he vowed his children memorized during recess:

> "Half an inch, half an inch, half an inch shorter,
> The skirts are the same of Mother and daughter.
> When the wind blows, each one of them shows,
> Half an inch, half an inch, more than she oughter."

Minds ran to skirt length in the early 1800's; for this was his second recitation.

> "Mary had a little' skirt, so neat, so bright, so airy,
> It never showed a speck of dirt, but it surely did show Mary."

The following ode he reserved, a moral for green apple season; lest any thirsty, or hungry child be tempted to partake.

> "There was a young lady of Rhyde, of eating green apples she died. Within the lamented, they quickly fermented, and made cider, inside her insides."

It was easy to see why Great-Uncle Hosea Clarke had no problem in securing ample field hands, from among the village children.

Each of the youngsters had his own special use for the change he earned. Most parents demanded the lion's share of his wages; but generously allotted their offspring enough of his earnings to thoroughly enjoy the Brookfield Fair. Without doubt the fair was the most colossal event of the year. It was chartered in 1839, but in '56 it had been incorporated, and much improved since that date.

Fordy, Mae, Meal and I attended opening day that year together. We did not have far to go, since the "grounds" were Oliver Babcock's meadow, bounded North by the Academy, and south by Uncle Hosea's meadow. Concessions and stands were filled by local people. One of them had installed herself in a fortune telling tent, just for fun. Dressed in gypsy garb, she stood outside her carpet doorway, drumming up trade, as we strolled by.

"Come on in, young lady!" she cackled, looking me straight in the eye. "Have your fortune told! It won't cost you a penny!"

I was tempted. Mama had warned me that real gypsies tried to take your money. But this costumed person had stated it would cost nothing! Free! How could Mama possibly object! But just to be on the safe side, I would leave Meal in possession of my handkerchief; for in its corner were my remaining coins, securely tied. Acting entirely upon impulse, I dashed inside, while the gaily bedecked old woman pulled the carpet behind us.

"Give me your hand," she directed; after seating me. She turned my palm upward and gasped. "Young lady! Your palm is so clear—the lines so distinct! But let me explain; these lines are your life's mirror—for the future, of course. Yours will be no ordinary life —you will see your share of joys; but more than your share of tragedy. You must learn, now, to place your faith in someone greater than yourself; for you, alone, will have to bridge life's gaps. Now this particular line tells me you will travel; while this one represents the men, who will play an important part in your life. Now—if you wish me to continue—to read the other lines—and there are many—I must have silver; with which to cross my palm."

"No—no, thank you" I quavered, "that's enough." A strange fear of the future, coupled with fear of the present, for having disregarded Mama's admonition, had overtaken me. I yanked my hand from the gnarled old one, bolted from the chair, and ducked under the carpet curtain. To my relief, Fordy, Mae, and Meal were keeping vigil just outside the tent.

My hurried exit brought a barrage of questions. "What ever dic' she say?" "How much did she charge?" "Why are you so white, Do.;h? Are you scared?"

"Oh, it's all just a lot of hokus-pokus, pure stupid nonsense," I returned casually, attempting to dismiss the disturbing encounter from my mind.—But that night, in the quiet of my room, even long after the echo of Papa's nocturnal snoring had commenced it's peculiar rhythm, I wondered, as I was destined to wonder through the coming years—*Was* it just pure stupid nonsense?

» » » » » » « « « « « «

In August I dashed home with a letter from Loganville, then waited, breathlessly, while Mama scanned it; and finally decided to read it aloud. "Dear Mama," she read, with a strange mixture of pleasure and worry mirrored on her face. "I'm writing this to you alone, since we'd like you and Papa to be the first to know. You are going to be grandparents! Hank is proud as a peacock, hoping for a boy, of course. But Mama, I'm scared. There's no doctor around here for miles, only a midwife. And I've heard so many tales! If only we could come back home, so I could be near you, and Dr. Bailey! All these women out here are so brave, that I'm afraid to tell anyone, even Hank, how scared I really am. I pretend I'm brave, too, but when Hank's gone, and I'm alone, I get to thinking about what could happen, when the baby comes.

Hank is doing right well on the farm. Our grain and garden look first rate. His harness business is doing great, and I dassn't say anything to upset him. He is so good to me.

I'm getting quite a stock of baby things sewed up, and some knitted sweaters and booties, too. It's a January baby, so he'll need them. Say hello to all the girls and tell them they're going to be aunts! I miss you all.

Love from Francie

Mama's brow furrowed a little more deeply, as she laid the letter aside, and murmured, "I guess you never quit worrying about them; even when they're grown women, and half-way across the country." Next day she penned the following:

Clarkville, N. Y.
August 25, 1858

Dear Francie;

Rec'd your welcome letter yesterday. Papa could hardly wait to get to the fork shop this morning and tell the boys. The girls are all excited, and of course I'm pleased. I'm only sorry that you don't take more after Grandma, and a little less after me. Papa and I agree that if you can get acquainted with the midwife, (and even tell her of your fears, you are not the first mother-to-be to be afraid, you know) you will probably rest much easier. It's natural to want to come home, but if you can manage to adjust to your surroundings until after the baby comes, we're sure you can be more than happy right out there. A child will be your crowning joy, Francie, and upon its birth, you, yourself, will cease to be a child. A whole new generation will have been born, with you and Hank at the head. Look at it as a glorious beginning, and the fear will cease with the joy of anticipation. Try to think of Hannah as if she were your own mother; confide in her. She must have known many such trials.

You are a fortunate girl. Lute's heart aches for a baby; though no doubt it's best they don't have one. They are staying with old George now, and George helps out in the mill, when he's a mind to. Lute keeps busy with her millinery and sewing. So count your blessings. The rest of us are well. Give my regards to Hank and all the Spooners.

With love, from your Mother

Francie concealed the letter from Hank, and courageously tried to follow its good advice. But try as she might, rather than subsiding, her fears mounted daily. She labored tirelessly in their garden, and in the harvest of its products. Often she hiked into the village, for they were still leasing the tiny log cabin. Now and again Hank took her, for the day, out to the Spooner household. But nothing, not even the good natured joshing of Hank's kid brothers, Beaman and Leonard, seemed to dispell her cloud of gloom.

Hank watched the saddened, thinning features with concern. Slowly came the realization that there was something inside her being; which so longed for family and the hills of home; a something so deeply rooted, that even his love was powerless to overcome. At this point, he arose early one morning, and upon opening the shop, went directly to the work shelf, where he took out a sheet of paper, and laboriously began to write:

Loganville, Wis.
Oct. 17, 1858

Dear Folks;

I hope this letter will not get you all upset, but Francie has not been well. Last week I decided to take her to Lone Rock for a visit to the Dr. He calls it nostalgia, fancy word for homesick, and says it's complicated by her condition. My folks, the boys, Nett, and everyone have tired to jolly her up, but she's in a world of her own. Doc advised us to return east, at least until after baby's born. Otherwise, he says, neither one may make it.

I calculate to let out my ox-yoke until spring; and in case I don't make it back then, Johnson will lease my farm. We have our harvest all in, so as soon as we can pack, we'll be heading east. If you know of any places for hire back there, I would be obliged if you would make arrangements about one of them for us. This from—Hank"

He finished the day's chores with a heart fully as heavy as Francie's, then made his weary way homeward. All his hopes and dreams were securely tied in and about this little mid-western town; the rail fence, so straight and strong, the pile of lumber for the house, which he had hoped to erect during the winter, in time for the birth of the child, the ten-acre chunk, which held the still golden stubbles of the greatest wheat crop he'd ever feasted his eyes on, and the oxen, dumb animals which he, with pardonable pride, had broken to command until they seemed nearly human. Well, hopes and dreams were only fading things, subject to changes over the years, and subject also to the well-being of humans. Certainly no dreams or material objectives were as important as his wife and child to be. He threw open the cabin door, and with a brightness that perpetrated one of the greatest lies he had ever told his beloved mate, related to her his uncontrollable joy, at being able to make arrangements for his possessions, that they might enjoy a much needed vacation back east.

» » » » » » « « « « « «

Thanksgiving, 1858, was indeed a day to be thankful, for we were all together again! Even Grandpa came down from the farm, to recite the annual prayer, now slightly re-worded, since Grandma's passing.

We were unprepared for the drastic change in Francie, despite the advance communication from Hank. Indeed, she looked as if she were at the very threshold of death's door; and that with only the slightest breeze she might slip through the tiny chink which separated the two. But soon, amongst her loved ones and accustomed surroundings, the bloom began to return to her cheeks, and the sparkle to her eyes; so that at the Thanksgiving table we felt we truly had much for which to be grateful.

Papa had located a house for Francie and Hank.° It was really half a house, for Mr. Daboll occupied the other half. George Daboll was a partner in the cheese factory and tannery with Samuel Jordan, a huge building which also housed the fork factory (Brookfield Manufacturing Co.), of which Papa was the foreman. Mr. Daboll had come here from Rensselaer Co., with his son, Sherman, who was my age. Papa figured that better man than George Daboll never lived. We were certain Hank and Francie would have no problems with him.

» » » » » » « « « « « «

° Present home of Frances W. Palmer, Main St.

The excitement of the holidays had barely subsided when Francie presented Hank with his son, born on Jan. 6th, 1859. They named him Frank, a clever combination of both their names. With four doting aunts, plus a set of brand new grandparents, I doubt if any baby ever fell heir to more attention.

Francie and the baby got along fine, but as spring approached, we sensed the mounting uneasiness in Hank. Since Mr. Daboll's dwelling was immense, and the three of them required much less than their half of the mansion, Francie decided to take in some boarders, men who worked in the tannery, and factories just behind their house. The extra change they could well use, for the trip west had deleted their resources.

The first of April crept ever closer, and Hank attempted, time and again, to broach the subject of Wisconsin; but each time Francie managed to avoid the issue. Finally came the day of reckoning, in the form of a soft spring dawn. The smell of damp earth, freshly exposed beneath the tattered remnants of its soiled winter blanket, floated through the open chamber window on a warm south breeze; while the newly arrived goldfinch and robins twitted and sang incessantly, announcing their incomparable joy. Every fiber of Hank's being strained to be out on the land, breaking, dragging, seeding, plodding along in the wake of the sturdy oxen. "Francie," he burst forth, unable to contain himself any longer, "we can't go on like this, avoiding issues. Don't you have any idea of going home?"

"Home?" repeated Francie, bewildered.

"Yes, home, Francie. *Home,* where our stack of lumber is drying, for the house we are supposed to raise, on our *own* ninety acres, home with our wheat field, our oxen, and the wide open spaces."

"Home?" re-echoed Francie, a far-away look in her eye. "Home —home, they say, is where the heart is. Oh, Hank, I tried so hard to put my heart in Wisconsin, so very hard to make it become home. The little lilac slip your Mother gave me, and I planted—I watered it every day, and watched it, trying to make it seem like home. But it was dying—I don't know why—I guess it couldn't bear being transplanted. It was dying—just like me. Oh, Hank, I'm so terribly, terribly sorry, I know that's where your heart is. I've known it for some time now; but I kept hoping—hoping against hope—that you'd be happy to be back here, as I was, and someday you'd forget. I know it's a beautiful land out there, I'm not denying it for a minute, and I'd love that little new house. Oh, Hank, if I had Alladin's lamp, I'd pick that chunk of earth up and set it back here in the twinkling of an eye, and we could be happy forever after. Once I was foolish enough to believe that life would be like that—you'd get married, and live happily ever after—that's what the story books all said. Oh, why did they mislead us so? Why didn't they tell us that life is an eternal struggle, a struggle to do right, to please others, and to try to maintain some vestige of self-happiness in the process? Oh, Hank, dearest Hank, if I thought for one minute I could go west again, and manage to retain my sanity, I'd go—but I'm so afraid— all I can remember is those dark, dark days—and I never did like the dark!"

"There, there honey, dry those tears," he comforted her, dabbing clumsily at the streams rolling down her cheeks. I didn't mean to start your day off like this, and such a lovely day at that. Maybe it's still too soon after the baby, and you've been doing so much, what with the boarders and all. We'll just drop the subject, and maybe someday you'll feel differently. So come on, honey, I'll make the toast, while you fry the eggs and potatoes, and forget I opened my big mouth." He placed an arm about her shoulders, and drew her toward the kitchen.

It was soon apparent that Hank did not plan on heading west during 1859. He rented a building to use as a harness shop, and before long was doing a thriving business, not only in the village, but in Leonardsville and North Brookfield as well.

Hank's enterprise grew until he was forced to employ the services of both his brother-in-laws, the Georges White and Woodworth. As he journeyed about the countryside, in the trips necessary to his business, he became intimately acquainted with a great number of its residents. His easy approach to life, and interested manner, led others to often confide in him, some of their most personal problems. To these persons, he usually managed to come up with a wise and knowing answer, or, at least, a word of comfort.

While Hank was engrossed with his contacts in the business world, Francie was equally engrossed with the social world. Each Sabbath found her in the choir loft, an activity which required one or two evenings a week to be consumed in practice. Bailey's singing school was holding forth at the time, a lively session which we girls all attended. Once a week Stott's shows were held at the Gantrovert (Ganny) Clarke opera house. Dances, also regularly featured there, most often were patronized by the James Hills daughers. Due in part to the boarders, callers at the Spooner household were continous. Rare was the moment they had to themselves.

Outwardly Hank appeared satisfied with his business and new-found role in the community, but how little we know of the inner man! By pushing himself, keeping always on the go, and involving himself in the perplexities of his fellow companions, he strove to exclude the little place in the west from his thoughts. But there were always the reminders from his mother, who wrote with regularity to report on their progress, the excellence of the corps, and so on. In January of 1860 the following news arrived from Hannah Spooner:

Dear Children;

I wish you happy New Year, and the baby, too. We are well as common. It is awful out today. We have got some snow and our folks are splitting and drawing rails.

Albert and William was here to Christmas. Well, we have seen Johnson about your land, and he says he will give up the two fortys and will break the ten acres or pay the hundred dollars. He thinks he can break part of it in the spring, and all of it, if he can, and he will pay the interest, but he thinks you did not mean to have him pay interest, only from the time you made the last bargain. You won't get it very soon, I guess. He has let out his house and land for two years to Bliven's brother. Johnsons is agoing to move on his circuit when Bliven comes and it ain't likely he will ever come back here to live again. One of your steers you let out to Colvin got sick and lame and want good for nothing. It was the Johnny Smith one. He has bought a good one to mate the other, and now they are a pretty good yoke of oxen. Colvin says you may have them for what he owes you.

Tell Allen Green I think he would find him some land out here that would suit him fine, unless you have told him such a shocking story about the west that he don't durst to come. We have heard of some more friends living out here. John Eaton, Henry Eaton, and Joseph Thomas all live between here and Lone Rock. Albert and William stayed there all night when they came up here last week and they was going to stay there when they went back. They have been there three years. Goodbye from your Mother Hannah Spooner

And in the latter part of February this one followed:

Dear Children: We received your letter and was glad to hear from you once more. We are well and hope you are the same.

Our folks have worked pretty hard this winter. They have got about a thousand rails and have got enough logs for two thousand pickets. We are agoing to have picket fence on the road before the house and around the garden. I expect you won't hardly know the place when you come out here, it will look so nice.

I wish you was out here, fixing up your place. Johnson was in here the other day, pleased enough he had found out how he could get out of debt, or thought he had. He said he would let you have the forty back that joins us, and he would take the south forty, and let you have that ten acres next to Barkers; and have you throw in that hundred dollars and the Bliven forty and all the interest; and then he would be out of debt to you. That was smart, wan't it. That would be giving him a hundred dollars right out, for any fool would rather have the south forty than that ten acres.

I told him you wouldn't do no such thing, for you can get that hundred dollars anyhow, but the interest I don't expect you will ever get. We have got the place, and that is all we can get, for he hain't got nothing nor never will have. He had to turn out his wife to pay the taxes. He didn't mean to pay them, but they drove him right up and made out to get it. He owes everybody and hasn't got nothing. He, like a fool, swapt his old mare that was agoing to have a colt for an old white horse and a saddle and now he is going out. He looks like one of the futes. He says he has got forty converts and twentyfive dollars for his winter's work. If his converts are as good as his word, they are some of 'emm, don't you think so? He said he would break up that ten acres in the spring, but he will never do it, and I hope he won't, for he wouldn't half do it, if he pretended to.

You said you should like to stop in and get something good to eat. I should like to have you come to supper. I will get you some good Indian bread and some ham and eggs, and custard pie, and a good cup of tea with sugar and cream in it, so come right along, for it is all ready waiting for you.

I can tell you what I think will be best for you to do. You know I am a pretty good farmer. I think you had better take your land back and go to work on it. You can make a pretty good farm of it, and you want a home, and there is no way that a man can live so independent as on a farm, and you can clear off a few acres every year, and then you can live just as you please. If you stay there and drill away and make out to get a livin, and by and by your constitution will be broke down, and your health gone, and then you won't have no home. There is no work so healthy as farming. The little boy can help some, you know. We have sent that mortgage to Baraboo to have it recorded. I won't write no more. So goodbye. Johnson is agoing to move next week. This from your Mother, Hannah Spooner

"Never mind answering that letter, I'll take care of it," offered Hank, placing himself at the round table, beside the flickering candle. Talking was one of his favorite pastimes, but writing a difficult chore. Tediously he began to pencil:

Clarkville, N.Y.
February 26, 1860

Dear Ma, Pa, and Leonard;

Thought I'd better answer your letter, so you'd know what to do. We are fine. Frank is growing good, but it will be some time before he will be much help on a farm, and Francie isn't really strong enough to do much heavy work. She is doing well with the boarders, though, and seems happy.

My business here is improving daily, though of course it was a little slack throught the winter. I have grown more attached to this town than I ever thought possible, and have made many new friends here.

You had best let out my land for another year, if you can. Maybe when Frank is a bit older we shall be able to come out and farm it for ourselves again.

Give my love to Albert, William and Beaman. Tell Antionette not to kill herself running that school!

That supper you offered us sounds pretty good, lucky I just ate, or I'd probably be on my way out after it! Francie sends her love. Love from-Hank

Chapter Eight

I was fifteen at last! Childishly—I awaited each milestone in my quest for adulthood. Spring of 1860; also Sate's expected baby, were just around the corner. It was daily custom for one of the family to look in on her. On a sloppy March 14th I cleared the Woodworth steps with a running jump, landing squarely in front of the window, only to discover Sate, peering anxiously through that same pane.

"Dosh! Don't bother to take your boots off—I've been watching —pains have started—fetch Doc Bailey, will you? And Mama, too!" she called after my disappearing figure.

I galloped toward Main Street, ducked a couple of buggies sloshing along, and dashed to Dr. Bailey's corner residence. My message delivered, I proceeded, top speed, to relate developments to Mama. She flipped on a clean apron, threw her cape over her shoulders, and hustled upstreet, where she soon assisted the good doctor in the delivery of her first grand-daughter, Minnie Myrtle.

Feeling the importance of sudden adulthood, I dispatched Meal to the harness shop, with the pronouncement that George was momentarily to become a father. This done, responsibility rested heavily on my young shoulders, as I sought to prepare the evening meal for Papa; one I deemed worthy of this important occasion. Far from an expert cook in those days, I rejoiced that excitement of the moment was such that Papa seemed only dimly aware of my concoctions!

» » » » » » « « « « « «

Except for the fact that Meal, Frankie, and Minnie Myrtle were growing like weeds, the next year flew by, for our family, quite uneventfully.

At sixteen I graduated from the Academy,° and in April of that year, the Confederates fired on Fort Sumter. Seven states immediately seceded. Speculation over the tea cups, round the cheese vats and pot-bellied stoves ran high on the possible implications of these developments, yet in our quiet valley, it all seemed a trifle remote. So our lives continued on, full of gaiety, in the blissful ignorance of the young.

Sherm Daboll, Albert Nichols and I haunted "the boarding house", as Francie's establishment was termed. It always had some excitement. Frank Leonard, (Francie's girlhood beau), and his wife, Fanny, were two of its most frequent visitors. Though I had long looked upon Frank as a sort of older brother, he possessed one major shortcoming, a red-hot temper. Fanny, whom he married on the rebound, was a natural born henpecker. As might be expected, their spats were frequent, and ill-concealed from the public. One

° Present Hotel Brookfield.

evening, while visiting at the Spooner's, the inevitable battle over some trifling matter began. Frank, egged on by Fanny, shortly stalked in anger from the house. Oh, but what a secret smile curled Fanny's lips, as she pursed her husband down the front steps. They continued their quibble for the length of Main Street, with Fanny screaming, for the world to hear, that she was sick to death of watching Frank stare "sheeps eyes" at Francie, followed by the warning that if he didn't mend his ways, she had a good mind to up and leave him! Frank returned that he didn't give a damn, the sooner she did, the better.

Hank was unfortunately absent during that episode, or perhaps the matter might have been peaceably settled. But it seemed Hank was seldom home during those days, so seldom, in fact, that his seemingly rare presence received special notation in Francie's diary. An inner force appeared to drive him, and I privately presumed that he was attempting to compensate for the loss of his place in the west in the only manner that he knew, by losing himself in his work and associated contacts.

For Francie the situation was heartbreaking. One day, after Hank had been unusually abrupt, she made the first move. "Hank," she hesitated, "What is the trouble?"

"Nothing."

"I know that isn't true. Are you happy, Hank?"

"Of course. Why all these questions?"

"Because you don't act as if you care for me anymore. I only see you at mealtime, sometimes not that, don't you love me like you did?"

"Now that *is* a foolish question, downright foolish."

She tried again. "Hank, is it because I dissuaded you from returning west? Because if that's the reason, I just want to say, I'm ready to go back anytime you say the word. Soon it will be spring, and we can start all over again. I-I guess I didn't realize how happy we actually were out west, where you were all mine. Here, I have to share you with everyone in the township, who has a problem. Hank, *say* you will go back, we'll build our new house, and fix up our yard pretty, like your folks have done. You know—last year Mother Spooner wrote that the little lilac slip I planted had finally sprung to life—oh, dearest, if the lilac can make it, I can, too. And don't forget, Frankie is three years old now; he'll be a lot of help pretty soon."

"Gosh, I'd sure like to believe you, Francie, I'd like to think

65

you would be satisfied out there, and never become homesick again. But how can I give up all this a second time, and take the chance of not having it work out? I thought my life was in the west, as a farmer. But here I've come to know a new kind of life, a life of service and dedication to my fellow man, and I like it. The folks around these parts hold respect for me, more than I've ever held for myself. They come to me with their problems and heartaches, though Lord knows I don't know why. I'm no answer man, but if I can lighten some man's load, I'm willing to try."

"Oh, Hank, I'm *so* proud of you, and I'm so happy that things are going well for you. But *can't* you see that you need just a little time away from our neighbors' problems; a little time to solve our own?

"*We* have problems? Now what problems could we *possibly* have, you silly girl!" he bantered, gathering her in his arms. He held her at arm's length then, and studied her blue eyes intently. "You can stay right here, in your very own home town, with your folks and friends, and be happy forever after, like the stories say. You aren't fooling me none, you're just trying to be selfsacrificing about moving west. Well, don't worry your pretty little head about it any longer, we're staying here, and you can write and tell Ma and Pa that's my final decision. Tell 'em we'll try to visit them and settle up our business out there this summer. And maybe I'll even buy a few acres here, just to be sure it'll be permanent. I know of thirty-five for sale right now. Now how's about a great big kiss to seal the bargain?"

Little Frank, who'd been standing on the sidelines, dashed up at that moment, arms wide stretched to embrace the legs of father and mother. "Mama, Papa, kiss Frankie, too!"

"Oh, so you want to be kissed too?" laughed Hank, smacking the small boy soundly, then tossing him upon his shoulders for a piggy-back ride.

"Hank, oh, Hank, if only you would understand that we *do* have problems," though Francie miserably. But there was no use in supposing he might grasp the situation, or of the widening gap which yawned between their lines of communication.

The Friday following was Feb. 29th, Leap Year Day. I was at Francie's, scheming over what boy I might scare out of his wits by a fake proposal, when Frank and Fanny Leonard appeared. Frank began the conversation with profuse apologies, for the argument which had previously taken place in the Spooner home. Francie

66

beamed at them, said there was nothing to forgive, and we chatted as if nothing had happened, even making plans to attend Stott's shows and dance together the following week.

"Would you care to dance, Mrs. Spooner?" queried Frank grandly, bowing full from the waist, on the appointed evening. Once on the floor, a lively conversation ensued. "I'm terribly sorry about that darn rumpus," he apologized, for the second time.

"Oh, Frank, Fanny started it, we both know that. I get the feeling she doesn't care much for me, though."

"I suppose she's a mite jealous, after all, it's common knowledge that we used to go steady."

"She ought to know that's water over the dam—Suppose I shouldn't ask—but confidentially, Frank—how do you two get along?"

"It would be best if you *didn't* ask."

"It's really that bad? 'Course everybody knows she henpecks you to death. You'd better learn to stand up for your own rights."

"I do."

"I'll bet! Once in a coon's age, when you get fighting mad, like you did down at our house!"

"So—well, alright, have it your way, but it's easier just to put up with it sometimes. I'll admit I probably made a mistake. Easy enough to do, when you marry on the rebound, so they say." He glanced significantly at Francie, who colored slightly. "You know the old adage, "Marry in haste—repent in leisure?" He sighed, and shrugged his shoulders. "By the way, long as we're getting personal —what gives with you and Hank? You hardly go anywhere together."

"Well—he watches Frankie for me when I go out. What's wrong with that?" she replied defiantly.

"Francie, don't try to pretend with me! We're old friends—as true as the Bible, remember? He doesn't spend one solitary evening out of the week with you! Your marriage is in trouble, so don't try to tell this old boy any different! Well, all I've got to say is this—if *I* had you, it sure wouldn't be like that!"

"Please, Frank, don't say anymore," Francie pleaded, blushing a deep red. "It's way too late for us, and you know it."

"Just tell me one thing, then," he countered, looking directly into her face, "and I'll be satisfied; quick, before this dance is done, the truth—do you *wish* it was different?"

"Oh, please, Frank, Fanny is watching, and so is Dosh, and

there's the end of the number," she begged, and headed gratefully for her seat, followed by a puzzled Frank.

Though Francie earnestly hoped her words would put an end to this dangerous conversation, she was unprepared for the effect they would exert on her, personally, in the forth coming days. The opinions to which Frank had given voice were only the echoes of her own fears; fears she had attempted to convey to Hank when she had begged for their return to Loganville. But now, here those anxieties were, mirrored back at her almost as clearly as if she stood in front of a huge looking glass; her innermost thoughts all plainly lettered across her face—magnified—for all the world to read. Her deepest concerns—tossed back at her by an outsider—or *was* Frank an outsider? Hadn't he told her long ago that if she **was** ever in trouble, she could always count on him? It was plain that Frank still cared, deeply. He was much too nice a fellow to be henpecked by that Fanny. *Had* she been mistaken in marrying Hank, blinded by love at first sight? Of course not, Hank was her one and *only*. Then why did Frank's words run circles through her mind, repeating over and over again, "Tell me, do you *wish* it was different?" Oh, *why* wouldn't Hank try to understand? Why is it that we can perceive others' problems, and their solutions, so clearly, but never our own? she thought grimly.

A few days later Francie had callers; Albert Nichols, Mandale and Julius Franklin, who carried with them a juicy bone. According to Julius, the Leonards had been overheard to have quite a quibble following the dance; the upshot of it being that Fanny had repeated her erst-while threat to leave Frank. Julius, noted town gossip that he was, observed Francie cleverly, for some reaction to his tale, but she wisely concealed her face behind her cup of tea, and said nothing.

Frank's visits now became the more frequent, and since he usually timed his calls to coincide with the times when he knew Hank would be present, he confided his trials to them both. If Hank suspected any ulterior motive, he relayed none of it to either Frank or Francie, but attempted to counsel with Frank to the best of his ability. Poor Frank was nearly distraught, for in his heart he carried not only the burden that his marriage to Fanny was on the rocks, but that he seemed doomed to be forever in love with the wife of another man, and one of his best friends, at that.

One morning he was affronted at the door of the boarding house, by a furious Fanny. "Ahaa!" she shrieked, "*I* thought I'd find you here, you good for nothing, woman chasing, poor excuse for a man! Run right down to tell all your troubles to dear little Francie, will you? Well, if it wasn't for her, maybe we'd be able to make a go of it! Git along home with you! I'll be along soon's I tell this hussy once and for all just what I think of her!"

"Please, Fanny," Francie begged, wishing for all the world that Hank were present. "Won't you come in, sit down, and try to talk this over calmly?" Heads of neighbors who had witnessed Act I a short time before were now appearing, in eager anticipation of the 2nd, yet Fanny's voice shrilled ever higher. She sailed behind Francie into the house, but refused to sit. "Just what is it you want with my husband?" she demanded. "You have one, and a mighty good one. Doesn't *one* satisfy you?"

"You are so right," returned Francie, ignoring her last nasty implication, "and I don't suppose you'd believe me if I told you that as far as Frank and I are concerned, we are only the best of friends, as we have always been. Search your own soul, and perhaps you can discover where *you* are at fault, with your eternal henpecking, your stupid jealousy and accusations! You, too, have one of the best of husbands, but you don't know enough to appreciate him, and I'm sorry to tell you this, but I doubt if you can mend the widening breach."

"Well, I never!" gasped Fanny, "When I take advice from the likes of you, *that* will be the day!" She flounced through the heavy front door and slammed it behind her, while housewives and store-keepers alike raised eyebrows, and nodded knowingly.

Several hours later, under cover of darkness, Francie answered a timid knock on the door. The lamplight through the doorway revealed the swollen, downcast features of a totally crestfallen Fanny. Her abject appearance aroused immediate pity in Francie, and she spoke warmly, "Why Fanny, come in."

"May I?" Fanny hesitated.

"Of course," said Francie, who had passed the day mentally re-counting its events, as well as those of the preceding months, trying to ascertain, to her own satisfaction, if she were, indeed, guilty as accused, in some small measure.

"Francie—Francie—it's hard to eat crow—but I guess that's what I'm doing. Francie—you're right—I'm wrong—I've been wrong right straight down the line. I—still love him—in spite of what I said—but now he's leaving—he's *really* leaving me." Tears rolled down her cheeks as she continued. "He said this afternoon was the last straw—said I'd humiliated him for the last time. He's getting his things together now—What can I do to stop him?" She broke into near-hysterical laughter. "Funny, isn't it, me coming to *you* for help —Francie, I don't know where else to turn—I'm so ashamed—oh, please Francie, you've got to help me!"

"Fanny—poor Fanny," Francie soothed, placing an arm 'round her quivering body; meantime attempting to assess the unexpected turn of events. "Here, sit in Hank's rocker, I'll bring us some tea. I was just about to have a cup; I'll share it with you. That's it, sip it good and slow, t'will calm you." Oh, dear, I wish Hank was here. He always knows how to handle everything," she murmured, as she racked her brain for some bit of wisdom, by which she might guide this desperate woman. "All I can advise you to do now, Fanny, she began, haltingly, "is to pray. Ask The Good Lord to show you where you have been wrong, to remove suspicion and hatred from your heart and replace it with trust and love for your fellow man. God will give you a chance, if you are sincere. I can't say about Frank, but miracles do happen. But you see, Fanny, most of our troubles are within ourselves, and therefore within our power to control. When we learn to control our thinking, to become more concerned for others than for ourselves, our own troubles seem to automatically fade away. And—gloriously—when this has happened— we find that beautiful peace has taken over in the place where misery formerly held sway. There is a verse I've always liked which says this: Philippians 4–6 and 7; "Be careful for nothing, but in everything by prayer and supplication with thanksgiving let your requests be known unto God. And the peace of God, which passeth all understanding, shall keep your hearts and minds through Christ Jesus."

"Oh, Francie" tremored Fanny, that's beautiful. You've forgiven me for wronging you, and that's beautiful, too. And Hank couldn't have advised me any better, if he'd been here."

Sudden tears filled Francie's eyes. "Thank you Fanny," she whispered, "it sometimes takes one woman to understand another, but, at any rate, that is the greatest compliment I have ever received."

Two days later, Hank made a routine trip to Utica, for harness trimmings, And along with Hank rode Frank, plus his belongings. Frank had arrived at a decision—to seek employment in the city, until such time as he might be able to reconcile himself to life with Fanny. Fanny, Hank, and Francie prayed for that day.

» » » » » » « « « « « «

Chapter Nine

Epidemics were a common occurrence when I was young, but in the spring of 1862 the outbreak was more severe than usual. Perhaps the war was contributing its share, since the troops were constantly on the move, and carrying contagion with them as they went. Smallpox, diphtheria, and an epidemic of measles settled in that season. Children were harder hit by disease than oldsters, and scarcely a day passed that spring without a new grave or two. We sorrowed with Albert and Mary Dennison, when two of their children were laid away that year, and wept with James Hibbard and wife, whose children were all claimed by the pestilences.

Frankie and Minnie Myrtle passed safely through the measles with no after effects; Daboll contracted measles, Hank was sick, and Francie, though suffering a sore throat, kept up both the work of the boarding house, and nursing the indisposed.

The Leonards called briefly on the Spooners during this period. Frank and Fannie had decided to try again, and were moving, permanently, to Utica.

In the face of all afflictions, activities, except for churches, were at a minimum. It was a Sabbath afternoon in May. I dangled my feet from the old wooden swing board in the horsechestnut, for lack of something better to do, when I spied a strange horse and rider approaching. "Fordy!" I exclaimed.

He tipped his hat. "Doshie!" Aren't you a little large for that thing?"

"Just killing time. And you?"

"Same here. No, really, just got a new horse, thought I'd ride him over; see how Auntie and all you folks are doing."

"It's not too good a town to come to. Everybody's sick."

"It's the same all over. Everybody's sick in Clayville, too."

Fordy's father was proprietor of the Murray House in Clayville, and Fordy was kept pretty busy there. It had been quite a time since we'd laid eyes on each other.

Fordy tied the horse to the hitching post, and stood by the swing, then gave me a few shoves. "Just like old times!" he yelled.

The faint odor of liquor floated above the apple blossoms. I dragged a toe on the ground, and questioned, "Fordyce Hickox, have you been *drinking?*"

He looked at my toe. "Well, yes, ma'm. Just one little one."

I was dismayed. "Oh, Fordy! You know how I feel about that! You're too nice a fellow to take a liking to that stuff!"

"So you do think I'm a nice fellow! Well, I'm awful glad to hear that, 'cause I think you're a pretty nice *girl*. Always did." The taste of alcohol had furnished him with the necessary bravado to speak his mind. "Matter of fact, I think you're the *nicest* girl." He rushed on, as if in his eagerness he'd forget something. "Do you care about me, too, Dosh? Oh, say you do, you're the only girl I've ever cared for, ever since that day we picked the first spring beauties, and I had to help you home. Matter of fact, I've been savin' for this horse all winter, just so's I could come help you look for them now. You do remember, don't you?" He was standing close beside me, so close that all I could think of was how much I despised the odor of the liquor.

"Of course I remember," I replied, stepping backward. "And you're still my very best friend."

"Friendship's not enough for me, Dosh. I thought I was in love with you, and now that I've seen you again, I *know* it. Is friendship *all* it is?"

"I don't know what love is, Fordy, and—I don't think I'm ready to find out yet."

"Is there someone else? You must have lots of fellows, you're so pretty."

"Pshaw! I'm *not* pretty, though it is nice of you to say so."

"Well, you are to me. 'Haven't you heard—beauty is in the eye of the beholder? Come on, let me touch that pretty auburn hair just once," he begged, reaching for a stray lock, and running the length of it between his fingers.

"Really, Fordy, I'm serious about that drinking," I scolded. "I don't see how I could ever love you, long as you drink that stuff!"

"Kind of hard not to, in my position. But I *could* stop it, for you."

"What do you mean, in your position?"

"You mean you hadn't heard that I tend bar now, for my father?"

"Bartender!" I gasped. To my prejudiced mind, he might as well have said thief, so strict had been my upbringing. "Fordy, you're too good for that!"

"So you do care!"

"Of course I care, didn't I just tell you that you are my very best friend?"

"So that's the way the wind blows." His face fell. "Never a lover, but always a friend. Well, I may as well tell you, I probably won't be seeing you again right off. My old man is moving, taking over the management of "The Old American" on Bagg's Square, in the city. But if things don't get better soon, I figure on enlisting."

"Enlisting! Oh, Fordy, everybody is thinking of it! Is it really getting that bad?"

"I'm afraid so. You will write me, just the same, won't you?" He grasped both my hands, and searched my face intently.

"Of course I will," I quivered, aware of many sudden mixed emotions, most of which I could not define at that moment. "I'll write you as often as I can, and I'll give you a kiss right now," I added on impulse, as standing on tip-toe, I kissed him tenderly on the cheek. "Take care," I murmured, "and give up that drinking for me? Please?"

"I'll try; I think for you I could give up eating."

"Eating! Say, why don't you come in to supper? Mama, Papa, and Meal will be *so* glad to see you, besides, we've got steamed molasses pudding!"

He followed me inside the house, thankful for the hospitality, while I was doubly thankful for the inspiration which had delivered me from a ticklish situation. Much as I loved to see the familiar, tousled, red head, somehow things seemed far more comfortable, when he was at a safe distance.

» » » » » « « « « «

Spring rolled into summer. Sherm Daboll and Albert Nichols were still around, to squire me to dances, but I missed Fordy's occasional visits more than I cared to admit.

The times were changing rapidly. It was in the very air, in the snatches of conversations heard about the village, serious talk, which engulfed old and young alike. The North had sent five-hundred thousand men to the field of battle, and of these not more than three-hundred thousand remained fit for duty.

In the midst of the deepest gloom our nation had ever experienced, the following call was issued by President Lincoln on July 1st, 1862: "Gentlemen: Fully concurring in the wisdom of the views expressed to me in so patriotic a manner by you in the communication of the 28th day of June, I have decided to call into the service an additional force of three-hundred thousand men. I trust that they may be enrolled without delay, so as to bring this unnecessary and injurious civil war to a speedy and satisfactory conclusion.— Abraham Lincoln."

On the following day, Governor Morgan issued the following proclamation: "This appeal is to the State of New York: It is to each citizen. Let it come to every fireside. Let the glorious example of the Revolutionary period be our emulation. Let each feel that the commonwealth now counts upon his individual strength and influence, to meet the demands of the government. The period has come when all must aid. New York had not thus far stood back. Ready, and more than willing, she has met every summons to duty. Let not her history be falsified, nor her position lowered."

Although by this time some of the country had the wireless, to dispatch news about the nation at unprecedented speed, so we were well aware that the organizational ground work was being laid, such as dividing the state into regimental districts, and appointing committees to head up the rendezvous camps in each; it was the 28th day of July before the true seriousness of our situation hit home. On that memorable day Sherm Daboll enlisted at Clayville, the first of our close friends to do so. And that very evening, our first war meeting, conducted by Captain Tucker and two other speakers from Hamilton, was held in the opera house. Martial music by our own Clarkeville band, never in better form, the Hamilton Glee Club, and rousing speeches stirred the soul of each one gathered there.

Added to the fact that it was the patriotic duty of every able man to support his country in her hour of need, was the bonus offered as an incentive for rapid enlistment. This consisted of a fifty dollar bounty from the county, fifty dollars from the state, twenty-five of the one-hundred due each man at the end of his service from the national government, thirteen dollars (one month's pay in advance), plus a two dollar recruiting fund for each man, making a total due each man upon enlistment of one-hundred and forty-two dollars. At a time when eggs sold for 12 cents a dozen, potatoes for 38 cents a bushel, and ham for eight cents a pound, this sum was indeed persuasive!

On August 2nd, a similar meeting was held in the village of Leonardsville, which Hank and some of the fellows also attended. On the fifth I dropped in at Francie's, where I found her going through the motions of preparing the noon-day meal. The word that three-hundred thousand men were to be drafted had finally reached her ears. "Oh, Dosh," she wailed, have you heard the report, about the men being drafted? That's all Hank and Julius talked of last night. Hank will surely have to go, if he doesn't enlist."

I nodded. "Yes, the talk is the same everywhere. Sherm is going, and I wonder about Fordy. I haven't heard from him lately, but they say this is just the beginning. How many more will have to go the Lord alone knows. But we don't have a choice, do we? Things look very bad."

"Dosh is right," agreed Hank, who, coming through the woodshed door, had overheard our discussion. "We have no choice. I guess times have been too good, things going along too smooth. We can't expect to accept all of life's benefits, and give nothing in return. My grandfather, Corp. Benjamin Spooner, served in the Revolution, and so did your great-grandfathers, Capt. James Hills, and Capt. Samuel Clarke. What do you suppose they and the others who fought to create this nation would think of our generation, if we were to shirk our duty? And you women have a duty, too, to be brave and bear with us just as your great-grandmothers did.

A silence fell, during which Francie swallowed his words, then formed her own, piece by piece. "You're right—just as right as Grandma Clarke was on that Christmas Day, when she told us she was plum ashamed of us—and of how soft we'd always had it. Remember?" Hank and I nodded silently. "Well, maybe she had reason to be ashamed—but Hank, I swear to you, from this moment on, I'm going to grow up—and make you proud of me—no matter what happens!"

"I've always been proud of you, honey," Hank returned softly, pushing aside a stray curl which had fallen down across her forehead, then kissing the spot where it had laid. "So now I guess you're ready to hear that come Monday morning, a bunch of us are planning to enlist."

Our hearts sank, but we put up a brave front, as we questioned simultaneously, "Who?"

"Well, Julius Franklin, Ran Spencer, George White, Henry Kellogg, Jerry Murphy and myself are some of them, he returned steadily, "and we'll be in an outfit known as Bates Battery."

I could see Francie battling to restrain tears, especially since her little speech about being brave. I came to her rescue by interrupting, "Say, Francie, these potatoes are about to boil dry—and if you'll take up the ham, I'll stir up some milk gravy. The guys will be in to dinner in a minute."

She turned gratefully, wiped her eyes upon her apron corner, and heaped the thick ham slices upon the platter.

Monday, the fellows left to enlist. Francie and little Frank, at loose ends, went to see Sate and Minnie Myrtle. But that day there was no pleasant chit-chat, no laughter over the children's antics. "I just couldn't stay home today, Sate. I'd have worn a hole in the floor," Francie confessed.

Sate stretched forth a hand to touch her sister's arm. "Let's find Lute and go to prayer meeting," she suggested gently. "There is a special service this afternoon. I heard it in the store."

The following Sunday an excellent farewell sermon was preached by Rev. Frost. On Monday we went to Leonardsville, to send Sherm and some other fellows, leaving in Captain Tucker's company, off. Beside the row of waiting stagecoaches an enterprising photographer had set up his camera, and all of us grasped the opportunity to have our likenesses taken. One of Frankie and herself Francie gravely presented to Hank, "in order that we may never be far from you."

Two more days, and the fellows in Bates Battery were also gone; however, it was but a short stay, for they were allowed to return almost immediately. Their return was but of a week's duration, and for the express purpose that the abundant harvest of hops might be assured. While elated by the reprieve, most felt that parting twice in this manner only prolonged the agony of the final leave-taking.

Following that reprieve, on the morning of the second departure, Hank was taken ill, but assured Francie that he believed it to be nothing more than an attack of nerves. To add to his gloom, it rained steadily all that day, as well as the next two.

On the first nice day, Lute journeyed to Utica, where the boys were still encamped, to visit George. She returned with a note from Hank, stating that he wished to see Francie in the worst way before the group left for Albany. She made the trip, which was to be their last reunion for some time.

Most of Francie's boarders had been among those enlisted recruits, and a cousin, Lucinda, now came to stay with her and Frankie. Rather than stay at home and mourn, the ladies decided to tour the country fairs, including events at Columbus, West Winfield, and North Brookfield.

Soon our vacation was over, for it was teasel trimming time. This, and stitching jockeys for the soldiers, whiled away many an otherwise lonely hour.

» » » » » » « « « « « «

Mail from most of the boys came through at snail's pace. In Hank's case, the probable reason for his infrequent letters was because he never fully recovered from the illness he contracted upon his return to Utica.

Sickness was prevalent among the troops, "both real and feigned. Among the former were fever and bowel affectations, and among the latter, lumbago, epilepsy, and hip disease."

On October 18th Francie received a welcome communication from her husband: My darling Francie,

I have just received your letter and Oh, Francie, how glad I was to hear from you! It seems as though I must have a letter from you every day. Francie, you said you were sorry I was sick. I know you are, Francie. You said it seemed so bad to have me sick away from home. I guess I realize that myself, but I will try and get along without you, but Francie, it is hard to be away from the one you love when you are well, much more when you are sick. But we will hope for the best, Francie.

You wanted to know what you should say to me. Say you love me, that will do me as much good as anything, but Francie, I feel better today. My shoulders are lame yet, otherwise I feel a good deal better. Every letter I get from you does me more good than a dose of medicine. You wanted to know if I slept in the barracks and what kind of a bed I have. I have slept in the barracks all of the time since I have been here. The boys have tried to have me go to the hospital, but I did not want to go, it is so lonesome there. I hope I shall get along without going there. As for my bed, I have a straw tick to sleep on, with my blanket to cover me up. Last night I slept rather cold, but most of the time I have slept warm.

You wanted to know what time we got the trains that day we left Utica. We got it about eight o'clock in the evening, but it did not make much difference to me for I did not have any appetite when we got here, neither have I had since. That is one trouble with me, I do not have any appetite, but you know it saves Uncle Sam something, so there is no great loss, but what there is some small gain.

You wanted to know when we were going to leave. I don't know anything about it, Francie. You must not worry about me, for

I guess I shall come out alright. Francie, you thought I was very good. Francie, I try to be good, I have not been down to the city once since I have been here, nor drunk any liquor. The rest of the boys are out every night, but you must not say anything about it, all but Luke. You said Lute feels bad because George does not write to her. I told him yesterday he ought to write her and I believe he has commenced one, but has not finished it yet. I pity her, but don't say anything about it, because George would be mad if he knew it.

Well, Francie, I must close. Give my love to Lute, Dosh, Meal and your folks and Frankie and all the boys. Tell Daboll I wish he would write me a letter. If I felt well I would write him one today. Write often. Kiss little Frankie a hundred times for me. You said you put a kiss on the letter for me. I will put fifty on this for you, great big ones. This from one who loves you dearly, Hank"

Having digested this disturbing letter, Francie, upon hearing that Doctor Augustus Saunders planned to visit the boys in Albany, promptly sent along with him a certain medicine; which, she explained to the good doctor, had always done Hank a world of good whenever he was indisposed. On October 24th, Dr. Saunders returned to the village, with the announcement that Hank was worse, and confined to the hospital.

» » » » » » « « « « « «

In late October, Grandpa David Clarke sent word down by Mama that he should like to see Lute and Francie; and I decided to tag along. In his prime Grandpa had been fully six feet tall, and weighed over two-hundred pounds, but now he had shriveled up into a rather diminutive old man. He had been sickly of late, though in the still remaining pride of his manhood, he endeavored to disguise his ailments as best he could.

We found him seated in the Boston Rocker, on his south porch; it being a gorgeous autumn day. He rose to greet us with obvious effort. "Doggone rheumatiz," he explained. "Kind a gets to me now and then. Such a nice day, kind a thought it'd do these old bones good to soak up some of this warm sunshine. 'Sides that, I like to set here, gaze out over these meadows to the hills and just kind a ponder on the past. You know, Lyddy and I *built* this house, and raised all our younguns here. She was sweet sixteen when we got hitched, and I warn't but nineteen. Never's been the same since she's been gone, five long, lonely years last July third. Never did believe I'd miss her so much. Allus thought she was kind of an old battleax. Doggone it, she was, too. Had a right sharp tongue in her head, you girls know that, I reckon. Kind a wished she'd shut up a good share of the time. But it's too *durn* quiet since she left, nobody here to jaw at me no more. Any of you girls take after her, be ye good at jawin?"

We smiled secretly between ourselves, while Grandpa scratched his balding head, then continued, "Well, I be seventy-seven now. My Pa, Captain Samuel, was seventy-five when he passed on to his reward. Tough old critter, he was, never thought I'd live longer than Pa. He was already forty-eight, when he brought us into this territory—But gettin' back to Lyddy. She hankered to quote to me from the Good Book when I was a young feller. Well, now, I had just about a belly-full of that when I was young, I figured, from Ma. Her people was the Maxons, most all Seventh Day Baptist ministers, back in Rhode Island. So natcherly I didn't cotton much to the idea when Lyddy started in on me; but to please her and keep her from that infernal jawin', I kind a went along with it. Lip service, I guess that's what they call it, and it came easy for me, on account of Ma."

We girls glanced sharply at one another, shocked surprise on our faces. To hear this sort of a confession from the Grandfather who had delivered those beautiful blessings at Thanksgiving and other occasions was incredulous.

He paused a moment, apparently deep in thought, then continued, "Lyddy was always remindin' me that everything happened for a purpose, and then she'd say, "If ye don't believe it, look it up! Romans 8:28." So after she was gone, I set myself down one day to do just that, and this is what I found. "And we know that all things work together for good to them that love God, to them who are the called, according to His purpose." So I pondered on that quite a spell, for I'd been awonderin' why he called her home before me, and I concluded it was because I'd never really believed her, when she was allus apreachin'. I figured then, and rightly, I reckon, that the reason she was taken first was so's I could think awhile on these things, and come to believe in it, so's I could go to be with her, when it be my time. Now somethin's been atellin' me that I should pass this on to you girls, afore it be too late—that no matter what should come to pass in your lives, look at it like it happened for some purpose, believing in God, and sure enough, some day ye'll find out that it did."

79

"I declare, Lute, ye look more like yer Ma every day." Poor Lute winced. Mama was not a handsome woman, by any means, and the fact that she insisted on pulling her straight black hair back tightly to her head in the strict Victorian manner, did not compliment her one bit. "Ye've a good look, and wholesome."

Lute puzzled over this statement, undecided as to whether she should thank him, for this supposed compliment, but was spared from answering anything as Grandpa carried on with his soliloquy. "So you girls' husbands have gone off to war," he remarked, apparently unmindful of my presence. A visit with Grandpa was always like this, he visited, you listened. "And I suppose you're wondering what possible purpose that could have. Well, I don't hold to wars much, reckon nobody does, except a scoundrel out to profit by it somehow. Can't say I go along with the idea of slavery, though, I say every man's got a right to be free, got a right to make somethin' of himself, on his own. Durn shame we have to fight our own blood like this, though, but they's the ones what asked for it! Been a long time since our country's seen a real war, 'bout eighty years, if I reckon right. 'Cep't for the skirmishes we had in 1812, when my brother, Joseph, was stationed at Sackett's Harbor. Joe went quite a ways, got to be quite a politician, you know. Quite an honor to get a village named after you, but Judge Joe did it! (Grandpa spoke with pardonable pride, apparently unmindful, for the moment, that we were Judge Joseph's great-nieces.) 'Fraid this war is going to be a bad one, and I be doubtful that I'll be around to see the outcome, but no matter what might happen to ye in the years ahead, just remember that your old Granpappy Clarke told ye to search for the reason." With this Grandpa settled back into the rocker, closed his eyes, and began a steady rhythm that seemed almost unconscious of our presence.

A little later, we kissed him goodbye, unhitched Hank's rig from the post, and Francie drove us back to town, while I pondered his words. Hank was terribly sick. What purpose could that have? And Lute, who didn't get even one small note from George—what possible purpose could there be in that?

» » » » » » « « « « « «

Either the medicine that Francie sent by Dr. Saunders, or the hospital stay was beneficial to Hank, for he was able to return, in company with all the other Battery boys, on the eve of November third, for the purpose of voting on the fourth. On Nov. sixth all but

Hank and Randall Spencer returned to their barracks in Albany. Hank had been extended a leave of two weeks, in the hope that his health would improve amongst the familiar surroundings. Upon expiration of his leave, he journeyed back to Albany; but after thorough examination, the doctors agreed it best to discharge him, due to his continual ill-health.

On December 9th, a weakened but contented Hank returned to the home town; and on December 12th, he and Francie commenced living by themselves, for the first time since their years in the log cabin out west.

As I beheld their so nearly complete happiness, I recalled that I had wondered what possible purpose could come from Hank's severe illness. Well, it was because of his enlistment that Francie had relinquished the boarders, and because of his illness that he was now discharged, and because of the combination of these two situations, that they at last had a home to themselves. Through his absence they had come to a new realization of the love they held for each other. Gone were all the problems, the barriers and misunderstandings melted away, and seeing them in their new found happiness, I doubted that any such barriers could ever again be established.

Chapter Ten

As my eighteenth birthday approached, I realized that I must be pursuing some more secure profession for my livelihood, since no prospect for marriage loomed on the horizon. Nor did I have any desire for such. Sherm Daboll wrote from the war, when he was able; and I heard occasionally from Fordy, who was still employed by his father, in the city. Though for both I felt genuine fondness, neither had aroused in me that latent desire loosely defined as love. I whiled away many an hour wondering about this elusive thing. Would I recognize love, if it should appear? The many songs and stories written concerning the subject would lead one to believe it was as easy to fall into as it was recognizable, but of both I had my doubts.

Lute had her talent for sewing, Francie her's for cooking and fancy-work, Sate was an accomplished pianist, while I apparently had none. My favorite pastime was to wander through the woods and fields, exploring the wonders of Mother Nature. When, by chance, I would discover a particularly lovely spot, or one which I desired to entrench more firmly in my memory, I would seat myself upon the grass, a rock or log, and with my small sketch pad and pencil or charcoal, create a reasonable facsimile. Many an otherwise desperately dull day I idled away in this worthless endeavor, as Mama was wont to speak of it.

Papa was more tolerant, and once even went so far as to mention that one of his aunts was particularly gifted along this line; however, hastening to add, "Doshie, ye'd best marry yourself a rich man, and pretty soon; as it ain't many that make a living from drawing pictures." His words were kindly spoken, but they held the bitter truth.

So one day I approached Lute on an inspiration. "Could you teach me how to turn out bonnets? I've got to learn some worthwhile trade to support myself."

"If you will put your mind to it, I've an idea you'll be a rather accomplished pupil," she assented.

Within a short time I was turning out bonnets, of which anyone could be proud; and even Mama had to admit that my artistry stood me in good stead when it came to decorating a headpiece.

Throughout that winter, we could see that Grandpa was failing rapidly; and it came as no surprise to hear that he had suffered a stroke. Mama, and her sisters, Polly Fitch, and Thede Green, stood watch over him, and on February 23rd, his final breath was caught up on the wings of the icy North wind, which came screaming, swooping down upon the tiny household; as if in bitter revenge it now demanded the life of the venerable man who had conquered this portion of its elements, in the clearing and erection of his homestead.

We girls, mindful of Grandpa's long conversation with us the previous fall, wept for the loss of the pioneer patriot; though our grief was assuaged in the knowledge of his firm belief in the reconciliation he would experience with his life's partner, Lydia.

It seems that whenever a soul passes into the great beyond, there is another to take its place; even as it is in the animal kingdom, so it is with us humans, intent on our own race preservation. On March 31st, Sate's second child entered the world, a son, named Edgar Lamott Woodworth.

» »» » » » «« «« «« « «

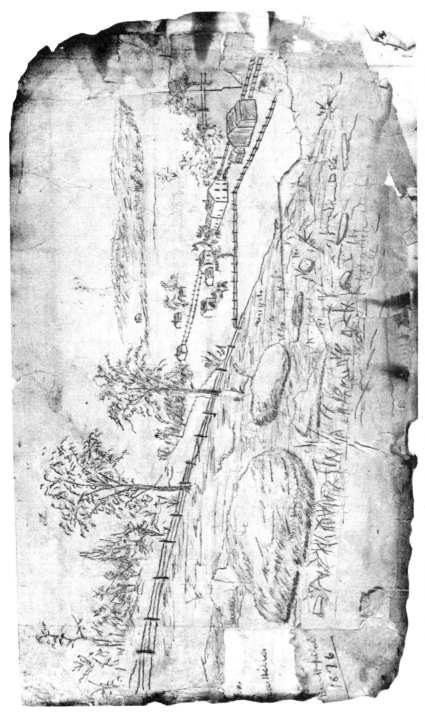

Father Hills' home, as seen from Oliver Babcock's pasture. Sketched by Eudocia Hills Knapp, 1876

Spring came again to our hillsides; but with it came a gnawing, clutching fear. From ages eighteen through forty-four, our men were largely gone, involved, in many cases, in the thick of the fighting. Reports persisted that black men had been seen skulking about the village, under cover of night. It was whispered that the underground railroad was operating under our very noses. One of our most prominent citizens, Calvin Whitford, went so far as to support the movement openly, even entertaining, with sumptuous dinner and band accompaniment, the renowned freedman, orator Frederick Douglass, and humanitarian Gerrit Smith.

In July of that year the battle of Gettysburg took place, and in it, the lives of twenty-three thousand Union men, as well as about twenty-thousand Confederate lives were lost. The South fell into a more or less steady decline after this, although the final outcome was uncertain for some time, as evidenced by the following, from the Joshua Spooners.

Loganville, Wisconsin
Nov. 6th, 1863

Dear Children:

It being election day and I am alone, I thought I would write you a few lines to let you know that we are well. William and Nett have gone at last. They have been here since last May and had the little girl with them. She is as pretty a child as ever I see but Nett will spoil her, I expect. William is selling seeding machines. He has sold his house and shop at Loganville and is agoing to take his pay in machines. He has bought the right of three counties. He asks ninety dollars apiece for them.

We are building a barn. We raised it yesterday. I don't know when we shall get it done.

We have got done husking and plowed some. We have raised about nine hundred bushels of corn, and about ninety of wheat, and fifty of potatoes, and we are fatting two large hogs and got three pigs to keep over.

There is not much news. Old Dan Newell is dead and Elezer Newell's wife is dead. The folks are well around here generally, what are left. There has gone from Sauk County six-hundred to the war. It don't seem as though there was many left. There was over one-hundred went through Loganville last week and they got up a splendid dinner for them. There has a great many gone from here. I had a letter from Albert a week ago, but I don't know whether he is alive now or not. They have had another battle since that. He is in a pretty dangerous place. I expect he will get killed, and I don't know but they all will, and the North get whipped.

We have not got the wheat from Johnson and I don't know whether we shall or not. He sent his brother down here last week to sell the wheat, but we told him he had promised it to you. I don't know if he will sell it, if he does we shant take the oxen. I don't care if he does or not, for Mr. Medd was here last week, and he said you should have your pay, every cent of it, for the land is in his hands, and his word is as good as money, so you are safe enough. About that money of Colvins, I think you had better wait till next month, then all the banks that are good will remain good, and we shall have to pay the taxes, and send you the rest. That will be the safest way. Bill Stewart wants you to come and make harnesses with him this winter.

Give my love to Francie and Frankie. Tell him Grandma wants to see him and see if he is as pretty as his little cousin Etta. Write soon.

Hannah Spooner

Hank and Francie were a happy couple in those days, and seldom did a disagreement of more than passing nature come between them. Frankie had developed into a serious little fellow, mature beyond his five years. Francie was wont to dress him extravagantly, in the fashion of the day, and especially on the Sabbath. Ordinarily a well-behaved child, he rebelled, exhibiting his masculine nature by throwing a tantrum when she compelled him to wear a small gold locket to church. The pendant was worn but once, having been mysteriously "lost" on the way home; and he henceforth, for the balance of his life, refused to wear jewelry of any sort. Perhaps for the first time, Francie became aware that she had a young gentleman on her hands, instead of her baby.

Hank restrained himself from entering upon the discussion, but remained close by in order to enjoy the performance, while reveling privately, in the fact that he had raised a manly son, despite his Mother's protestations.

Truth was, Francie longed for a daughter, on which she might lavish her jewelry and furbelows, but another child was never forthcoming.

Minnie Myrtle was plain, but talented, and at four, Sate started her on the piano. The three children, Frankie, Minnie, and Edgar spent a good deal of time together, for they lived only two blocks apart. Frankie thought it jolly fun to visit Uncle George's horse stables. George Woodworth boarded horses, and also ran a stage, from Brookfield to Bridgewater. (During the early 1860's the village name of Clarkeville was changed to Brookfield, since the mail was being confused with that bound for Clocksville, also in Madison County. Nevertheless, there were those who persisted in referring to the village as Clarkville, until nearly 1900.

Life was hum-drum, and fearful for us during those war years. Most of the young men were at the war; I was now nineteen, and rapidly on the way to becoming an old maid. The cloud of gloom hung heavily over all of us, and even in the few new bonnets I created for others, it became increasingly difficult to exact an air of gaiety. It was as if each of us waited daily for the next awful news to filter through the wireless; and be related by those coming into the community on the next stage. As the casualty lists mounted we mourned for our boys and their families; the Clarkes, Washburns, Simons, Gardners, Beebes, Browns, Burches, Conklins, Crandalls, Holmes, Loomis, Parkers, Sanders, Stones, Thompsons, and many others, who gave their sons to lie, dead and wounded, upon the battlefield.

And in Loganville, Joshua and Hannah were not spared, for word came, in Jan. 1864, of the death of their next to youngest son, Beaman, a member of the 23rd. Regt. of the Wisconsin Infantry. And Antionette, wife of William Spooner, also of the 23rd. Regiment, took ill in an aftermath of concern for her husband, and was laid to rest in September of that same year.

But bad as they were, our losses were small by comparison with the ravaged South. *Why* didn't they give up?

I passed those days by helping with the teasels, often in the fields, when need arose, since we were desperately short of man power. And many times when a helping hand was needed in a home beseiged by illness, I rendered my services until the emergency was over. Soon it was spring, 1865, and the looked for periodic letter from Hannah Spooner, arrived, dated Mar. the ninth.

Young folks at home,
    I thought I would write a few lines to let you know how we are getting along. We are well and hope this will

86

Antionette Spooner, shortly before her death, in 1863

Ettie Spooner, daughter of William & Antionette York Spooner

Stone of Antionette in Loganville, Wis. Taken 1970

find you the same. We got a letter from you the other day, and was glad to hear from you. It had been so long since you wrote I thought you had forgotten your old Father and Mother, but we have not forgotten you. We think of you often and want to see you and your family very much. I should be glad to have you come out here and live, but I suppose you can do better where you are.

We are very lonesome living here alone. Albert is to the village, to be sure, but then we have to live alone, back here. It is hard for us, to get along, and we don't know as we can let our farm this year or not. We did let it to Charley Floothfield, but he has gone to the war, and now we don't know what we will do.

Albert will stay in the village if the mills stays, and if it goes away he will go with it. We talk some of buying a house in the village, and if the mill stays I think we shall buy it, and move down there, and let our farm out, if we can.

William will go away from here, soon, I think. He will make his home at Mr. York's, for his little girl, Ettie, has been there since Nett has gone, and he wants to be near

Home of Henry L. & Frances Spooner, Brookfield. "The boarding house"

her, and if Albert should go away, we should be left alone. We can't stay alone much longer for Pa can't do much. He has a good many sick spells and he is so lame he can't hardly get around. He makes out to do the chores, and cut the wood, and that is all he is able to do.

We shant try to live alone here another winter. If Albert stays and we move to the village we shall be alright. We have got enough of everything we want to live on, and money enough to use. We have got wheat enough to last till next winter and three acres of winter wheat on the ground and corn and oats. We have sold fifty bushels of oats at fifty cents a bushel and have got enough to sow, and corn all we want and two good cows. We have made twenty dollars worth of butter this winter. We have got the best hog there is in town, so we shant starve. It is as cold as Greenland but not much snow.

The folks are all well around here, what there is left. They have most all gone to the war. You may tell that man that bought your place that we received the money, and paid the taxes, and got a receipt, and if he wants it, we will send it to him, and if not, we will keep it safe.

I will close for it is about time to get dinner, and I wish you and Francie and Frankie was here to eat with us. I hope you will come sometime. Give my love to all my friends, Goodbye, from your Mother, Hannah Spooner"

"I wonder," Mama spoke thoughtfully, "if Hannah still is as enthusiastic over the west as she was when they went out, some eleven years ago. I thought our life was a bit hard, what with pinching pennies, and so on. But we've held on to this little place, and it means security. Hannah and Josh have fought for security, too, but a rolling stone gathers no moss, so I've always been told. And now they're old, none of their five sons are left to them, but Albert, and he may soon be gone. Their relation and friends are scattered to the four winds—Well, I thank God I'm not in Hannah's shoes!"

» » » » » » « « « « « «

On the ninth of April came the greatest piece of information that had reached our ears in five long years—the news of Lee's surrender; and hardly had we finished rejoicing than the tragedy of President Lincoln's assassination transpired, shaking our little town to its foundations.

In June the remnants of our boys came home, amidst cheers and celebrations. Upon the final count our township had furnished three-hundred and thirty soldiers, and twelve sailors; of these sixty were from Clarkville village; while two-thirds of the total were enlisted men. In a short time most of the lives were back nearly to normal. Those who were tillers of the soil set about the season's crops with an enthusiasm they had seldom before possessed, so happy were they to be home at last.

Many of the boys had married, prior to enlistment, and it was a joyful reunion indeed, for them with their brides. Several of our boys would never return.

At this point life became, at least for me, singularly dull. While the others reveled in their new found joy, I was left to my solitary existence. It occurred to me one day, that I was now fully twenty years of age; with absolutely no prospects of marriage in view. Nor were there any likely unattached young men in the village.

I saw Fordy but once, that summer. He had not eased up on his drinking, and I realized it was probably next to impossible for him to do so, as long as he continued in his Father's employ. Happy as I was to renew our old acquaintance I could find nothing but friendship in my heart for him. He appeared to resign himself to this, and it was many years before I heard from him again.

The continuing days of '65 and '66 were drab and monotonous. I plodded along at my usual perennial activities, while the accumulation of a wardrobe became my mainstay in life. Nearly every cent I earned was invested in material, until I became one of the best-dressed young ladies in the territory. "But of what avail is a wardrobe to the wearer, without one of the opposite sex to pay an occasional compliment?" I thought glumly.

On November 16th of that year, there occurred an event destined to adversely affect our township for a long, long time. Some years prior to this date, Papa and his partner in the fork factory had sold the delinquent business to Mr. Samuel Jordan, a former wagon maker and tanner. Being an excellent business man, Mr. Jordan had expanded his operations to include his tannery, which was housed in one end of the buildings, and was newly fitted with vats, leaches, bark mill, etc. In another section he had established a grist mill, which contained two runs of stones. The main portion of the structures housed the cheese factory, in the store room of which lay curing some three-thousand dollars worth of cheese, owned by dairymen of the vicinity. The south wing was occupied by the blacksmith shop, which Papa had reserved for his trade.

George Woodworth, kept a livery and drove Brookfield stage, with his wife, Sarah (Sate).

Minnie Myrtle, daughter of George and "Sate" Woodworth

George Daboll, Brookfield, partner with Jordan. Inscription—"A better man never lived."

Eudocia (Dosh) Hills, in the eighteen-sixties.

This entire establishment was but a few short rods behind Hank's dwelling, and it was from the workmen employed in these buildings that Francie had drawn her boarders. Awakened in the night, by a brilliant light streaming from the structures, through her kitchen window, she screamed to Hank, who turned in the alarm, then raced to the south wing, which the flames had not yet engulfed. Papa's loss was only about $100.00, since they were able to save most of his tools, but Mr. Jordan's was set at $7,000.00, only $2,000.00 of which was covered by insurance. For the workers in the enterprises, the area farmers, Mr. Jordan, Papa, and the township at large, it was a bitter blow.

Before the coals had cooled from the conflagration of the evening before, news of the New York State election reached us. Sherman Daboll and Eugene Hall, preparing to celebrate the election by a salute of the old fifty-six, were injured when it accidentally discharged. Sherm lost one thumb and finger, and was severely burned. Following this mishap, Sherm, the grown man, returned to the Academy, and graduated, with highest honors. From this basic education he proceeded to law school, and eventually was elected to the office of Madison County District Attorney.

In March of 1867 we were invaded by another epidemic of diphtheria, and this time it claimed, among others, the life of Sate's seven year old Minnie Myrtle. She was laid to slumber beneath the figure of a sleeping lamb. At this point I again recalled the words of old Grandpa Clarke, and wondered what purpose God could possibly have in the taking of this sweet and innocent life.

Chapter Eleven

It was July, 1868, and Uncle Hosea was out for an early morning call. Though he was then seventy-one years of age; he continued about his business, but perhaps on a bit smaller scale. I noticed it was difficult for him to swing his huge body in and out of the carriage. "How are you today, Chloe?" he addressed my mother. Things look pretty quiet around here. You're not working today, Doshie? How about tomorrow? I'm looking for a chauffeur again, goin' off over the hill to South Hamilton, to bargain for some wool."

I knew Uncle was really looking for company, and I eagerly agreed to go.

Next morning dawned a bit cloudy, with a hint of thunderstorms in the air. Uncle Hosea squinted at the cloud formations, estimated the wind, and said he figured it would pass us by. I was grateful for the breeze, as without it, the day would have been unbearable. I further suspected, that could faithful Maggie talk, she would have agreed. Still a beautiful, proud horse, she was graying now about her forelocks, though her step was as brisk as ever.

I dressed carefully for the day, in one of my latest costumes. "Land sakes!" ejaculated Mama, "Looks like you're dressed up fit to kill! If your Grandmother could only see you now!"

"Well, Mama," I countered, "I might as well wear them as to let them hang in the closet. Where else do I get a chance to go, except to church?"

"I know, dear," sympathized Mama, in an uncommon moment. Now you run along and try to have a good time. I just hope it doesn't rain on your new outfit. Better take the big umbrella, don't you think?"

We started off, Uncle Hosea cheerful and chatty as ever; Maggie taking an easy trot. "Guess we'll take the direct route today," he prattled. "Straight over the hill."

We rolled southward down the East Beaver Creek Road for about a mile, and turned to the right at Kenyon's Corners, onto the road which led past White's Mills.

"You know," Uncle spoke up, your Grandmother's niece, Esther Frink, was killed right here. She was a couple of years older than me; probably just about your age when she died. Real strange, it was. Folks say she had a premonition, heard a voice a callin' her name, "Esther, Esther," 'bout three weeks before it happened. And then the very night before the accident the neighbors claimed they heard strange groanings outside in the darkness. Folks put a good deal of stock in such "signs" back then."

"I've heard about it from Grandma," I admitted. "It always sounded pretty weird to me. How exactly did it happen?"

"Well, young Tom York was her cousin, on her Mother's side. He'd spent the night with his Aunt Thede, and the next morning Esther decided she'd like to go to the religious services they was holdin' in the new Waterman school house. Tom says she'd be welcome to use his horse. They fitted her up with a side-saddle, as was proper, and she set off. Snow was light on the ground, but enough so's there was sleddin'. Just past that corner was the first school house, used before Waterman was built. Fellow by the name of Dudley Hall was livin' in it then. Apparently the snow was just quiet enough so's Esther didn't hear him comin' with his cutter. He passed her easy enough, he said, but her horse was a mite skittish, and reared. Threw Esther off that danged side-saddle, but her foot was caught in the stirrup. Dudley didn't see what had happened for a minute, and when he did, 't was too late. Her mount kept right on agoin', draggin' her 'twixt the stumps and brush. Then the horse, scared to death by the thing a thumpin' at its side, crossed the mill bridge, where it suddenly whirled and jumped clean off the bridge, straight into the middle of the creek. They got Esther right out, but 't was no use, she was good as gone then."

"How horrible!" I shuddered.

"That it was. That old stream's claimed quite a few lives, you recollect some of them, I reckon."

I nodded, and we rode on in silence till we reached Page Road, where Uncle pointed out the old homestead of the Usher family, whose son, John P., he well remembered, and who'd gone on to become Secretary of Interior in the cabinet of Abe Lincoln.

We continued on, straight up one side and down the other of Usher Hill, passed the Harvey Holmes farmstead,° and crossed the Giles Road. "This road crosses the entire township," explained Uncle, and it runs from the river road, below Leonardsville, past Button's Falls, through Five Corners, Kenyon's Corners, and from where we are now, straight over to the Sherburne town line.

We stopped at Lambs, Palmers, Browns, and Warners, among others, and Uncle purchased a couple of lots of wool. By the time we approached South Hamilton the clouds were thickening. "We're callin' at Sam Tuttle's next," announced Uncle. "Sam has the biggest spread in the whole township, 'cept for the Faulkner boys, cattle dealers at North Brookfield. There's four-hundred acres here. Sam raises sheep, southdowns mostly, and a few merinos. If I can buy his wool right, it will finish us up for today. See that big house off over on the hill? That's the Tuttle place."

"Golly," I ventured, "that does look like a big outfit! I can see why they raise sheep!" The side hill was mountainous. Here and there a few sparse grasses struggled for existence between the rocky ledges. The sky had by now darkened, and the wind suddenly increased, as thick, deep purple clouds swirled overhead at an un-

° Present home of John Ray.

precedented speed. Despite its ominous overtones, I felt an artist's urge to capture the moment on canvas. Maggie, sensing the approaching storm, quickened her hoof-beats, even though the rutty, narrow road appeared to climb almost perpendicularly over the near mountainside.

"Believe we're in for a real blow!" yelled Uncle. "We'll try to make Tuttles before she hits!"

The last few feet of the roadway leveled off to skirt a well-kept lawn between the house and outbuildings. As Maggie skimmed across the drive, I noticed some men scurrying about to bolt the barn doors tightly. One of them, struggling with an enormous shed door, spied us and shouted, above the mounting gale, "Helloooooooooo! Better pull that rig in here!"

Uncle immediately swung Maggie in that direction and she unhesitatingly rolled us in. While Uncle jumped down to calm the snorting Maggie, the fellow secured the door from the inside, and joined Uncle.

The shed was long and dark, darker than usual, I knew, for it was almost as black as night outside, and bore that peculiar odor, common only to horses. In the dim light I could barely distinguish the heads of several horses in stalls on the lower end, as they turned and whinnied, curious to know what the commotion was all about.

"Picked a kind 'o rough day for traveling, didn't you, Hosea?" observed the young man.

In the half light I estimated his age as somewhere near mine. Outside I heard the rain commence, lashing at the shed as if determined to either twist, dissolve, or otherwise demolish it. An involuntary shudder shook me.

"Pretty bad, ain't it?" commented our host. "Not often it gets this bad even up here on the peak. The old place don't show off too well on a day like this. What brings you folks out on such a day?"

"My yearly rounds," replied Uncle, "Must say I didn't expect this! 'Twas a bit cloudy when we left; I concluded it would blow over. Which goes to prove," he grinned at me, "the weather is just as unpredictable as a woman."

The pandemonium from without was dying now.

"By the way, young fellow, this is my niece, Eudocia Hills, from Clarkeville. Don't believe I recollect your name, but you look like Sam, so I s'pose you must be one of his boys."

"I'm his nephew, but he's been like a father to me since my folks died", explained the young man, plainly relieved that the storm was over. "I'm Edwin Tuttle, and I'm pleased to make your acquaintance, Miss Hills. How about us going in the house for a spell? I bet you folks could use a cup of tea, and I'm sure I could! That air cooled off pretty sudden," he observed, with a slight shiver, as we followed him gratefully.

The Tuttle house was relatively new, constructed in the large, sprawling style of the times. The kitchen we entered was all of twenty feet in length, and nearly as wide; boasting of a nine foot ceiling, while instead of the customary fireplace, there reposed at the far end of the room a large, shining black cast iron stove. Apparently this family was rather well off. I contrasted it in my mind to our little Cape Cod cottage, comprised of small, low-ceilinged rooms, and the huge fireplace about which my mother labored tirelessly. In spite of four enormous windows, the room was dreary, for the clouds had not yet lifted; the only cheerful article in sight being the cast iron teakettle, which steamed a genial welcome.

"Aunt Lovina," began Edwin, "You know Hosea Clarke, from Brookfield, and this is his niece, Eudocia Hills."

"Nice to see you again, Hosea," returned Mrs. Tuttle, "and I'm pleased to make your acquaintance, Miss Hills. Won't you set over by the stove and have a cup of tea?" She pulled a rocker nearer to the stove, as she spoke. "That air is a bit chilly, I believe it will be more cozy here than in the parlor. Did you folks get caught in that blow?"

"Just missed it," replied Uncle. "Your nephew was kind enough to open the stable doors and give us shelter till it passed. Sure surprised me, it blew up so sudden. Kind of a whirlwind; guess the worst of it missed here, though. What confuses me, is that durned leech I've got at home, in the bottle."

"Leech?" puzzled Mrs. Tuttle.

"My weather barometer," explained Uncle. "Had him for a long time; faithful as the devil. You take a small bottle, fill it three quarters full of water, and just put a good healthy leech in it. Simple as that, just have to change the water once a fortnight. He's pretty dependable, don't quite understand how he slipped up this time. If it's to rain, he'll come up to the top of the bottle, slow like, and just stay there, 'till the weather settles down again. If it's to be a bad storm, he'll be most out of the water for days ahead. Well, he was up to the top of the bottle alright, staring me right in the face, but he sure didn't say nothin' about such a blow as this!" He chortled then, while we smiled in polite amusement. Uncle could break the ice in any situation.

Mrs. Tuttle poured our tea. "And how is everything else over in Clarkeville?" she inquired. "That is, besides the leech! I never get that way, but once a year, when the fair is on. Guess by rights I should say Brookfield, only we've called it Clarkville for so long."

"Oh, nothing's changed much in Brookfield, except the name," I laughed, then added impulsively, "My, but this is certainly a beautiful place you have here."

Mrs. Tuttle beamed with pride. "Why, thank you. I like to say that it's the culmination of years of dreams, plans, and toil, but," she hastened to add, "It was worth every bit of it. We just built a couple of years ago, after we were able to buy the land, through Wait Clark. Until then we lived in that old cabin, which Sam's grandfather raised, when he settled these acres." She pointed to the side of the house opposite the barns, toward a tiny old time log house, which undoubtedly had been enlarged at least a couple of times. "I love this new house, but you know," she lowered her voice confidentially, "I sometimes get homesick, even yet, for the old house, especially in the winter, when the wind is howling, and I think about those pleasant evenings, just sitting round the fireplace, warming our feet, and talking over the day's affairs. Didn't even need a candle—the snap and crackle of the logs; the tinge of smoke in the air, and if you needed to freshen it up a bit, you could toss in a pine cone. And then summertimes—the old rambler rose, twining up the walls, clean to the roof!" Her voice trailed away.

"I only wish I could paint the approach in oils, as it was at that moment when we came up through," I interrupted her reverie. "That barren hillside, this mansion setting on its summit, silhouetted against deep purple sky, and the three towering elms swaying over all. It was breathtaking! But such a hill to live on!"

"No worse than your Beaver Hill!" interrupted Edwin, who had apparently been eavesdropping, from the far end of the room.

"True, but we live *under* Beaver," I countered, "almost in its shadow."

"So that's why your name is Hills," he teased.

"Please, don't let Ed bother you," apologized Mrs. Tuttle. "He's always been like this."

"Well," observed Uncle Hosea, "look at that sun shine, sky's as blue and clear as ever I see! Never'd know we had a storm, cep'tn for the wet grass. Guess I'd better meander down and take a gander at that wool you folks aim to sell."

"Uncle must be out in the barn," offered Edwin. "Probably

stayed out with the stock to make sure everything was alright. Looks like he's headed toward the house now," and he nodded his head in the direction of the windows. He turned toward me. "You seem to have an artist's eye, Miss Hills. Would you like to admire our view in the sunlight?"

"I'd love to," I replied. "It was so nice making your acquaintance, Mrs. Tuttle, and thank you for the tea. It'd be a pleasure if you'd stop in at our house, when you are in the village, and meet Mama."

"Perhaps I shall," she smiled, "and do come back with your Uncle, when he comes this way again."

"Take a look at that!" boasted Edwin, as we neared the edge of the lawn, where the ground dropped away sharply. "Now what do you say?"

"It almost takes my breath away!" I gasped. From our height, the opposite hillsides appeared dotted with buildings and neat little squares of fields, surrounded by walls of hand picked stone, painstakingly laid up, straight across the gullies and hilltops alike.

"Some view! Isn't it? Great-Grandpa built up here in the beginning; he believed the crops did better high up, where the frost didn't touch quite so early. Said he wanted an eagle's eye view of things, and up here he sure got that! Always have a nice breeze up here—Summers are nice and cool, the air is always stirring. Got to admit, though, it does quite a bit more than stir in the winter! 'Course the new house is pretty tight. Tight as a man can make it, I reckon. Exactly where do *you* live, Miss Hills?"

"South of the Academy, a few houses, on the East Beaver Creek Road. Why don't you call me Eudocia?" I added impulsively.

"What's the matter, don't you like your name, either?" he teased.

"Let's just say I've withstood a lot of kidding about it over the years," I replied.

"Confidentially, you and me, too. They used to call me Tittle-Tattle Tuttle, that is, until I got big enough to put a stop to it. Darn, there comes your Uncle, and just as we were getting acquainted. By the way, do you dance?"

"I love to."

"Well, it looks as if I've been traveling in the wrong direction," he muttered.

"I beg your pardon, what did you say?"

"Just that I should have been attending Brookfield's dances, instead of Sherburne's. Do they hold dances on Saturday nights over there?"

"Every Saturday."

"Gosh, I always supposed that was a Seventh Day town."

"Well, it pretty much is, though I guess in numbers they are about evenly divided; between the Methodists, the First and Seventh Day Baptists. But our Sabbath commences at sundown, Friday night, and ends on Saturday, at sundown, so you see, Saturday evening is still our big night."

"Maybe I'll see you around then," he returned hurriedly, just as Uncle drove Maggie up to where we stood, conversing. "Goodbye, Eudocia, really nice meeting you," he spoke casually, for Uncle's benefit, meanwhile grasping my arm and assisting me up onto the high carriage step. "See you next year, Hosea."

"Well," remarked Uncle, as we crept slowly down the steep, winding descent, "looks as if you two hit it off pretty well," and he grinned, slyly.

"Uncle, you brought me here on purpose, didn't you?"

His grin opened a little wider.

"Didn't you?"

"Well, you've got to admit, you're a heap more cheerful than I've seen you in quite a spell. I bought Sam's wool," he switched the subject abruptly, signifying that the preceding subject was closed. "Guess we'll be aheading home." Now on the main highway, Maggie leaped as if she recognized the word, and the carriage began to roll along at its fastest pace of the day.

Chapter Twelve

Since it was highly improper for a young lady to attend a dance unescorted, I frequently planned to go with my baby sister, Amelia, and her squire, Hiram Beebe, whom everyone knew as "Hi." He hailed from Gorton Hill vicinity, son of Lyman Beebe, the master carpenter. Hi and Meal had been keeping company for a year, which made my lack of male companionship seem even more tragic.

On the Saturday evening following our visit at the Tuttle farm,

I made certain to tag along with them, taking extra pains in the choice of my apparel and hairstyle. I was not disappointed, for during the second number I spied Edwin, standing alone, at the opposite end of the hall. It took me a moment to be positive it was he, for in his dress clothes he bore little resemblance to the farmer who had welcomed us into his stable. For the first time I noticed how tall and straight he stood, as he gazed about the opera house. At last his eyes alighted upon me, and he commenced to pick his way down the side of the dance floor. His shoulders loomed, wide and muscular, beneath a jet black beard, while his smile of recognition revealed a set of broad, even teeth, and dark placid eyes which sprang to life at sight of me. I gasped, appreciating, for the first time, how handsome he actually was. Apparently some of the other young ladies also held similar views, for I observed a great many eyes fastened upon his figure.

"Eudocia!" he bowed. "I was afraid you mightn't be here tonight."

"Edwin!" I returned. "I really didn't expect to see you over here amongst *our* hills. And speaking of hills," I motioned to the couple standing beside me, "this is my sister, Amelia Hills, and her beau, Hiram Beebe. This is Edwin Tuttle, who rescued Uncle and me the day of the storm."

"Pleased to meet you," he replied, bowing to Amelia, then shaking hands with Hi. The music began. "May I have the honor?" he addressed me.

He was an accomplished dancer, and I remarked that he must have had quite a bit of practice.

"I've been around a few years," was his nonchalant reply.

"Then you weren't in the war?"

"I turned eighteen after the Shenandoah Valley campaign, and Sam said long as the war was just dying a slow death then, I should stay up on the hill with him."

"You've lived with him quite a while, then."

"Long enough so they both seem almost like parents."

"Do you like farming?"

"It's really all I know," he said, neatly avoiding the question. "Now let's talk about *you*."

"There's not much to talk about, you know where I live. I attended the Academy. There are five of us girls, and we are all married, except Amelia and me. I have no brothers."

"How about beaus?" he grinned.

"Oh, some, but none serious at the moment," I replied airily, unwilling to disclose the nearly total lack of male companionship I had experienced during the past few years. "How does it happen *you're* not married?"

He laughed. "Let's just say I've been lucky enough to escape so far!"

"Then you are not an advocate of marriage."

"Oh, I wouldn't go so far as to say that, let's just leave it that I've never found the one I'd like to devote the rest of my life to."

He was distinctly charming, I decided, with perhaps just a bit of conceit showing about the edges. Perhaps this, too, accounted for his strange fascination, a fascination I felt positive many young ladies had fallen victim to. His attire was immaculate and expensive. Candidly speaking, though I knew he fell in the hired hand category; he looked the part of the young man about town, the perennial hero in the novels my sister Francie doted upon reading.

The remainder of the evening was a whirl of dancing and conversation. He asked to take me home. His buggy was a fast one seated model, and his horse young and beautiful. Her name, he explained, was Ginger, not only because she bore that color, but also because she was just as snappy. She was a Hambletonian, a breed newly introduced into the county. No doubt about it, his tastes ran in the same vein as mine, I mused. He asked if he might escort me to the next week's dance, and I consented.

All during that week, which seemed uncommonly drawn out, I found myself day-dreaming dangerously of Edwin Tuttle. I scolded myself severely for this deviation, since I was certain I was only one in a procession of girls who had done likewise.

The 2nd dance date was as pleasant as the first, with Edwin at all times a perfect gentleman and agreeable companion. That night he asked if we might have a Sunday ride together, and again I agreed, though with reluctance, for I could feel myself being drawn inevitably closer to this remarkable man, and with no conviction in my heart that he might feel the same.

I discovered a mutual interest with Ed, in our love of fine horses, and in fact in all of the finer things of life. He confided that he really aspired to go beyond the boundaries of the hill farm in his life's work; but that he had not the remotest idea of how to do so. "So—" he concluded, "It looks as if I'm stuck, little education, what else is there for me?"

"You never know when opportunity is going to strike," I

101

scolded him. "In the meantime, read, and study, that's how Abraham Lincoln got ahead, and you certainly have many material advantages over him."

» » » » » « « « « « «

So the remainder of the summer passed away, and fall moved in all too swiftly to take its place. On a lovely Saturday in late October, Edwin appeared during the early morning hours. "How about donning your best bib and tucker?" he asked. "We'll take a ride off over the hill into Sherburne; have dinner at the hotel, and stop by to see the folks on the way home."

"I sure will!" I replied, "Just give me a few minutes," and I hustled up the stairs into the little bedroom I had called my very own, ever since sister Sate had married. Between the slanting ceilings and the one tiny window, it could be likened to an oven in the summer, and an icebox in the winter; but on this autumn day it was cozy and quiet, except for the persistent buzzing of a few near dormant chamber flies, sunning themselves in the warmth of the south window.

I dressed carefully, in my miller's gray light cassimere dress, white cashmere shawl, my black cloak, best black shoes, white gloves, bag and bonnet of black felt, with a long scarlet feather in the latter, and completed the transformation with a touch of rouge and powder.

Ed was chatting with Mama and Papa when I returned, enjoying a second cup of coffee round the old kitchen table. He bounced to his feet, whistled, bowed, and commented, "They'll never know!"

"Who—will never know—what?" I demanded.

"That you are from the hills of Brookfield!"

"Take that back!" I commanded, laughing, and shaking a finger in his face. "Lucky that was said in jest! We Brookfielders are a proud lot! Seems to me you're from the hills, too, Mr. Tuttle!"

"I apologize, dear lady, he grinned, glancing surreptitiously at Mama. From the way she returned his smile, I surmised that Mama, too, had fallen under the spell of his particular wiles.

The trip to Sherburne was much more swift than with the aging Maggie. Ginger was really snappy, as he demonstrated well. We reached Sherburne at precisely one o'clock, and found the noon rush partially dispersed. Ed selected a corner table for us. "By ourselves, but not *too* secluded," he instructed the waiter, and remarked, aside to me, "I want to show you off a little bit!"

I smiled in return, reflecting that this must account for a great deal of his charm; for what woman is there, who does not thrive on compliments? Again I admired the chandeliers, and decided that during the ensuing eleven years, since I had first visited the Medbury house with Uncle, my tastes had not changed. I should still like to own a house with chandeliers such as those.

We ordered our meal, and while waiting, enjoyed a bit of a debate, concerning the merits of Brookfield versus those of Sherburne. Although Brookfield, I argued, was a thriving township, which had placed first in number of milk cows, second in butter production, and bushels of potatoes harvested, and ran a close third in number of horses, according to the Madison County census of 1865, I had to admit that it lacked the excellent location the village of Sherburne possessed. "What Sherburne has had," I acknowledged, "is the Chenango Canal, and now that they have just opened the Chenango and Susquehanna Valley Railroad, your town is bound to be way ahead of ours. Now tell me—just why can't *we* have a branch railroad coming over the hill, from North Brookfield?"

"Do you realize the hills they'd have to contend with?" countered Ed.

"I realize they are pretty bad," I conceded, "but have you heard about the near-impossible Cazenovia and Canastota Railroad they began last year? From what I hear, that must be a lot worse terrain than Brookfield's!"

"That may be true," he admitted, "but do you also realize that the presence of a few wealthy individuals in Brookfield, such as some in Cazenovia, would benefit your township a great deal?"

I was just dipping my fingers in the bowl, preparatory to wiping on the large white linen napkin, when I was startled by the approach of a well-dressed young woman, who appeared to be near my own age. "Why, Edwin Tuttle," she cooed, "How are you? It does seem like *ages* since I saw you last!"

"How are you, Doll?" he returned smoothly.

"Well, aren't you going to introduce me to your newest affair?" she demanded.

"Sorry, Doll—this is Eudocia Hills, from Brookfield," mumbled Ed, flushing a deep red.

"So *this* is where you've been spending your time!" Turning toward me, she spoke, "I'm truly sorry, Miss Hills, I don't suppose you would have any way of knowing what Ed is *really* like. So why don't you tell her sometime, dearie?" she re-addressed Ed, who by this time had nearly stirred a hole through his teacup. "Well, I really *must* run along. *So* nice to see you once more." She swished, dramatically, from the dining hall.

We sat, in total, embarrassed silence; until Ed rose to pay the bill; and I was vastly relieved when we were once again in the privacy of the buggy seat, headed toward home.

On the outskirts of town Ed broached the subject. Staring straight at Ginger, he muttered, "Well, I suppose you must think the worst of me now, Eudocia."

Completely disillusioned, I returned, "Does it really matter?"

"Very much," he answered, earnestly. "Would you believe, now, that today I had planned to ask you to marry me?"

"I didn't suppose you were the marrying kind," I countered, fingering the cashmere, while a hundred unrelated thoughts raced through my mind.

"To be absolutely truthful, neither did I, but you have changed all that. I know it sounds bad—but hear me out. Let me tell you a little of my past. True—I knew that girl—Doll, as a matter of fact, I knew her *very* well." His voice was low, unsure, but I caught the inflection on "very." He continued, haltingly. "And—she told the truth, she *was* only one of many. You see, during the war, there weren't many fellows around, and I sort of had my pick of the crop, so to speak."

I nodded silently, how well *I* knew.

"But as I told you the night we first danced together, I'd never found the one I'd like to devote my life to. But now I have, Eudocia," and he pulled the buggy to a halt on the road shoulder, alongside a pair of slender old cedar trees. He wrapped the lines about the whip socket, grasped my hands in his, and pleaded, desperately, "Eudocia, *you* are the only girl I have ever loved. At first, I'll admit, it was only attraction, towards a new girl, but as I've come to know you better, I've fallen in love—for the first time. I'm so proud of you, your bearing, your gracious and kindly ways. I thought we had a lot in common, and hoped we might have a good life together. Could we still?" His voice was imploring me, in a tone I had never before heard him use.

One instant, and a wild, mad impulse seized me; I threw my arms about him, and kissed his cheek.

His lips found mine then, as he whispered, "Oh, my dearest, I do love you so! I was so afraid I had lost you!"

And I murmured, without even stopping to question the consequences, the simplest, but most meaningful words in the English language, "I love you, too."

At the inopportune approach of another carriage, Ed grabbed the reins, spoke to Ginger, and we were off, laughing like crazy, and both trying to talk at once. It seemed but no time until we reached the Tuttle homestead. Ed tied Ginger out front, while he drew me into the house. "Aunt Lovina," he called, Come here! I want you to meet someone!"

Mrs. Tuttle appeared from the other room, wearing a question on her face, since we had, of course, met many times.

"Aunt Lovina, I want you to meet Eudocia Hills," he repeated dramatically, "the girl who is going to be my wife!"

Mrs. Tuttle smiled broadly, answering only, "I believe I knew that quite some time ago."

"How could you!"

At this Mrs. Tuttle laughed outright. "Just call it that undefinable thing—woman's intuition! Eudocia, you know Ed is not our own son, but he's been here so long, we treat him as one, and I hope to become a mother to you, too." She hugged me, in a welcoming embrace.

One moment later, Mr. Tuttle entered the kitchen, curious as to what had gone wrong, that Ginger should be tied outside. Upon hearing our tidings, he shook hands with us both, saying, "Congratulations! My boy, couldn't have done better if I'd picked her myself! Now Ed, don't worry none about chores tonight, the rest of us'll do them, and if you want to take my horse and give Ginger a rest, you're welcome. 'Tisn't every day a man get's himself engaged!"

"Well," began Ed, as we rolled down West Hill, approaching the village, "Where do you want to stop first?"

Without a moment's hesitation, I replied, "Uncle Hosea's!"

We found Uncle on his front steps, soaking up the late afternoon sun, and stroking his favorite black cat, which was comfortably curled upon his lap. "What brings you two here, on a day such as this?" he inquired, squinting up at us.

"Good news, Uncle!" I burst forth. "Ed and I are going to be married!"

"By golly, that *is* good news," he repeated, "I always knew you was a salesman, boy. When I saw how you wound Chloe around your little finger, I said to myself, now there's a boy who could sell anything!" He chuckled. "Have you set the date, Doshie?"

"Not yet," I answered, "but it will be soon. Well, Uncle, I hope you'll excuse us for running along, but we have to tell the folks yet. We just wanted you to be the first to know, after all, it it wasn't for you, we probably would never have met."

"Pshaw!" he returned, his big bass voice booming with laughter. "I'd have done it for anybody! Now git along home with you and tell Jimmy and Chloe! They'll be right glad to be gittin' rid of you at last!"

We jumped in the buggy then, Ed still chuckling over Uncle Hosea. "He's always been like that," I revealed, "I guess probably that's why he's my favorite Uncle."

Mama smiled, in the same manner as had Mrs. Tuttle; and Papa danced a little jig to celebrate, at our announcement. A few days later I disclosed that we had set the date—for Christmas eve 1868; so that all the families might be present; and upon that pronouncement, all the girls and even Mama, rallied round excitedly to offer their services toward the event.

Mama declared that with me marrying into such a well-to-do family as the Tuttles, we should endeavor to make this wedding as special as possible, so while we girls set about readying my trousseau, Mama was extra busy in the kitchen. Into the bee-hive oven went tins of fruitcake, baked well in advance, in order that it might have ample time to ripen. Papa butchered one of our hogs early; and tended, twice daily, the maple twigs smoldering in the smoke house, where hung the hams and bacon. As the great day approached; Francie, Lute, and Sate began to plan for the tasty dishes each would bring for the wedding supper. Neighbors and friends who had pewter and silver teapots, platters, tureens, serving dishes, and flatware, offered to lend their best for the occasion.

Mama, Meal, and I polished the house from top to bottom. The carpet for which Mama had hoarded rags for so many years, and which we girls had cut and sewed together on countless winter evenings, then wound into balls and stored away, had at last been hurriedly woven on the loom of a townswoman, and laid, in all its bright new beauty, on the parlor floor.

Lastly came the Christmas trimmings, strings of creeping cedar, wound into rope garlands, lacing the archway between the front rooms; boughs of pine and fragrant spruce cones upon the mantle, accented with native red barberries; wicker basket bouquets overflowing with princess pine and rose hips, intermingled with teasels dipped in gilt paint. Newly molded candles, some in borrowed candlesticks, replaced the half burned ones, and flickered in every corner; while in the fireplaces, the choicest apple tree wood snapped, dispensing its own delightful aroma. Never had the little Cape Cod cottage been so resplendent.

For my part, there was no time for meditation. I did recall briefly, how I had once speculated as to whether I would recognize love, when it came. All doubts were removed from my mind as I stood beside my beloved, in the company of our assembled relatives, and unfalteringly repeated my wedding vows.

Chapter Thirteen

The months following our wedding were among the happiest of my life. Since Ed was still employed on the farm, we lived in the old house, built by his great-grandfather.

Between our two families and the Tuttle youngsters, there was plenty enough excitement to keep life from becoming dull, even when winter's storms severed us, temporarily, from the rest of the world below. A blizzard upon that hilltop was something to remember. Its arrival was always signaled, hours in advance, by a blanket of morose gray clouds, which steadily unloaded their flaky white burden upon us. The constantly wailing wind increased its tempo to a howl, sweeping over the hilltop, lashing at the windows, while setting about with a vengeance to sweep the plateau clean of its newly fallen coverlet, and re-deposit it in the valley below. The worn brick hearth struggled beneath the very weight of the logs piled upon it, and in response to the increased draft, roared and blazed the brighter, as if endeavoring to compete with the incessant clamor from without. But when the storm had at last abated, a period of calm prevailed. Then the farm teams, taking turns, labored to break through the belly high drifts. The roads again opened, Ed would likely hitch Ginger to the cutter, for a trip to town. I dare say our Ginger had as many bells as any horse around, and when she set out for town, bells clamoring, and snow balls flying from her hooves, most folks around dashed to their windows, to gape at us speeding past.

On one such excursion, we stopped by Uncle Hosea's. He stood in his open doorway ° while Ed blanketed the horse. "Heard you acomin', all the way down West Hill," he greeted us. Following preliminaries, the conversation turned to spring's work, close at hand. "Somehow you don't seem over-enthusiastic about it, boy!" chided Uncle.

"By gosh, Hosea," blurted Ed, "I don't know as I was cut out to be a farmer. I just don't have it in my blood, like Sam and his boys."

"Why do you stay there, then?" demanded Uncle, shaking his finger. "You're young, boy! Now's the time to make your move!" A man's got to find contentment, satisfaction in his work! It's a mighty long road ahead of you, and 'twill be a heap sight longer if you're unhappy in it!"

"Eudocia keeps saying almost the same things," returned Ed. "Tells me to read and study, and some day maybe something better will come along. As a matter of fact, she's been helping me study all winter. You see, I left school young, to help Sam; figured I didn't need all that education on the farm."

"And a right smart pupil he's been, too," I added.

"Have you anything special in mind, you'd like to do?" questioned Uncle.

"Well," Ed hesitated, "I've thought about selling, not in a store, mind you, but traveling, about the country, maybe some line of farm machinery. I think I could do it; I know farming; but it's a big jump to make with no experience at salesmanship."

"By golly," exploded Uncle, whacking his knee, "I said a long time ago you was a born salesman!" He scratched his head, packed his pipe, lit it on the third try, and with a long draw, settled into his wing backed chair, deep in thought. At last he spoke. "It's acomin' spring," he stated, "and I'm acomin' seventy-two. The black shop, and all the buyin' and sellin' of wool, hops, and teasels, is gettin' most too much for me. I need younger blood. My boys has all got their own business. I didn't want to give up the reins when I was younger; I don't believe in it. And they didn't want to wait for me to grow old and die, before they took over." He drew on the pipe, then continued. "So here it 'tis. I'm a rattlin' around in this big house, alone, course I got La-Fayette and Norm next door, but it'd be kind 'o nice to have somebody around to cook and tidy up the place." He shifted his huge body in the chair, to face Ed directly. "Now if you can see your way clear to leave the farm; I'll furnish

° Present home of Miss Elizabeth Avery.

108

you folks with a place to live, and you can help me out in the shop, 'till it's buyin' time again. Then you can go out with me a couple of times, and after that you'll be on your own, abuyin' on a percentage, for me. In the meantime, you can be feelin' out prospects for machinery or what have you, and iff'n you can't get a start with that offer, then you aren't no salesman a'tall, and I've plum wasted seventy years o' judgin' human nature!"

"Hosea," exclaimed Ed, springing to his feet, to stride across the room to Uncle's chair, and grasp his hand, "A salesman knows when he has just been offered one whale of a good deal, so I'm ready to start anytime you are; that is; if it's alright with you, honey!"

"What can I say," I ejaculated, "except that I always told you opportunity would strike someday; and here it is, sooner than even I had expected!"

Sam and Lovina received the news graciously; and wished us well. By the time of the robin's return, Ed and I were also nesting in my home town village. Uncle's place was just around the corner from Francie and Hank, on Clark Street; and within walking distance of both Sate's and Mama's.

Ed took to buying and selling from the first. As for the black shop; the work was hum-drum, but it supplied our bread and butter. Ed looked so good on his first couple of trips out with Uncle Hosea, that Uncle immediately put him on his own. Due largely to his youth, he soon traversed much more territory than Uncle had ever done; consequently they purchased more wool than the warehouses which Uncle contracted with, in New England, could handle. It was decided then that Ed should journey to Syracuse, where Uncle heard the highest going prices, west of New England, were being paid, by the Hayden Brother's Woolen Mills; who were also proprieters of the Onondaga County Store, on Warren Street. On his return trip, Ed planned to stop at the Bramer and Pierce Agricultural Works in Fabius, manufacturers of "The Young Warrior Mower", and other farming implements.

"But Ed," I worried, "how can you hope to sell their line of machinery? It takes money to buy a demonstrator, or at least an agency, neither of which we have. Perhaps they already have someone selling in this locality."

"Well, little lady," he rejoined, "this is where we shall see just how good a salesman I am; for if I can sell myself to this outfit without any money, we just might have a chance!"

"You really think so! Oh, but it's going to be a long trip," I fretted, "I'll miss you terribly!"

"Oh, I don't believe so," he chuckled, "because you're going with me!" At this pronouncement, he grabbed me in his arms, and we did an impromptu whirl about the room.

"I'm going?" I was incredulous. "But how can two of us afford to go, Ed?"

"With the extra percentage I made buying so much wool, that's how! By all rights we probably shouldn't spend the money, but I look at it this way. We never had a honeymoon, and I figure it's high time we did."

"But people in our class just don't have honeymoons," I countered.

"Class! Class!" he mimicked. "Just what class do you think we're in, lady locket! Just wait until I get my feet on the ground in this machinery business, we'll *be* class! You don't fool me one bit, with all these objections, you're dying to go, but you figure we've got to be thrifty. *Now* start making plans for your packing, because *we* are leaving Monday morning!"

Very early on the appointed day, we climbed aboard brother-in-law George Woodworth's stage, which carried mail and passengers between Brookfield, Leonardsville, and Bridgewater, (North Brookfield Station still being under construction). At Bridgewater we caught a second stage which took us to the depot for the New York Central and Hudson River Railroad. Despite the smoke and soot we swallowed, my first train ride bid fair as a rival to my first buggy ride behind old Maggie. The drunken, lurching sway of the cars, the rhythm of the clacking wheels upon the rails, the mournful wail of the whistle at every tiny crossing, and the glory of the ever changing scenery from my window seat; was equalled only by the fact that my beloved and I were together, on what seemed indeed, to be as genuine a honeymoon, as if we had been married that very day.

It was late evening when we checked in at our hotel, a welcome haven for two very tired and sticky people. We slept late, and after a hearty breakfast I accompanied Ed to the Onondaga County Store, where he had an appointment with a Mr. J. W. Gates. Shortly they came to a satisfactory bargain on the wool; which left us free for the remainder of the day. We window-shopped, and made a few small purchases. "Souvenirs," Ed said, "of our honeymoon."

We rose at day break on the following morning, and took a train for LaFayette, from which village we caught the stage that traversed the famous Cherry Valley Turnpike. I was aghast as the vehicle, drawn by six panting horses, trundled up first one side and down another of their so-called hills, which, by comparison, made our Beaver Hill back home resemble a mere ant hill. At Pompey we ate an early lunch, and changed stages to one bound for Fabius, arriving there in time for Ed to contact Mr. Bramer, while I waited apprehensively outside his office.

"Well?" I questioned, scarcely able to speak, as Ed emerged, smiling, from the office of Bramer and Pierce.

"Did you doubt for one moment that I would get the contract?" he scolded, and I, suddenly remembering how he had won over Mama, replied firmly, "Oh, never! But what about money for collateral?"

"Well, I know it's hard to believe, but after hearing my story, and checking out the wool contract I made in Syracuse yesterday, they said they'd be pleased to give a promising young fellow a chance. Therefore they are trusting me with the first couple of machines!"

"Oh, I believe you, I *do* believe you!" I exclaimed hurriedly, giving him a great bear squeeze, but seeing only Mama's completely sold and smiling face.

"I also inquired of Mr. Bramer about coach service out of town," he continued. "There are no more stages today, but there is a good hotel here. Early in the morning there will be a stage which travels most of the Skaneatles Turnpike."

"You mean to say that this is the *same* turnpike which crosses Brookfield, and runs through Plainfield Center?"

"That it is. It cuts down, on a southerly route, from the Cherry Valley, in Richfield Springs, and rejoins the Cherry Valley turnpike at Skaneatles. Back a few years, these roads were the main thoroughfares for hordes of cattle, sheep, pigs, turkeys and what have you; as they were driven east, on their way to market in Albany. And of course, the settlers heading westward used them, too."

"Uncle Hosea told me about that once," I replied thoughtfully.

Dawn of the next day found us rolling along on the stage, a ride which was doubly enjoyable, due to the success of Ed's mission. Along our route were scattered the several glittering bodies of water which served as reservoirs for the Chenango and Erie Canal; while between the villages of Eaton and Hamilton we noted extensive construction underway for the Midland Railway. Again I stated my consternation about Brookfield's lack of a railroad. "If we don't get it soon, Ed," I worried, "our little town is going to shrivel up and die!"

'I fear that is only too true," he replied. We'll have to see what we can do about it."

Dusk was gathering as we rumbled down West Hill into the village, and staggered, on sea sick legs, the last few yards to Uncle's house. He was waiting up, expecting, he said, that we just might get back tonight, with good news. I left Ed to relate the details of our trip, while I took the big blue flowered pitcher which matched the washbowl Aunt Luranda had always kept on the guest chamber washstand; filled it with warm water, and retired, gratefully, to our room, for a much needed bath.

In the morning, after sudsing and airing most of the clothing we had worn on our trip, I scurried around the corner to see Francie. I had no more than said good morning; when Frankie dashed in, so excited he scarcely noticed me.

"Well, are you in such a hurry that you can't speak to your Aunt Dosh?" scolded Francie.

"Oh, sorry, hello, Aunt Dosh," Frankie apologized, then turned, grabbing a breath, "Mama, did you know they found Moses Johnson?"

"No!" Francie replied. "Where?"

"Down in an old dug well, over in the Giles district!" (Moses Johnson's disappearance had been of more than ordinary concern to us, since his daughter, Lurinda, was the wife of Hosea Moreau, Uncle's next to youngest son.)

We gasped in unison—"What?"

"It's true, somebody just rode down into town and said so! They need help to get the body out. Mama, some of the men are leaving right away with ropes and tackles to draw him out! Please, can I go along, please?"

"What—go with those men? No, you most certainly may *not!* He must have been down in that well for weeks! How you could want to see such a thing as that is beyond me!"

Frankie slumped out then, and I watched him make his way, dejectedly, back upstreet. What I didn't see was that Frankie's curiosity soon got the better of his judgment, as he met up with a bunch of fellows in a lumber wagon, who were going along "just to see the excitement." Frankie jumped in, hiding under the seat while the conveyance made its way past his parent's home.

The sun hung low in the western sky, when Frankie appeared at our door. "Aunt Dosh," he pleaded, "you got anything handy for a sick stomach?"

One glance told me he *was* sick. "Oh, oh, you didn't mind your mother, did you?"

"Noooo—but I wish I had," he groaned, rubbing his stomach while he downed a cup of catnip tea. "We got there just as they were pulling him out. I only took one look, and oo-ooooh, why did I do it—I've been sick ever since!"

"Nothing like experience as a teacher," I muttered. "What do they figure happened?"

He shrugged. "They all figure it was murder, no idea who did it, or why; but some say he probably showed off his gold pieces once too often!"

The suffering Frankie then begged me not to relate the tale to his mother, who had by this time noted her son's prolonged absence. Upon putting two and two together, she surmised where he had been. However, upon viewing his condition, she concluded his illness to be punishment enough for his disobedience.

About two weeks after the Moses Johnson episode, which murder was never solved, our baby sister, Amelia, and Hi Beebe were married, in a pretty August ceremony. Congratulations were in order for the happy couple, but even more so for Papa, who had at last succeeded in marrying off all five of his daughters!

Ed presently sold the machines which Bramer and Pierce had entrusted to him, plus a few smaller implements. Since he had begun this venture late in the season, it seemed doubtful he would make any more sales until the following year; at which time he voiced confidence that "we will see our ship come in!"

Chapter Fourteen

We enjoyed winter in the village; it being spiced by dances in Keith's ballroom, shows at the opera house, choir practice, and just socializing. Uncle Hosea was a mainstay in the church choir. He was also on the board of the Madison County Musical Society, which was specifically organized for the improvement of sacred music. A public minded citizen, he was for higher education; and served on the Academy board as well.

One persistent topic of conversation between Ed, Hank, and Uncle was the railroad; which all deemed necessary for the continued prosperity of the community. The question of how to obtain enough interest in the project to raise the necessary funds, was the one which plagued them.

But there were quiet, uneventful winter evenings, and these were the most precious of them all. Uncle often retired early, and we were left alone, to visit about the day's affairs, or past events, with me curled upon Ed's lap, before the roaring fire. In such a manner the season passed away, and it was spring again; time for Ed to make his contacts for possible sales. As soon as the roads were passable, he did so, and when convenient, I accompanied him. Early that May, our joy was complete, for not only did it seem that Ed had been correct in his hunch about "our ship coming in," but I discovered we were to have a "stork coming in," just about in time for our second anniversary. "Our Christmas present," we termed it, in joyous anticipation of the expected event.

Doctor Saunders advised me to forego any long buggy rides, as the roads were much too rough and bumpy for my condition; so I busied myself with the sewing of a layette for our little one. Tiny stitches, all hand done, on the finest of cotton and flannelette, were stowed away, as well as crotcheted sweaters, booties, and embroidered blankets. Our baby should not want for anything.

It was August, and once more Ed had purchased a bumper crop of wool. Since he wished to observe some new machines in action in Fabius, he arranged to go by way of Syracuse, to dicker over the surplus wool; thereby planning almost the identical journey we had made the previous year. Certain of the stage connections had been discontinued as railroads had become more prevalent; and he therefore planned to come from Fabius home, by way of Cazenovia and Canastota, to the New York Central tracks. In this manner, he reasoned, he should make better time; since he would drive Ginger to Utica, leave her in a livery near the Dudley House Hotel, and pick her up on his return. He left me on a Sunday afternoon, intending to spend the night at the hotel near Baggs Square. If luck were with him he might return late Wednesday evening; if it were not, he should at least make it home by Thursday.

It was the first time since our marriage that we had been apart for overnight, and I dreaded it. I reminded myself that this was best for our child to be, and that it would be only for a couple of days, four, at most. Certainly this could be no comparison to a lengthy absence, or, sending a husband off to war; so as a sudden, unexplainable shiver shook me, I threw it off, mentally tagging myself as a silly, spoiled fool, and smiled a forced goodbye to Ed's whispered "Take care, Eudocia." I watched, motionless, while he and Ginger disappeared around the corner of Clark Street onto Main, headed toward Beaver Hill, on the first lap of their journey.

I busied myself patiently until Wednesday night. When it appeared that Ed was not going to make it back that evening, I climbed the stairs to bed, still listening for the clap of Ginger's hoofs to round the corner. After this manner I fell to sleep, arising in the morning with the joyful certainty that Ed would be home that day. Thursday's darkness fell. I sat alone on the front porch, rocking slowly in Uncle's favorite outdoor chair; my eyes fixed on the myriad stars hung in infinity. From time to time a buggy clattered down Main Street, one even turned our corner, and my heart skipped, but the vehicle continued on toward Nashville. At last my weary eyes closed fast, and when I awakened some time later, I methodically climbed the stairs and tumbled into bed; just as the mantle clock struck twice.

Friday brought no communication from my husband. I paced the floors, unable to concentrate on anything, except the stark fact of my beloved's absence; while Francie and Uncle Hosea attempted to quiet me, insisting there was "nothing to worry about" and "that he must have been merely detained longer than he had expected."

When Saturday dawned with still no message, Uncle quietly hitched old Maggie to the buggy, and without a word to me, drove off in the direction of North Brookfield. He returned some time later, with the information that he had dispatched a wireless to the Onondaga County Store, and in return, had received the reply that Ed had arrived there on Tuesday, as scheduled. Since there was no way possible to contact Bramer and Pierce that day; he next consulted with Hank, who confided to Hosea that he also, was terribly concerned. "If he doesn't show up tonight," said Hank, "I'll leave for Utica about dawn, to check the Dudley House, and the livery where he should have left his horse."

"Well, now, I'm not lettin' you make that trip alone," Uncle stated.

"It'll be a long, hard trip, Hosea."

"I've stood 'em before," insisted Uncle. "It's part of my business, too, you know."

The men were up long before the sun rose. I was frantic, and announced my intention to accompany them.

"But there is nothing you can do, Dosh," Hank reminded me gently.

"Please, Hank, I can't bear to sit here alone and just wait!" I was begging.

"Francie will come and stay with you, or you can go to our house."

"Oh, no, Hank, please, *please* don't try to stop me! Francie can go with us, if she likes."

"But what of the baby?" Francie tried to reason with me. "Dosh, you are so beside yourself with worry, that you are not thinking clearly. You know Doctor Saunders warned you about riding!"

"I will be worse off if I don't go," I rebutted, and reluctantly, Hank conceded I might as well ride along. Francie dispatched Frankie down to Papa's for the day, with instructions to "put him to work," since Sunday was the beginning of the work week for Seventh Day Baptists.

At a livery near the New York Central tracks we located Ginger; and the irate livery owner, who sputtered that the fellow who left her had informed him he'd call for his horse Wednesday or Thursday. "She's run up quite a bill," he fussed.

"Don't worry about it," replied Uncle, shortly. "I'll take care of it."

On a bench outside the livery we spied a couple of bums who appeared to be part of the establishment. One of them spoke. "Folks, it ain't none o' my business, but did I hear you talkin' about thet Hambletonian? Dang nice lookin' horse. 'Course you can tell me to mind my own affairs iff'n you want to, but I was jest kind o' curious as to what became of the feller who brought her in."

"Did you see him?" Hank pounced upon them.

"Sure I saw 'im. There ain't much goes on around here *we* don't know about." He squared his shoulders, and leaned back against the livery wall, to eye Hank directly. "Isn't that so, Bub?" he addressed his silent, slumping partner, who merely nodded. "Saw 'im when he come after her, too."

"What? What's that you said?"

"Said we saw 'im when he come after her, but 'sa funny thing!

The next time me and Bub went in the stable thet Hambletonian was still there. "I says, "Jim, (he's the livery man), how come thet feller didn't take his horse, when he was here?" And Jim says, "I didn't see nobody come after no horse." But me and Bub sure did. Say, are you lookin' for thet guy? He in some kind o' trouble? Better check the saloons, thet's where they thet's got troubles hangs out. Ain't in the one me and Bub hang out in, though. Is he, Bub?" Bub shook his head.

"You *positive* it was the same fellow who brought her in?" Hank questioned.

"Sure as shootin'. Young feller, mebbe twentyfive, tall, dark hair and beard, good lookin' feller. Never ferget a face—Mebbe I don't look too smart, but I never ferget a face! Do I, Bub?" Bub waggled his head loosely. "Say, thet feller ain't wanted by the police, is he?"

"Not yet," Hank returned. "I'm his brother-in-law, and we're just trying to find out what in thunder has become of him."

"Well, I'm right sorry to hear thet, ain't we, Bub? But like I said, I'd try the saloons. Many's the man got lost in them!"

"Here," offered Uncle Hosea, digging into his pocket, "you fellows have helped us a lot," and he handed each a fifty cent piece.

"Well," puzzled Hank, while I struggled to control my mounting fear, "I can't imagine Ed hanging out in a bar all this time, but since I can't think of any other place to look, I suppose we might as well make the rounds."

A search of every known saloon and surrounding alleys in the vicinity of Utica turned up no Ed, nor had anyone on the premises seen anyone answering his description in the past few days. We contacted the police, who in turn questioned the livery owner, also Bub and his friend, whom they discovered at their saloon hang-out, congratulating themselves on their great good fortune.

The story remained unchanged. The city police assured us they would do everything in their power to follow even the slightest lead; but in the meantime, they advised, "You folks had better start for home. You look pretty beat, and there's a long trip ahead of you."

Hank and Uncle, resigned to failure, agreed; and I, too sick at heart to assimilate what had taken place, trailed behind, my hand tightly clasped in Francie's.

Uncle paid Ginger's board bill wordlessly; took her, and the buggy up Genessee Street, branching off on Oneida at the Square.

Hank, Francie and I brought up the rear, in Hank's rig. Then it was that the finality of the situation first hit me, watching Uncle drive Ed's rig home, without him, and knowing that only *God* knew where Ed was.

Francie huddled close beside me, whispering, "Don't give up hope, Dosh, Ed is young and strong; he knows how to take care of himself; he'll be back in a day or two, you just wait and see!"

Though I knew she was putting forth everything at her command to convince me; I think we *both* knew in our hearts that it was only idle chatter, designed for the sole purpose of consuming time, until the inescapable truth hit home to all of us. The dry, hard lump in my throat grew to a choking sensation; until it seemed as though I could not grasp another breath; as tight lipped and tearless I sat stiffly through the long, dark ride back home.

As the night wore on, my teeth commenced to chatter; Francie placed the lap robe and her arm about me to ward off the evening's chill. No other sound escaped my lips, until a sudden small abdominal cramp brought me into focus with reality; and a second fear; almost as awesome as the first, clutched relentlessly at my being. We started the descent of our familiar Beaver Hill; and I whispered to Francie the first words I had spoken all during the long ordeal. "Take me to Mama's. I'm afraid. I can't go back to Uncle's tonight."

Hank nodded as Francie directed him down the street toward Mama's, and as Uncle noticed us turn down East Beaver Creek Road, he reversed his route and followed. Hank half carried me out of the buggy, assisted by Francie on one side.

Mama was standing in the open door, explaining, "Papa and I just couldn't go to bed, knowing that you folks were still out on the road." She opened her arms to me then, as the wisdom of her years took in the situation at a glance; Ed's horse and buggy, driven by her aged Uncle, the hour of the night; the weary, hopeless expression on our faces. I fell into her arms, and for the first time since Ed's leave, the choking gave way to tears, and the tears led to sobs which racked my body; while Mama tried to pat me as she had done when I was but a baby. She and Papa led me to the couch, while Francie hustled to the kitchen, to make a pot of tea.

"Mama," I choked, between sobs, "come here." As she leaned over me, I murmured, "Mama, I think I'm about to lose the baby!"

Mama sprang into action. "Hank-quick! Go fetch Dr. Saunders! This girl has taken more than a body can stand. James—fetch me all the blankets and pillows you can find! Hosea—poke up the fire!

Francie—good, you've got the tea. Get more water into the kettles. We might need lots of it. Here, Dosh, sip this tea. That's right, James, help me take this pillow out from under her head, and place those extra ones under her feet. Now lay those blankets here; then go out in the kitchen to see how Francie is coming with the water."

As Mama loosened my clothing, I noticed the loving concern written on her weathered face; a concern she usually was able to conceal from her daughters. "Francie," she called, "we need bottles filled with good warm water, and wrapped, to lay at her feet and legs. This girl has taken an awful chill." Once the bottles were tucked snugly in place and the blankets were weighting down my body, Mama held the tea cup to my trembling lips, forcing me to drink the scalding liquid.

Hank returned then, with Dr. Saunders, whom he had been obliged to raise up out of bed. He made a quick examination, then commended Mama for her swift command of the situation, saying, "We'll try our best to stop it, but I'm afraid we're too late. Draw some fresh cold water from the well," he directed Hank, and to Francie, "Wring some cloths out of the well water, place them on her abdomen, and change them as fast as they become the least bit warmed. I'll give her something to quiet her down a bit. Would you step outside a moment, Chloe? Now tell me, just what has happened here?"

Briefly Mama described the situation, Ed's disappearance, our resultant trip to the city, and of our failure to find him. Doc shook his head.

"I tell you frankly, Chloe, that girl hasn't one chance in a million to save that baby now, and it's going to be tough sledding to bring *her* out of it. She's in danger of shock, both physical and mental; but it's up to us to keep it from happening! I don't want her left alone, not for one moment!"

Mama and Doctor Saunders stepped back into the room. Upon re-examination, he shook his head, muttering, "Well, I guess that's it. All we can do now is try to control the hemorrhage." Some time later, he deemed they had the situation in hand, whereupon he advised Mama and Francie to continue the same treatment until morning, at which time he believed the immediate danger would be past. "But," he warned them, if you feel there is *any* change for the worse during the night, send for me without delay." He took his leave then, and as I heard Hank's rig rolling back upstreet, carrying the good doctor, I inquired faintly, "Mama, I lost the baby, didn't I?" She turned her face away from me, in a masked expression; 'twas then I knew, for the second time that day, the awful clutching fear of certainty.

The quieting medicine Doctor Saunders had left for me, plus the warmth of the blankets and bottles, were too much for my exhausted body; and I dozed thankfully, only dimly aware of Mama and Francie as they took turns changing my dressings, and watching me throughout the remainder of the night.

Morning arrived—a mere continuation of the endless night. Mama darkened the windows in the parlor where I was lying, "almost like a corpse in state," I thought grimly.

Doctor Saunders arrived early, again praising Mama's nursing skill, crediting her with preventing me from entering into severe shock. "The only shock we have to fear now is mental," he stated, supposing he was outside of my hearing, "and it may be an uphill climb."

During the daylight hours, Mama and Francie took turns sleeping, until Sate arrived to relieve them both, ordering Francie to go home, get some rest, and tend to her family; that she would supervise for the remainder of the day.

Mama retired gratefully to her room; while Francie posted notes to Lute and Amelia that morning, on her way past the post-office.

Thus it happened that on the third evening after our unfruitful trip, the entire family gathered in the parlor, where I was still confined to bed; my physical condition much improved, but the mental in its beginning stages. They milled about me, speaking in hushed tones, all of them obviously at a loss for words, but their very presence was gratifying, since I knew they were endeavoring to comfort me in the only way they knew.

"Lute," my voice cut through the quiet, "will you help me make over Mama's old black dress?"

Total silence fell on the assemblage, as they caught the full implication of my request, and recognized my acceptance as final. George White, always able to prattle when it would have been best not to, was the first to speak. He meant, I'm sure, to jolly me up, but George's line of thinking differed from the average person's. "Why, Dosh, you *can't* mean to mourn for a man, when you don't even know——Why, maybe he's found a good lookin' skirt somewhere, and he'll be home yet!"

Lute's face was pained; the others, shocked; and as I scanned the family circle, I replied, firmly, "I mean just that—to mourn for my husband, and my baby. There will be no funeral, no formal ceremony, for saying of goodbyes. How can there be a funeral without a corpse? For I have nothing left, nothing, even to bury." I spoke bitterly. "Nothing but the corpse of my own dead body, alive, but indeed, living in death, devoid of feeling. Now allow me, please, without protest, to clothe it in black, as a symbol of devotion to my loved ones, and my own living decease." I sank back then, my eyes expressionless, while the family filed slowly from the room, almost as if they were indeed filing past my coffin.

Only Lute lingered behind, to touch my hand, in the only gesture of sympathy she knew how to express. After a long moment she spoke; and raised her tear filled eyes to mine. "Dosh, oh, Dosh, if only I could help you!"

"You can—help me with the dress," I persisted. "Will you?"

"If it will help in some small way, to make you well and happy again, I will do anything," she promised. "I'll get it from the closet now. Are you sure you feel well enough to try it on?"

I asserted that I did, and from that moment on, the reconstruction of that black dress was my only touch with the world of reality. Once it was finished, I placed it on my body, pinned my curls back closely to my head, and sat daily, with folded hands, in the big arm chair, which Papa ordinarily occupied. All attempts by Mama or any of the family by way of conversation, I answered as briefly as possible. Sam and Lovina called, and informed me that they had also checked in the city, but that no new evidence had been uncovered.

Poor old Uncle Hosea hobbled in, looking as if he had aged five years since I saw him last. "Doshie, Doshie," he repeated brokenly, wrestling to control his emotions, "if only it had been me to go. I should never have let that boy leave alone; things goes on in the cities we don't have no idea of, out here in the hills. And now to see you sittin' here like this, agrievin', it 'most breaks my heart!" A single sob escaped his throat; he rose, turned, and scuffled from the room. I tried to follow him, to assure him that it was not his fault, that he could in no way be blamed for what had happened; but the power to move from that chair was not within me, and I sat, unmoving, as before.

Doctor Saunders came again. "She's fine, physically," he informed Mama, "but as I told you before, it's likely to be an uphill climb. We've got to try to draw her out of this depression before it's too deep set. I believe it is time she returns to her own bedroom, her old familiar surroundings, and I'd advise you to try and coax her to help you around the house some."

And so it was that I found myself back in the little upstairs bedroom, with its slanting ceilings and the chamber flies buzzing in the window, searching for a warm place to pass the winter; and I would awaken in the morning, and for one brief moment it would seem as if none of it had ever happened, and I was a girl again, and that everything which had transpired was but a terrible dream, which I would soon forget. And then I would realize that it *was* true, and that no matter how horrible these last weeks seemed; there were portions of the last two years, even if they had been but a dream, that were beautiful, and too wonderful to forget. And so the remembering would start all over again, and the grief with it, and each day seemed exactly like the one which preceded it. And I would go downstairs to help Mama as she asked me to, exactly as I had when I was still a child; awaiting each order that she gave, and unable to do anything on my own accord, but sit, unmoving, in Papa's chair.

Chapter Fifteen

There came a day in early November, one of those rare, warm ones, left over from the summertime; when I felt moved to venture outside the house on my own volition. I circled the lawn, the young maples in the front yard, and the horse chestnut at the side. The trees were barren then, stripped of their few remaining leaves by a lusty fall gale a couple of nights before. As I glanced past the slender maples, their summer clothing strung in crumpled disarray upon the sod, spongy with the prolongated autumn rains, it occurred to me that here was a reasonable facsimile of myself, stripped of all that a woman holds dear; my body sodden with my own tears. My feet led me onward then, up the narrow path, out past Mama's garden plot, stripped also for the winter, over the fence, and up through Oliver Babcock's pasture, where I turned to the right, and, still climbing, I found myself eventually at the foot of the first ledge. Carefully I placed my feet, one above the other, following the steps nature had cut into the side of the huge rock by millions of years of erosion, until I was standing upon the topmost side of it. Here I paused to catch my breath, for I was not accustomed to this kind of exertion. Above this ledge, were the two higher ones. I would climb farther. Coaxed onward by a strange impulse I could not understand, I ascended the second, and finally, the third.

The dark, towering forest above me stood quiet and tomb like, defiant of time, and untouched by humanity, except for the occasional hunter. Bereft of its foliage, the village below had become clearly visible; and the sounds of activities therein wafted on the breeze as if the hamlet were a stage, the performance being amplified by a huge megaphone; and I the lone audience. Now and then a hound dog lifted his voice to bay an announcement in melancholy tones, and I shivered. The sun abruptly disappeared, and a sudden cool breeze blew stiffly across the cliff face.

I approached, fearlessly, the edge of the precipice where the sheer drop off was some twenty-five or thirty feet high. Then it was that the first dangerous thoughts occurred to me. Could I only be sure that the fall would be fatal from such a place, I should try it. Of what good was I, barren, useless, a burden and a worry to my parents? Why should I not lie in death along with my dear ones, rather than the living death I experienced from day to day? How happy must they be who lie under the ground, their troubles over at last! Oh, to be like them; and I reflected on Jesus, as he hung on the cross, crying in agony, "My God, My God, why hast Thou forsaken Me?" But the only answer I received was the whine of the wind and my own muffled sob.

But the taking of a life, even of one's own, was against the commandments of our Lord, and as my sickened mind debated with the teachings of a lifetime, a snapping twig startled me from my transfixion. It was Hank's hound dog! Strange he should have followed me up here! A second figure blurred before my tear filled eyes. Frankie!

He was the first to speak. "Aunt Dosh! What are you doing way up here?"

"Oh, just viewing the scenery," I sniffled, desperately trying to appear nonchalant.

"Way up here?" he repeated wonderingly. "You better get away from the edge of that old rock—quick! S'possin' you should fall off from there! Or maybe those old stones would give way, why, gosh, you could even get killed!"

I shuddered.

"Why, Aunt Dosh, your lips are blue. You look like you're freezin'! How long have you been up here, anyway?"

"Golly, I don't know, Frankie. How come *you* are up here?"

"Jeb and I been huntin' squirrels," he returned proudly. "First time Pa ever let me go out alone."

I shivered.

"Say, Aunt Dosh, take my jacket and put it around you. It's too hot, anyway, but Ma made me bring it. We've been hikin' all over!"

"Do you think it will fit?" I managed a tremulous laugh.

"Aw, sure it will, you're not much bigger than I, after all I'm almost twelve years old now." He placed his jacket protectively across my shoulders. "There now, I guess you just needed somebody like me to come along and take care of you! Come on, I'll show you the easy way to get down over these rocks!"

I trailed him blindly, thankful that he had interrupted before it was too late. Once we were safely below the three cliffs, I attempted to pull myself together for Frankie's sake. "Say," I began shakily, "Have I ever told you about the time that Fordy, a boy I used to know, his sister, and I came up here? I wound up spraining my ankle. Fordy was just about your age then." I reflected, momentarily, "Fordy—dear little freckle faced Fordy—how many years has it been since I have thought of him? And of how he bragged, in boyish fashion, that he would take care of me. And now here is Frankie, offering the same thing, in almost identical words!" I continued with my tale, and by the time we had reached our yard, I was in better spirits than I had been for some time.

The improvement was temporary, for in the morning there was no appreciable change. If only I might know what had befallen Ed, in order that my mind could rest at ease! I had unnumbered recurring dreams, which haunted me nightly; and some of them lingered to consume my waking hours. One, in particular, though in reality I knew better, was persistent. I would envision Ed at the table where we had dined in Sherburne, and the young lady who had addressed us there. And Ed would state, matter of factly, "But she's only one of many, Eudocia, *many* girls of whom I had my choice." Then I would pose in a line, at his request, with the many girls, for his inspection. He'd eye me over, then pass me by, to review the others in that row. And then George White would appear from behind me, and laugh and laugh, as if to say, "I *told* you so!" Screaming, I would awaken, to find Ed missing from my side, and to realize my indescribable loneliness.

This nightmare alternated with another. There would be Frankie, rolling in agony, while describing with vivid detail the decomposed body of Moses Johnson, emerging from his dug well. And I would see, for myself, the horrible scene he depicted, but the emerging corpse would be that of Ed; and I would awaken, screaming.

So at last I commenced to pray, unceasingly, "Oh, Lord God, if You can do no other thing for me, at least remove these terrible imaginings from my mind, and show me, I pray Thee, what has become of my dearly beloved husband, for if You do not, I shall go stark, raving mad!"

After this manner fall passed bleakly into winter, and even the approach of the holidays could not cheer me, for remembering that Christmas Eve should have been our anniversary, even perhaps the birth date of our child, which now would never be.

On Christmas Eve the family gathered, as was our custom, in the parlor, but it was not the same; and even the traditional visit from Santa Claus, (played by Uncle Hosea), who came especially for the benefit of little Eddie Woodworth, since Frankie announced he had outgrown such foolishness; was a dismal failure.

The party broke up early, and upon taking to my bed, accompanied by my large, warm soapstone, I dozed fitfully, until the jangling of the sleigh bells on a fancy Hambletonian horse and cutter, driven by a very thin Santa, captured my attention. At once I recognized the driver as Ed, and with him rode one small passenger, a precious little girl, whom I knew as Minnie Myrtle. The doll she cradled in her arms whimpered, and reached toward me. I gasped. This was no doll, but a very tiny infant! My baby! *My* baby, with the black curly hair, and resembling so much his father! I struggled to reach the cutter, but my legs were powerless. I moaned, and the driver hesitated. "Oh, please, please help me in!" I begged.

"Sorry, but I cannot leave the cutter," was the answer, emanating across the chasm which yawned between us. "*You* will have to come to me."

Again I tried to move toward them, but to no avail. I could not reach them, and they were so close! "Oh, where have you been?" I cried. "And what happened to you?"

"Look! See here!" he replied, yanking away the Santa Cap, to reveal an ugly, gaping hole. Search the river, for part of me is there." And with that little word, he slapped the horse.

I screamed, "Wait—wait for me!", but the answer floated back,

"It is too soon—you are not ready—ready—ready—ready—" It echoed through my sleep clogged brain, finally arousing me into full awareness of what had just taken place. This dream had not been like the others—it had an ethereal quality—it was a vision! Without doubt it had been a vision, and I laboriously went over every minute detail of the panorama which had been enacted for me alone. Truly the personages had been sent from God in answer to my pleadings. All were safely in heaven now, but for that one brief moment, He had allowed them to penetrate the cloud which separates the earthlings from the immortals; and with tear-filled eyes I slid from my bed, to kneel beside it in the frosty night, and thank Him.

There was no more sleep for me; as I attempted to reconstruct the crime which had perpetrated Ed's death. We knew that he had been last seen at the livery, on his return trip. I also knew that he should have had on his person, about thirty dollars, and presumably, someone had seen that roll of money, when he opened it, to pay for Ginger's board. No doubt more than one person was involved, for after delivering the wound, which had been probably intended to merely render him unconscious, they had discovered it was mortal, and had tossed him into the Mohawk River, a favorite dumping off place for the disposal of bodies, and just a short distance from the livery. Now at last the nights of unknowing torment could come to an end, and I awoke on Christmas morn exhausted, but more at peace in my soul than I had been at any time since Ed's disappearance.

I debated whether to tell Mama, finally doing so only because there was no one else around in which to confide. Mama, practical minded person that she was, believed only that black was black and white was white, and there could be no in-between shade of gray. She smiled indulgently, and conceded that if believing that dream would bring peace to my soul, she guessed there would be no great harm in giving credit to it.

Later that day, when Hank and Francie arrived, I drew her upstairs to my room, where I related the unnatural happenings in my dream, and those which had preceded it. Francie was a woman of imagination, more like Papa, who was given to day-dreams, some of which were more impractical than others. "I am convinced," said Francie slowly, "that it was an answer, a supernatural appearance allowed by our heavenly Father in response to your continued prayers."

"Oh, Francie, I wanted to touch my baby. I wanted to explain to Ed, what happened to it."

"Don't you suppose that he knows?" inquired Francie, gently.

"Francie, do you suppose it possible for me to make contact with Ed again?" I suggested, warily.

"Contact?"

"It *has* been done before."

"Dosh, get hold of yourself!" She eyed me sternly. Be grateful for the experience which has been accorded you; accept it for what it is—but let it go at that!"

"I'm not so sure I should. I have been reading some of Hawthorne lately; here, let me read you this passage I have marked." I fingered through the book. "Here it is: 'When we shall be endowed with our spiritual bodies, I think that they will be so constituted that we may send thoughts and feelings any distance in no time at all, and transfer them warm and fresh *into* the consciousness of those we love.' Francie, have you heard of spiritualism, and mediums, who can make contact with the dead?"

"Who are *supposed* to make contact with the dead," repeated Francie grimly. "Are you aware that spiritualism, in that form, is against the teachings of the church, in fact, prohibited; as was also the fortune teller you visited at the fair many years ago? Do you recall the state of mind in which that short visit put you? Don't you suppose that is why our heavenly Father has forbidden such communications with the unknown? Our human minds were not constructed in such a manner, as to be able to withstand the knowledge we *might*, and I emphasize, *might*, gain. You have evidently secured the good Lord's favor through your continued belief and prayers, now would you destroy all that you have won through a greedy desire to pierce the veil of the unknown, which belongs to His realm alone?"

"I don't know, Francie, I just don't know," I moaned miserably, anxious to draw her lecture to a close; but knowing that in my own stubborn soul I had to persevere in this endeavor, no matter what the outcome.

New Year's Day found me with but one firm resolution; to continue at all costs, to re-communicate with Ed. Though I prayed fervently, as before, no answer was forth coming, but in my mind a plan began to formulate. As this scheme crystalized, I outwardly appeared much improved, but the facts were that I had but one desire, driving me to continue along life's path until the completion of my self-appointed task. To consummate my plan I would need money, and lots of it; so I proceeded to let it be known that I would once again be available for creative millinery, dressmaking, or what have you.

Since the home town folks all were acquainted with my plight, the word soon got around, and I had more contracts than I could handle. After fashioning an extra black dress for a spare, I had all the clothes I needed, and I proceeded to save my entire income, except for the portion which I gave Mama toward my board. Uncle asked me back to live with him, but I couldn't face the memories that house held for me. My only outside activity was to attend church, and I did that for appearances sake only. Though I was grateful to God for the vision I had been privileged to behold, I knew the plan formulating in my mind would not be in accordance with His will. Nevertheless I could not be dissuaded from that single purpose.

Chapter Sixteen

So the seasons followed one another, as the earth made its revolution about the sun, and I scarcely noticed. Three times in this complete rotation, and I was nearly ready. My sizable nest egg was hidden away from prying eyes and lips that asked too many questions. The one luxury I allowed myself was the daily paper, and an occasional book, should it pertain to spiritualism, the foremost matter on my mind.

In the early spring of 1874, a notice in the paper came to my attention. The advertisement was for a first class milliner in the town of Cazenovia. Now I knew that Cazenovia was little larger than the village of Brookfield, but it was established on a lake, and along with nearby Chittenango Falls, was a famous resort area. Situated as it was, on the famous Cherry Valley Turnpike, and with connections to Syracuse and Canastota by the Syracuse and Chenango Valley Railroad, and the Cazenovia and Canastota Railroads, respectively; as well as being the home of a long-established seminary, it could not help but grow, and should certainly be a fertile field for millinery and such.

"Why not," I reasoned, "give it a try?" Perhaps thereabouts I should even be able to learn of a practicing medium, with whom I might have consultations, apart from the inquisitive eyes of my family. I forthwith packed a few of my belongings, took the stage to Brookfield Station, and from there the train right into Cazenovia, changing only twice. Arriving late at night, and knowing no one, I secured lodging at the Lincklean House. Next morning I called at the millinery shop, and after displaying samples of my handiwork, they decided to give me a try. Later that day I located a room, to let with cooking privileges, in another section of the village. I then proceeded to write Mama of my safe arrival, and to direct her to forward my trunk.

I found my new position interesting; my employers agreeable. The atmosphere of the village and my new-found independence were good for my morale. I took much comfort in short walks about the streets, and more often, down by the lake. The beauty of the sun-set, behind the western hill, its varicolored lights reflected on the wind whipped waves; and the stately elms casting their long, dark shadows in the fading light of day, were imprinted indelibly upon my memory.

I believe a complete cure for my mind might at this time have been effected, had I not come across an article portraying the powers of a medium in Syracuse, called Madame X. I immediately wrote her a letter, requesting an appointment on my day off.

On the specified date I arrived in the city of Syracuse, frightened and lonely. This was the identical city where Ed and I had spent a portion of our honeymoon, but everything had been so different then! Memories flooded over and around me, renewing the bitterness and despair which had followed on the heels of those two precious years we had spent together. As I drew near the street number of the clairvoyant's place of business, I was shaking, filled with fear at my unfamiliar surroundings, as well as with a strange excitement which pulsated the blood through my temples, reminding me that I was about to come face to face with the person, whom, I hoped, would bridge the yawning chasm which separated my husband and me.

Madame X. listened sympathetically while I outlined briefly the purpose of my visit, then instructed me as to what my behavior should be during the forthcoming seance. The little cubicle was dark, except for a faint red glow, and as far as I could ascertain, we two were its only occupants. I held my breath as the medium began her chant, my eyes peering into the darkness, searching for some form, however microscopic. I saw none, but momentarily I heard the jangling of sleigh bells exactly as they had sounded on Ed's rig. I screamed, though I had been instructed in advance to be quiet. At that moment I distinguished the whinney of a horse, and as I cried, "Ed, Ed," in a semi-conscious state, Madame X. announced that the spell had been broken by my outburst, and that our session was over for the day. She then advised that I rest in her waiting room outside for a few moments, until I felt strong enough to venture into the street; and as she assisted me to it, she suggested that perhaps another meeting might bring further results, provided I could learn to restrain myself. Anxious as I was to continue the contact which had only begun, I eagerly agreed to another engagement with her the following week. As I rested in the foyer, striving to regain enough self-composure to re-enter the street, a large man entered the room and took a seat, apparently waiting for the medium.

I gathered my skirts about my ankles, rose from my chair, and hurried to the avenue, for it was a long, tiring journey back to my room in Cazenovia.

During the succeeding weeks, I found myself living for those appointments. The fact that I was placing nearly all my weekly savings in the visits, and the journey to and fro, worried me not in the least. My only concern was, "Will *this* be the time that I shall finally contact my beloved?"

The sorcerer assured me that we were making progress. During my third and fourth visits, there appeared an ectoplasmic phenomena, a filmy, white, shapeless substance, which floated in mid-air. Ectoplasm, as Madame X. explained to me later, is the visible substance in which the forces of the other world materialize. However, I heard and saw nothing as significant to me, as the sleigh bells had been on my initial visit.

Madame X. was able, as well, to perceive the auras surrounding certain individuals. On my fifth visit, she confronted me as follows: "My dear, I observed, when you first placed yourself in my hands for consultation, that your aura was brightly colored, in spite of the unbelievable anguish you had undergone; but today I find that it is beginning to shrivel, and darken. I had noticed this on your last visit, but was reluctant to speak of it to you."

"Yes?" I quavered. "What does it mean?"

"I denote from this," she continued, "that you are a very lonely person, and desperately in need of companionship. You are relying on yourself too much; you are becoming ingrown, instead of outgoing, which is your natural, vivacious nature. The shriveling of your aura designates only one thing; impending death of the personality you now possess, and eventual death of the body as well. Now you have a choice to make. You may continue in your present course, and join your husband and child within a short time, or you may reverse it, and live, to the fullest, the earthly journey to which you are entitled."

"And if I should choose the earthly journey?"

"Then you must begin, immediately, to make your own life your first concern; brood no more over the past, what is done, and cannot be undone. Reach out for others, cling to them if you must; it will be your only salvation."

"But you, and our consultations, are all I have to cling to!"

"My dear, I am not the one you need, though it is against my best interests to tell you so. It is only that I feel an affection, and a concern for your welfare, indeed almost as if you were my own daughter, that I place your well being above my own financial gain. Now try my prescription of mingling with others, and in three weeks come back and see me."

I took my leave then, more upset than I had been on any of the previous visits. As I wrestled with the heavy door, it swung suddenly open from the other side, and I recognized the same large man that I had seen on each of my other visits; holding it open for me. I thanked him as he nodded a greeting; and continued on my way.

The ensuing three weeks were interminable. Time had previously been counted from one to seven, but now it was from one to twenty-one. I tried desperately to communicate with my employers, but beyond good morning, good evening, and discussion of the weather and store conditions, there seemed to be no common meeting ground. The customers likewise had their own preoccupations, and after style, price and whether or not the model was becoming had been deliberated, they were not about to linger and make small talk with the milliner.

But it was nearly summer now, and I took comfort in the fact that I felt free to wander down by the lake shore, and mingle, unnoticed, with the crowd that gathered thereabouts. The lake was dotted now with great white birds—the billowing sails of lithesome crafts as they skimmed across the water, borne on the wings of the warm spring breeze. Grasping my sketch pad and pencil, and seating myself upon a hummock, I would sketch until the gathering dusk obliterated my pencil marks from the parchment, whereupon, I would arise from the grass, already wet with the evening's dew, and stroll slowly homeward.

On the twenty-first day I eagerly kept my date with Madame X.; but I was vastly disappointed when she informed me there would be no seance that day.

"Actually it is for your own good," she stated. "I denote little change in your aura from three weeks ago; mind you, it is no worse, but on the other hand, it is little improved. In your present condition, I do not feel it wise to try and contact the spirits again. I can only advise you to continue your present course of action.—My dear, I just had a thought. You are living away from home, are you not?"

I nodded.

"Then may I suggest that you return?"

"Oh, but if I do that, I cannot come to see you anymore!"

"Mrs. Tuttle, I am your physician, in a manner of speaking, and as such, I am *ordering* you to return home, or you will be returning in a manner which will *not* be of your own accord. This will be our last visit," she stated firmly, "Goodbye, and good luck."

I retained my composure until I was outside the building, when the full impact of the whole futile struggle suddenly struck home. My only reason for existence in the past four years had been to try to communicate with Ed; my single purpose in coming to Cazenovia to try and contact a medium. The months of fears and loneliness in that strange village paraded through my semi-conscious mind. To return home now—would be to admit defeat and failure to all the family. The world about me began to spin, and slowly darken; I clutched at a lamp-post, and the next thing I remember was of lying on the sidewalk, staring up into the face of the large man I had seen so often in Madame X's. waiting room.

"My dear Mrs. Tuttle, you are very ill. May I help you to wherever you might be going?"

He had to know my name from Madame X's. waiting room, I thought stupidly. "What am I doing here?" I mumbled.

"I was just about to enter Madame X's, when I noticed you staggering in the street, but by the time I reached you it was too late. Are you feeling better now?" he queried, as I pulled myself weakly into a sitting position. "Here, let me help you." He grasped me firmly by the arm. "Are you strong enough to stand? There is a tea room right next door, permit me to assist you to it."

Grateful for his intervention, and too helpless for protest, I accepted the proffered arm whereupon he led me to a quiet corner table. After tea had been served, and its stimulation had partially renewed the color in my cheeks, the large man leaned forward, inquiring gently, "Now would you like to tell me just what happened in there today?"

"Oh, Mister, oh, er, I'm sorry, I don't even know your name," I hesitated.

"Knapp—George Kasson Knapp."

"Mr. Knapp. I am most grateful for your having rescued me from the street, believe me, I truly am, but shouldn't you be at Madame X's? Your appointment, you know?"

"My appointment can go hang today, Mrs. Tuttle. I have a phobia for helping people in distress. Now, I repeat, what happened in there?"

Now the last thing that I intended in the world was to burden anyone with my troubles, let alone a complete stranger, but as in my debilitated state I raised my eyes beyond the full beard and mustache, to the shaggy brows and the piercing eyes which searched my very soul, and beheld there naught but complete concern for my well being; my wall of defense crumbled, and I unleashed the innermost secrets of my heavy heart, in a torrent of alternate words and tears. I do not know how long we might have remained thus, had not the ringing of a tower clock returned me to the present. "My train!" I exclaimed, horrified. "I've missed it!"

"You must return to Cazenovia tonight?"

"Yes, yes, I have to work tomorrow!" I replied frantically, gathering my purse and parasol.

"Is there another run today?"

"Oh, I don't know!" I cried miserably.

"My dear, you simply are in no condition to make that trip tonight, but if you insist, I will help you to the station, and we will see if there is another run."

Luckily we found another train was scheduled to leave that evening, which meant it would be extremely late by the time I reached home. Mr. Knapp was quite insistent that he should accompany me there, but at my several protests that I could keep out of harm's way, he finally wished me luck, and bade me goodbye at the station. The homeward trip was without incident, nevertheless,

I was vastly relieved when the door to my room was safely locked behind me.

» » » » » » « « « « « «

I slept well that night, too exhausted, I suppose, to do otherwise, but in the morning I was hard put to keep my mind on the job at hand. Between the medium's orders, and my meeting with Mr. Knapp, I, figuratively speaking, could scarcely tell a feather from a hat-pin. I had barely returned from lunch when a pretty little girl, her long, dark curls bobbing, came bouncing into the shop several steps ahead of her father. I gasped with surprise, as lifting my glance from the counter, I recognized the large man behind the prolific beard as Mr. Knapp. He beamed at me.

"Mrs. Tuttle, this is Fanny, my daughter, and we've come to find her a new summer bonnet. This bonnet business is a little beyond my talents," he apologized. It kind of takes a woman's touch for that sort of thing, and I thought maybe you'd be just the one to help us out. Besides, to be absolutely truthful, I just couldn't seem to concentrate on anything until I knew if you had made it home safely."

"All credit to you, Mr. Knapp," I replied, "everything went fine. Now let's see—Do you have any special color in mind for the bonnet?" For the succeeding few minutes our conversation centered on the selection of the bonnet. Fanny was a lovable child, and, I commented, must look like her mother.

"Yes," said Mr. Knapp, "I believe she does. Her mother was a beautiful woman."

"Was?" I queried, then, in response to his downcast expression, "Oh, I'm so sorry, I didn't know."

"She passed away last January 12th," he replied shortly. "A lingering death—consumption. Seems at times I can still hear her struggling to breathe and the coughing—" He turned away. "That's why I was at Madame X's. too," he confessed.

"And I made you miss your appointment," I apologized.

"So—perhaps it's just as well I did miss it," said he, squaring his shoulders. "We have to put these things aside after a while, and go on with the remnants of our lives."

"Strange, that's almost exactly what Madame X. said to me," I commented. "Tell me, do you have other children, Mr. Knapp?"

"Yes, a boy, George Albert, he'll be ten years old in a few days now," he responded, furrowing his brow. "He really took it hard, and it's been a bit of a problem to cope with him. Now Fanny was so small that I don't believe she remembers too much of her mother. Well, I see your employers are looking this way, no doubt I've consumed enough of your time. Tell me, Mrs. Tuttle, what time are you finished in the shop?"

"Five, as a rule," I replied, with surprise.

"Perhaps we shall see you later, then." He bowed, grasped Fanny firmly with one hand, the hat box in the other, and with steps befitting his size, strode from the shop.

At exactly five minutes past five, I emerged from the building. Immediately my eyes fell upon Mr. Knapp and Fanny standing just beyond the doorway. "Hello again, we've been window shopping while we watched for you. Would you condescend to have dinner with us tonight?"

"Well, I really shouldn't," I began; then, as I noted the disappointment slowly spreading across his face, I relented, "but I suppose I could."

Fanny at once grabbed me with her right hand, her father with her left, and in this fashion, we strolled to the Lincklean House to dine. After a sumptuous meal, which I confess, I ate with greater relish than any since Ed's disappearance; he suggested that we stroll on down towards the lake. I fell readily in with this proposal, and observed on the way that I frequented this same route upon returning from sketching the lake in the evenings.

He stopped short. "Well, what do you know?" he began. "You *really* sketch?"

"I love to."

"I haven't disclosed my occupation to you, have I?" I shook my head, as he continued. "By choice, I am a painter of landscapes, especially those of historic importance. I am also on the faculty of Fine Arts at Syracuse University, though serving without compensation at the present time. By means of my bread and butter, I am a portrait painter and sculptor. But scenery such as this is my 'piece de resistance', as they say. I did some sketches while we waited for you this afternoon. I have them in here," and he pointed toward the hatbox, with a silly grin.

We seated ourselves near the shoreline, while Fanny chased about in glee.

"I don't take her out often enough," he remarked. "Always too busy, just trying to make ends meet."

"It's not easy alone," I agreed, "and it must be ever so much more complicated with a couple of children."

"I expect it is," he sighed, "though I'm fortunate in that my

135

parents are with me, so at least they have a grandmother's care. But I will say, children do give you something to go on for, a reason for living, as it were."

"Then you have felt that way, too?"

"Oh, many a time; but as they say, time heals all wounds. I have a feeling that we are standing on the threshold of a new era for both of us. Do you feel it too, Mrs. Tuttle?"

The piercing eyes again, searching into my inner self. I dropped my eyes then, for the confusion in my mind at that moment I wished to keep within my secret heart.

"I'm sorry about that question, it's much too soon to ask it. Always the absent minded professor, I guess. Fanny, are you ready to leave? We mustn't miss our train back to the city."

Outside the door to my room he paused to inquire if he might come down again, perhaps on Sunday; and suggested that we might even make it a picnic with the children. To my great astonishment, I readily agreed to the following one; and when I thanked him for the pleasant evening, I meant every word.

I tossed and turned, trying every known possible position, but sleep would not come that night. Over and over again I pictured my beloved Ed, and my baby, as they had appeared in the vision, and my conscience stabbed me with pangs of remorse. Had I put another man and child in their place? No, never, *never*, would I be guilty of that offense! But then the medium's advice would creep into my consciousness: "Do not brood over the past, what is done and cannot be undone. Reach out for others, cling to them.—— Return home, or you will be returning, but not of your own accord."—Along toward morning, sleep finally blessed me with a few moments apart from my perplexities.

Saturday evening I put a pan of beans to soak, arising early in the morning to bake them along with a batch of molasses cookies, whilst I washed and arranged my hair, humming as I worked. "Perhaps it would not be so difficult to reach out for others, after all," I mused.

Our picnic was held under a giant elm tree, on the south side of the lake, a bit apart from the crowd gathered at the shore. Mr. Knapp had contributed sandwiches, pickles, and fruit. Along with a beverage procured from a nearby stand, we had a delicious meal. Fanny amused herself, as before, but George Albert was stand-offish, though finally commencing a charcoal scene. I was amazed at the talent he possessed for one so young; and at my favorable com-

"Original sketch by Eudocia Hills Knapp, probably done in 1874."

ment, he smiled, for the first time that day. "His grandmother tries to fill his Mother's shoes, but he still misses Jenette," observed Mr. Knapp. Though he asked me that day to call him George, I could not bring myself to such familiar terms with him, and I replied that perhaps if I referred to him as Mr. Knapp; it would save confusion between father and son.

While the children were thus entertaining themselves, we had our first long get-acquainted talk, a discussion of families, home towns, education and so on. Mr. Knapp had never heard of Brook-

137

field, but then, it was seldom that anyone to the west of Cazenovia had.

That Sunday outing was the first of a series of such events; and although Mr. Knapp spent the entire latter half of August in town at a resort; boating, fishing, and sketching, during which time we saw a great deal of each other; upon his return to Syracuse, my thoughts returned also to Ed.

About the middle of September, I chanced across an article describing the Spiritualistic meetings held weekly at the Ely homestead in Deansboro. As my eager mind consumed all the reported mystical occurances that took form there, my heart surged upward in the renewed hope that if I could but arrange to go there, perhaps it still might not be too late to contact my beloved.

The following Sunday was dreary and dismal. A strong north wind whipped the waves across the lake like speeding demons, bent on submurging everything in their path. A stinging, biting hail pounded down upon those crops still unharvested. Thus it was with astonishment that I opened my door to behold a dripping Mr. Knapp, who hastened to explain that he had left the children at home, for "it was so darn miserable." Under his large black umbrella, and well bundled against the premature autumn storm; we hurried to the Lincklean House for our Sunday dinner.

Unable to conceal my latest information any longer, I proceeded to divulge, in detail, all that I had gleaned from the article concerning the Spiritualists and their meetings. He stared at me, shocked unbelief registering on his face. "Eudocia," he shook his head, "you haven't given up yet! When are you going to commence living for the future, and let the dead bury their dead? You are twenty-nine years old now, and God willing, you should have another forty years ahead of you. I had thought perhaps we might share a portion of those years together. I know I cannot be your first love, and you know that you will not be mine. But we have companionship, Eudocia, our interests are somewhat the same, and I need you. The children need you. Consider carefully in your heart, Eudocia, who needs you the most, a spirit, whom you may never be able to contact, or the children and I? And beyond all that, my dear, you need us, though you are too stubborn and proud to admit it, even to yourself."

I raised my downcast eyes then, to look deeply into his sincere and sorrowing face, and I knew that he spoke the truth. "Mr. Knapp," I considered each word carefully, "if you are willing to take me, knowing all the facts as you have just now presented them, and—can be content with half a loaf, then—I will consent to become yours."

Returning my gaze steadily, he smiled, by slow degrees, as if unable to comprehend what I was saying; 'till finally he reached across the table to grasp my hand in a tight but tender squeeze; and repeated the old adage, "Half a loaf, my dear, is better than none."

Before he departed that day, he asked if I might set the date, saying, "Let's make it soon."

"How does the first of October sound?" I returned.

"That soon?" he answered happily, undisguised desire in his eyes. I lowered mine, that he might not read there the hesitation, and know the truth; that the real reason I had set the date so soon was for fear I might not be able to go through with my bargain.

Chapter Seventeen

The next morning I set about all the endless arrangements that go with even a quiet ceremony. First there was the matter of clothing, for I had never laid aside my mourning black. I would have to prepare my body for acceptance of its new garments, as well as my mind for the acceptance of a new husband. Mr. Knapp was very kind and considerate, but even so, he was not Ed, and the very thought of sharing his bed sent an involuntary shiver through me.

I would request an extra day off, and go home for the weekend, alone for the last time. I sent word to no one, so on Friday morning when I left the Utica, Chenango and Susquehanna Railroad at Brookfield Station, I caught the stage leaving for Brookfield village with passengers and mail. Once in the hamlet, I quickly took the few steps to Francie's house, and strolled, nonchalantly through her open kitchen door.

Startled, she stood stock still for a moment, then shrieked, "Dosh! Dosh! Is it *really* you?" as she threw her arms about me; then stepped back, exclaiming, "Oh, Dosh, how nice you look! Like you had just stepped off the cover of Godey's Lady's Book!"

"You do like it?" I turned around.

"Oh, yes, yes! You had been in that black much too long, you know that, don't you? Oh, dear, let me fix you a cup of tea and a bite to eat, you must have been traveling all night. You haven't been down to Mama's yet, have you?"

"No," I replied, pumping water from the cistern into the washbasin which stood in the kitchen sink; then washing the road grime from my hands and face. "Oh, does that ever feel good! Well, how is everyone?"

"Oh, fine. Lute is back in town again."

"And George?"

"Oh, well, you know George, here today and gone tomorrow, why she puts up with it I'll never know, but that's Lute, I guess."

"I guess. And Uncle Hosea?"

"Well, there's been quite a change there, he's failed considerably, but it's to be expected at seventy-seven."

"Francie," I interrupted, I've got to make this a hurried trip. I have to leave early Sunday, and Mama may be hurt if I don't get down there pretty soon, but I'd like to go over and see Uncle first. Can you spare a few minutes to run over with me?"

"Yes, I guess I can manage, just let me get these potatoes into the oven, and I'll be ready."

"Aunt Dosh!" yelled Frankie, bursting through the door. "Gosh, we haven't seen you since last spring!"

"How are you, Frankie? My goodness, but you have shot up! Maybe you'll be as tall as your father yet!"

"Yes," agreed Francie, "he's already informed us that we must call him Frank now, no more of that baby stuff!"

"I beg your humble pardon, *Mr.* Frank." I teased.

"Aunt Dosh, come see my calf, will you?"

"But Frank, she has her good clothes on!" interrupted Francie.

"Oh, Ma! She's out to pasture. Aunt Dosh won't get dirty just looking over the fence!"

"But of course I'll go see your calf," said I, hoisting my skirts as I followed him out to the thirty-five acres Hank owned, which laid behind the harness shop, and Jordan's and Daboll's Tannery. "Calf, did you say? She looks like a yearling to me!"

"She's big, alright!" agreed Frank. "Grandpa gave her to me in the spring, for helping him around the place. He said he didn't need her, and he'd like to help me get a start."

"Oh, then you are planning on going to farming."

"Well—" he hesitated.

"Don't you want to?" I queried.

"Well, it's *alright*."

"But there is something else you'd rather do," I interjected.

"Well, in a way, yes."

"Well, what is it?" I demanded. "Come on, you can tell your old Aunt Dosh!"

"Promise you won't laugh?"

"Of course not."

"Well, I like to write; I do real well in English at the Academy; and the preceptress, Miss Saunders, even said *she* thought I'd do well at it."

"Quit beating around the bush, what is it?" I repeated.

"Um—it's like this—there's no newspaper in town; and I think we need one; so—maybe if I could get a good price out of my calf I'd sell her, and get started in the printing business!" he burst out.

"Well!" I said, "Well!"

"You don't think it's a good idea, do you?" he said, disappointment registering on every word.

"On the contrary, I think it's a *very* good idea, only won't it take an awful lot of money?"

"That's what bothers me," he confided, "I know Mr. Whitford, or any other banker wouldn't lend money to anyone my age for what they'd term an uncertain venture."

"Then we'll just have to find another way," I responded, "for if you believe you can do it, then I believe you can; for your very youth and aspirations will make the venture successful. Have you discussed this with your father and mother?"

"A little, but I'm not certain they have any faith in it, either."

"Then I'll talk with them myself," I promised, "first chance I get."

While hurrying around the corner to Uncle Hosea's, I confided to Francie that I had something of a surprise to divulge; but that I intended to wait until we were in Uncle's company for the telling of it.

We found him out in his little barn, close beside the creek, where he kept his horse and a few chickens. He was "just aputterin' around," as he expressed it, brushing Maggie, after giving her the morning ration of sweet timothy hay. It was dim in the tiny stable, but even through the darkness, I ascertained the gleam leap into his eyes at sight of us. He grasped one side of the stall, eased himself out of it, and seized his cane when he reached the floor. "Well,

141

Doshie," was all he could say, and as I returned his greeting, Maggie turned, and whinnied, almost as if she recognized my voice.

"Hello, there, Maggie, do you still remember me?" I patted her flanks. "Goodness, but you are getting old."

"We both are," said Uncle, "Ain't either one of us good for nothin', but we sort of stick around to keep each other company. Well, this is a bit of a surprise, though I must say, at my age, takes a lot to surprise me! Kinda figured you'd forgot all about us back up here in the hills."

"Never, Uncle, *never!* But sometimes a body just has to get away from things to clear the cobwebs from her mind!"

"You're lookin' good, girl. Best I've seen you in many a year."

"I'm feeling better, too, Uncle; you see, I'm going to be married next week!"

"So that's the surprise!" exclaimed Francie, "I should have guessed it!"

"Well, thank the Good Lord," said Uncle, "I ain't had a moment's peace since I let Ed go alone on that trip, but now that I know you'll be taken care of, I'm ready to go anytime. So tell us about the lucky man!"

"Actually, I guess I'm the lucky one," I answered, "for without him, I would probably have been at the end of the road, myself. The strange part of it all is, that is exactly what I wanted at first, but awhile back I suddenly discovered that I had only just begun to taste of life, and I should like to stay around a while, to see what the future might hold for me."

"Saints be praised!" shouted Uncle, clapping his hands, "The girl is well at last!"

Francie asked me to stay for dinner, but I declined. My heart longed to surprise Mama and Papa. As my even tred drummed merrily along the board walks of home, my heart pounded with the excitement of returning after nearly six months. Even the village looked prettier and different somehow, in an unexplainable way. Or could be it was me, viewing it once more through the rose-colored glasses I had not worn since Ed had perished.

I peeked through our kitchen window to a long familiar sight, that of Mama placing heavy ironstone ware upon the table, in preparation for the noon-day meal. "Better set another place, I think we're having company," I advised her, as I stepped, unannounced, through the back door. She whirled about, nearly losing a platter of steaming golden ear corn, and stood, speechless, while I laughingly continued, "Golly, Mama, let me rescue that corn! I'm starving!"

Tears welled up in the corners of Mama's wrinkled old eyes then; something I had never before seen, as she recognized immediately that I had been completely healed. "Saints alive!" she gasped, recovering at last, and wiping her eyes on the corner of her apron, "You like to scared me half to death! We better break the news a little easier to Papa; his old heart might not take a shock like the one you just gave me!"

Papa arrived shortly, with face aglow at sight of me; and over the corn, a thick slice of Mama's bread spread with new churned butter and warm applesauce, served atop the old red-checkered tablecloth; I related my good news. "Where is Lute?" I inquired eventually. "Francie said she was back in town."

"She's up at Sate's today, I believe," offered Mama. "She's helping about town again, sewing and such like."

An inspiration hit me. "Say! Do you think maybe she'd like to go back with me, and try out for my job? I know she could do it; she's the one who taught me millinery in the first place, and I have only three days left. She could even let my room, if she wanted to!"

"She just might, at that," put in Papa. "I can't see any sense in her trying to stick it out with that George."

"Now, James, that's not for us to judge," spoke up Mama, "although I guess there's no law against drawing our own conclusions."

The noon hour over, Papa returned to the blacksmith shop; Mama and I finished up the dishes, and strolled upstreet to Sate's. She and Lute were not in the least surprised to see me, since George Woodworth had carried home at noon, the rumor that I had been seen in town. "We just thought we'd wait and see how long it would be until you'd remember that we still lived on this corner," commented Sate, just a bit hurt.

"Oh, I remembered, but it *does* take a while to make the rounds," I apologized, "and as it is, I'm nearly dead for lack of sleep; but I had to run up here to present you with a proposition, Lute," and I proceeded to tell both my news and to outline the opportunity she could have in my place.

"I'll certainly meditate on it, Dosh," she said thoughtfully, "and if I should decide to make the move, you'll have company on your way back."

On Saturday morning after church, I dropped in to Francie and Hank's. Frank was outside checking on his calf, which was just as well. I came swiftly to the main purpose of my visit. "Do you folks know just what Frank has in mind for that calf?"

"Oh, I see he has told you," remarked Hank, "rather far fetched, don't you think?"

"Not at all," I replied firmly. "You need a publication here in town."

"I'll grant you that," returned Hank, "but the boy is too young, immature, won't be sixteen until January; and he hasn't the vaguest idea of what editing a paper entails."

"But couldn't he start with just a very small sheet, so he could see how it would be accepted? In the meantime he would be gathering a lot of valuable experience. Francie, I haven't heard anything from you. What do you think?"

"I think Dosh has a point there, Hank. . Why don't we let him try?"

"You two are perfectly willing to let him be made a fool of? A thing like that could hurt the boy for the rest of his life! Well, all I know is, he'll have to earn quite a bit more than the market price of that calf, for the money going down the drain won't be mine!"

I switched the subject abruptly, as it was plain Hank was getting riled. It took a great deal to upset him, except as now, in the case of someone most dear to him. "Why," I mused wryly, "can we seldom see objectively those closest to our hearts?"

Very early on the following morning, while the little Cape Cod cottage which we called home slept peacefully in the shadow of our beloved Beaver Hill, we trundled out of our village once more. We had hired George Woodworth's stage to make a special trip to Earlville, where we could board the Syracuse and Chenango Valley Railroad, which would deliver us directly to Cazenovia, with no changes. We turned on West Hill, for one last homeward glance; to behold a gorgeous sunrise flooding the eastern sky. "A good omen," observed Lute, "for both of us. Let's hope all our days will be as bright as this one from now on."

Chapter Eighteen

The next three days were hectic. First there was the matter of getting Lute settled, since my employers were more than happy to locate an experienced milliner in my stead, with no trouble on their part. I shopped for the little odds and ends necessary to complete my trousseau; but after that had been accomplished, I still possessed a sizable nest egg. My savings had accumulated since the visits to Madame X. had been discontinued. "You know," I confided to Lute, "this money is my very own, to do with as I please; and I please to invest it in Frank."

"Frank?" Lute queried blankly.

I recounted then my discussion with Frank, as well as the subsequent one with Hank and Francie; and dear, sweet, unselfish Lute was so excited over our nephew's project that she offered to lay aside a portion of her weekly earnings, for, as she dubbed it, a "Frankie Fund." "I shouldn't be a bit surprised if Sate might even help out," she exclaimed, "you know she has her own income from the piano lessons!"

"Frankie, you don't know it, but you're as good as launched!" I cried, unmindful, in my excitement, that he had now progressed to "Frank."

On Thursday, October 1st., I became Mrs. Knapp, in a ceremony performed by the Reverend E. W. Mundy, and witnessed by Lute. Then, together, Mr. Knapp and I made the journey back to Brookfield, that he might become acquainted with my family.

The hills and valleys of home had exploded for their annual riot; the oranges, reds and yellows of our maples, elm, cherry, ash, and beech rivaling each other for first place in the beauty contest, as they fluttered placidly against a magnificent green backdrop, provided by courtesy of the stalwart pine, hemlock and cedars. "A place to do the soul of any artist good," breathed Mr. Knapp; who was impressed as well with the orderly appearance of our quiet little town, and vowed that if only his work were nearby, he should desire nothing more than to pass the rest of his days among our hills.

He had no more than met Mama and Papa than he took me aside, saying, "Do you think your parents would object if I were to paint them? I have painted many a celebrity—army generals—and persons of wealth as well—their position in life is written on their countenances. But your parents—*they* are my kind of people. Do you know I still long to wrestle with the plow handle; to watch the earth turn clean against the shining share? And that is what is written on the faces of them both, in every line and wrinkle—the feel of living, struggle, earth, and all humanity."

"They would be more than honored," I replied, "to think that such a celebrated artist would wish to paint them. Only tell me—when you so long for this same kind of life—why do you live in the city?"

"They say," he replied with a sigh, "that I have talent. And if a man has been so gifted, I believe that he should share of his gift. Each being I work with at the University is a being with talent, some less than others, of course. But who knows—perhaps a Rembrandt or a Corot is hidden in the group, and needs only some simple instructions to be discovered. But even if I never know the privilege of having a great artist study under me, I have at least the knowledge that I have brought satisfaction and pleasure to many, by training them to express themselves through the glory of the brush."

The new life to which I had committed myself entailed many adjustments. First of all was my new husband, and children, to say nothing of my new in-laws, Noah and Tamer Knapp. In no time little Fanny addressed me as Mother, and had become as dear as if she were my own. George Albert plainly felt neglected. Though I tried always to win his confidence, (it was evident he had outgrown mothering); he obviously felt that I had dispossessed him of his rightful place in his father's affections.

It came as quite a blow when I first discerned that our problems of family adjustment were complicated by serious financial stress; and that our home, on East Genesee, which Mr. Knapp had purchased a few years earlier, was in imminent danger of foreclosure.

Coupled with the circumstances at home was the situation created by the society with which we mingled. One must, at all times, be on one's best behavior, in readiness for the unanticipated callers. Society in Syracuse was on an entirely different level than in Brookfield, or even Cazenovia. Since Mr. Knapp was a college professor, we were expected to entertain others within our circle frequently, as well as those of means who presented themselves, in hopes that Mr. Knapp might condescend to paint their portraits.

As he became increasingly occupied with his obligations, I likewise felt the burden in the extension of my duties. Busy as I was, I cannot say that I did not enjoy it. There was a certain exhilaration to be derived from the prestige attached to my position, and now and then I felt it necessary to recall the incident with Uncle Hosea and the whipped cream, lest I become "too puffed up."

Though it was impossible to make the trip back home throughout the winter, we corresponded frequently. In January we managed to make the trip to Cazenovia, to see how Lute was progressing. She seemed content in her new environment, although, she disclosed, George had put in his appearance shortly after her arrival.

"And where is George today?" I inquired casually, while Mr. Knapp had taken the children downstreet, to buy them some stick candy.

"Well, I don't really know," she hesitated, "he left rather early this morning, but he'll be back tonight."

"Yes, I'm sure he will," I agreed icily, "he knows which side his bread is buttered on. Lute, when are you ever going to wake up, and tell him to get lost? This is your home, your opportunity for a new life. He has spoiled nearly every moment of your existence for the last twenty years! Must he always do so? Has he been working?"

"A little—by the day."

"Yes, and I'll bet my bottom dollar it has been darn little, too," I scolded.

"Dosh," Lute broke in gently, "I know you mean well, but George is the only man who ever looked twice at me. I know I'm not attractive like you, or pretty like Francie. I have eyes, I can see what's ahead of me in the looking glass. I was forty years old last spring, let's face facts; George is the only man I ever will have!"

"Well, long as you're facing facts, Lute," I interrupted, "face the one that the looking glass doesn't reflect everything, such as the soft-hearted, generous nature you possess. Oh, George knows a good thing when he sees one!"

"But Dosh, I've prayed all these twenty years that he would change!"

"Have you ever heard of a leopard changing his spots? Oh, you can go ahead and pray forever, if you want to, but you'd better pray for the strength to tell him to disappear, as without a decent man to support you, you may have a hard time keeping a roof over your head and food on the table. Have you given any thought to your old age, your security? How would you like to finish out your days in the county poor-house?"

"Please, Dosh, don't *say* such terrible things! I'd rather *die* than go to the poorhouse! But how can I make you understand, that without George, even if he *is* worthless, everything is just so empty and futile? I'm happy for just the little time he's here."

147

"Well, I guess it's your bed, and your business, Lute," I shrugged. "I should probably learn to keep my opinions to myself." At this point Mr. Knapp and the children conveniently returned, and I changed the subject abruptly.

"Francie wrote that Frank plans on selling his calf the latter part of March. Don't you think it is about time for us to disclose our secret, the Frankie Fund?"

She agreed, so a short time later, Lute, Sate, and I placed our accumulated and corporate savings into one bundle, which we presented, with our blessings, and best wishes, to our joyous nephew. Francie, too, had been saving; so it came to pass that when Frank sold the calf, he had nearly enough cash to commence. It was at this point that Hank surrendered, commenting, "You girls have displayed more faith in my son than I have." He forthwith delved into their reserve, and came up with the small amount of lacking capital.

Thus on May 1st, 1875, "The Young America," published semi-monthly, by Frank M. Spooner, its sixteen year old editor and proprietor, was born. Though it was only a four page paper, approximately the size of a hand bill, and sold for the sum of fifty cents a year, the response, for the most part, was overwhelming. News from all localities within the township, and some outlying communities as well, was contained therein.

In July of that same year Mama wrote that Uncle Hosea was very low. We decided to come home, pay him a visit, and enjoy a vacation in the country with the children. For the visit we were tardy; but we were present for his funeral. I well knew it would have pleased Uncle, termed as one of the town's oldest citizens, to eye the long, drawn out procession, led by Mr. Todd's hearse, resplendent in a brand new set of plumes, and drawn by two spanking ebony horses.

The ceremony proved too much for Papa, who suffered the first of a series of poor spells at this time. His affliction was convenient for Mr. Knapp, nevertheless, since he had ample opportunity during our sojourn to complete the portrait of Papa, while he recuperated. The period of recreation benefitted all of us, and through our wanderings, revisiting some of my favorite childhood haunts, we attained a closeness we had not previously enjoyed.

In October we welcomed our first company from home; Hank, Francie, and our cousin, Bill Dennison and wife, who were enroute to Niagara Falls and Rochester. I twitted Hank about their means of conveyance out of town. "I know what you're driving at, Dosh," he admitted, "but I guess the railroad is a dead issue. We just can't seem to drum up any further interest in it. I guess they all figure the village is doing alright without one. During the past six years we have built thirty-three new houses within our village limits, and there is not one decent lot available within the corporation. In fact, they are begging for persons residing in the suburbs of the village who have land suitable for the laying out of one or two new streets, to step forward and place the acreage upon the market. Business is flourishing and has never looked better. We're hoping to have our new Union School in operation this fall, and they are holding the fair on a new half-mile track right in back of your Father's place, on Oliver Babcock's flat. Sure hope the weather is decent, it's pretty late in the year, but they've postponed it once, due to rain. Why, we even have a brand new Clarkville Cornet Band! On the surface, times look as good as any the old village has ever seen, but I fear for the continuation of this prosperity, without a better tie to the outside world."

Hank and Francie, during those years, enjoyed many such excursions about the country, and it was a pleasure to watch their companionship. Often their outing would consist of a hunting or fishing expedition; sometimes to the North Woods, as we termed the Adirondacks; and usually in company with two or three other couples. As Francie confided: "Actually, Dosh, it's much more trouble than to do the cleaning and cooking at home, though it hardly seems it, for the happy moments make all the trouble worth while."

Hank was an excellent marksman, and one of his favorite sports was to take his hunting hound, and head for the hills. If he could secure a rare specimin, in good enough condition to be preserved, his day was complete, with delivery of same to the town taxidermist and druggist, Adelbert (Quad) Miller. A caged fox, caught in the act of devouring his rabbit dinner, and several cages, holding various species of birds, artistically mounted by Quad, were Hank's pride and joy.

We passed the winter busier than ever, as Mr. Knapp had contracted to restore a painting done in 1833 by Samuel F. B. Morse, the same who was credited with the invention of the telegraph. The painting portrayed a section of the Louvre, including the principal works of art in that gallery, but in miniature. It had been purchased by Mr. Allen Munroe of Syracuse, for $12,000.00, but had suffered fearfully from furnace heat, which had turned the varnish so brown, that the artist's work had been all but obscured. To Mr. Knapp this undertaking was not only a challenge, but an honor, and a salvation for the purse as well. Mr. Knapp's artistic ability never seemed to quite compensate for his inability to balance the budget; however, for that spring of 1876 our home was sold, by the sheriff, and we moved to a rented apartment.

Mr. Knapp was an earnest student of history, and strived for the preservation of such to the best of his ability. Thus it was only natural that he should commence a series of paintings encompassing much of the early history of Onondaga County and the city of Syracuse, which he faithfully executed. Most of these required extensive research, for they depicted events occuring fifty years prior to Mr. Knapp's birth, and this project was ever foremost in his heart.

Throughout the winter, Mama, supplemented by "the Young America," kept us informed on the little news items from home, the successful piano concert, given by Sate's pupils, at the Baptist Church—the birth of Amelia's third child, the three being Willie, Winifred, and James Hills Beebe; the latter, of course, named for Papa. In April Lute wrote from Cazenovia that she had purchased the millinery shop, and had employed Ettie Spencer, from back home, to assist her.

The same mail brought a letter from Francie, which said, in part, "You girls have really started something. Frank has been so successful with "The Young America" that he has decided to expand to a full page weekly, which will be known as "The Brookfield Courier." Since this will necessitate the buying of larger presses, Hank is remodeling the entire shop, placing the harness workroom in the rear, the New Home Sewing Machine show room in the front, (a business in which he held a partnership with Myron Bonfoy,) and raising the roof to allow for the presses and office room necessary for the publication of the Courier." Then, she continued, "Frank has taken on a partnership with Frank E. Mungor, of Oxford, N.Y., since he will require help in the printing of the larger sheet, and also to help share in the greater investment."

At this point Frank began advertising for all kinds of book and job printing, and it was apparent that the boy was well launched on the road toward success. The attachment with Mr. Munger lasted but one year. Hank then became a full partner in the business with his son, and Barton G. Stillman of De Ruyter was hired as an apprentice.

Chapter Nineteen

Frank was interested in a girl. Her name was Dennie, daughter of Daniel Brown, who was owner and proprietor of a large, modern cheese factory near Five Corners. She was lovely, talented, and a recent graduate of Cortland Normal.

Though greatly enamored of her charms, and desiring marriage on the one hand; Frank had also inherited, from both sides of his family, that grain of wanderlust which seeks for something better. So, as had his father before him, when he asked Francie's opinion prior to his initial visit to Wisconsin; Frank now posed almost the identical request of Dennie.

Perhaps the fact that his boyhood idol, the powerful and political newspaper leader of his day, Horace Greeley, had consistently and untireingly thundered at his vast audience of readers, "Go west, young man, go west"; was the contributing factor. Or maybe it was the discovery of silver-bearing lead carbonite ore in Colorado in 1875, and the consequent rush of speculators; perchance it was the result of the undeniable success he had attained at so early an age; or just possibly it was the natural desire of one whose heart and aspirations were so bound within the literary world. At any rate, in the spring of 1879, at the still tender age of twenty; while leaving the Courier in the capable hands of his father and Barton Stillman; Frank embarked on a trip which extended for some three months, and which encompassed much of the west, at a time when that country was still largely in its infancy.

The subsequent articles published in the "Courier" attested to the indelible impression made upon the young man, as, traveling upon the rails of the Atchison, Topeka, and the Santa Fe, and the Colorado Central, during the months of February and March; he wound his way through the states of Pennsylvania, Ohio, Missouri, Kansas, and Colorado, viewing in the meantime countless numbers of Prarie Schooners wending their way across the boundless plains, in search of new homesteads.

His final destination was the village of Leadville, Colorado, where he experienced the excitement common to all those traveling within the area at the time; when he wrote: "The veins are seemingly inexhaustible, and the ore is rich in either or both gold and silver, making the resources of the state incalculable. The unearthing of this vast storehouse of wealth will diffuse new life into the veins of our country, whose blood has moved so sluggishly for the past few years. Is Colorado invested with the power of extricating the government and the people from the "Slough of Despond?"

Having also explored the wonders of Colorado agriculture, which was accomplished largely by means of irrigation; as well as the majesties of her plains and mountains; Frank next tried his hand at ranching, after which he penned the following: "It is indeed a pleasant sensation that overcomes a person as he finds himself homeward bound after an extended absence from all the friends and places made dear by youthful pleasurable associations. And his reverie is still sweeter, if, in his sojourn as a stranger he has been braving some of the little incommodities, incident to life in the far west—such as using the soft side of a plank for a bed, a nail keg for a chair, and a mirror two by three—inches, to arrange toilet before, and other furnishings of like elegance, to say nothing of the table and its accompaniments—and is hurrying toward the land where people take some thought of personal comfort. My three weeks as a ranchman gave me the pure essence of frontier life, and fully satisfied my romantic nature. I am now convinced that ten-cent literature is founded on idealism altogether."

His homeward trip, which embraced the states of Illinois, Iowa, Indiana, and Wisconsin, afforded him a brief stop-over in the land of his grandparents, Josh and Hannah. The village of Loganville, once so excitingly pioneer and opportune filled, had settled into the routine existence which befalls most small towns following their initial spurt from baby to adulthood. Frank felt no greater opportunity, not even in the Loganville which had been so great a conversation piece during his childhood years, had presented itself during his entire trip, and he returned home, completely content. We heard little more then of his venture; except that he had undertaken to write a book of his escapades on the ranch, which he entitled, "Colorado Reminiscences."

That June Frank requested Dennie's answer to his proposal of marriage, but she parried, "Wait a while." For Dennie was a home loving girl, and Cortland was as far from family as she cared to wander.

Throughout the summer they kept steady company, and in August, Hank, Francie, Lute, Frank and cousin Ed, Dennie and Ed's girlfriend camped for a week on the Gulf Road, near Cedarville, at a spot which Lute dubbed "Hazel Dell." Fishing, roasting green corn, trout, and potatoes were the order of the day, while they camped under an ample tent, resting on beds of boughs, and warred with mosquitoes by night. It was during this sojourn that Dennie became convinced they should be wedded; for if they could get along agreeably 'midst such a primitive mode of living, they certainly should be much more compatible in their native habitat. They promptly set the date for November twelfth, 1879.

For four years Frank and Dennie knew happiness, and with the exception of one year passed in West Winfield, during which Frank lent his ability to the "West Winfield Star," they lived in one half of the house which Frank had known as home for his twenty-some year existence. On October eleventh, 1883, the old house rang with the wail of a new born babe, and the exuberant voices of both brand new parents and grandparents. The baby girl was named "Frances."

Although the delivery was performed with instruments, the baby did well, and for a few days the household smiled. But then a note of concern crept stealthily over their countenances, for Dennie was *not* doing as well as could be expected. The diagnosis revealed "childbed fever," a contagion introduced by unsterile instruments. Dennie's will to live was very strong, and her hope for her own ultimate recovery radiated to all those about her; nevertheless, God's will had the final say, and her spirit took its flight, to rest among the angels, on the fourth anniversary of their marriage.

Francie wrote me, one of the saddest letters I had ever received: "We miss her, so much we cannot say. Dennie was the daughter for whom I had longed. And now I have her daughter to bring up, at least for the time being. Pray that heaven will help me to do just half as well as her mother would have, and that He will raise and uplift Frank, for he is utterly lost in the aftermath of events. Though he had been more than successful in the years before his marriage, Dennie, in the past four, had become his inspiration and his guide."

I read the letter with tear-filled eyes. Who should know better than I, what hopelessness the untimely death of a partner can place in the remaining one's soul?

Frank felt the immediate need to vacate the locality, wherein all his fondest memories were stored. Hearing of the need for assistance on the "Canastota Herald," he persuaded Hank and Francie to rent the house which held so many sad reminders for all, and go with him to join in the publication.

Hank and Francie spent one year apart from the home town, when Papa's severe illness called them back. On October tenth, at the age of seventy-six, he left our family circle, all gathered together, in the little Cape Cod cottage, for the last time. Since Francie felt the entire responsibility of Mama should not be placed upon Sate's shoulders, she, Hank, and baby Frances remained in town.

Frank had by this time accepted his loss, and was able to carry on the Canastota project, without the support of his family. In 1885, he moved to Morrisville, then the Madison County seat, where he and Welcome Stillman, brother to Barton, established the "Morrisville Leader," which rose to a subscription rate of 2500 within a year. At the year's end, having launched the "Leader" firmly, he remigrated to his first love, "The Brookfield Courier," and incidentally, to his little daughter.

The home town folks bid Frank a warm welcome, and in this bustling village he was shortly attracted to a tiny, quiet, blue eyed school teacher who was employed on the East Beaver Creek Road, in the Burhyte district school. Her home was on the East Unadilla River Road, and her people, too, had been pioneers to this locality. On October 28th, 1886, Frank Spooner and Luetta Huntington were married. Luetta looked forward to raising her three-year old step-daughter, Frances, but at that early age, Frances had other ideas, and put up such a fuss that she continued to live with her grandparents, making only an occasional visit to her Father's household.

Chapter Twenty

The village of Brookfield had ambled along, literally speaking, in its same old rut. For nearly twenty years it had been serviced by Brookfield Station; at North Brookfield, some seven miles distant; apparently content to haul its passengers, freight, and mail by horse drawn vehicles.

But a new development was in the offing; a speculator from

New York City had happened along in Brookfield territory. This man was a contractor of sorts, or professed to be, and supposedly skilled in the engineering of railroads. He craftily disclosed to the town fathers his confidential information on the proposed Unadilla Valley Railroad, which was to run from New Berlin Junction, near Sidney, to Bridgewater. This, he forebode, would leave Brookfield village in isolation, sandwiched between the hills, with a railway on each side, and each bypassing it by some five or more miles. "But," said the opportunist, "there's a way to beat it, put Brookfield on the map forever, kill two birds with one stone, and have it cost you nearly nothing in the process."

Now by this time not only had a railroad become a necessity from the standpoint of prosperity, but also as a mark of status, for any town that amounted to a row of pins, either had, or was about to have, a railroad. Naturally the townsfolk were more than interested.

His proposition was this: Build the railway, approximately seven miles in length, from Brookfield to North Brookfield, where it would then connect with the Chenango and Susquehanna Valley R. R., which already spanned the distance between Utica and Binghamton. "Once done," he stated, " 'I' will be a simple matter to convince the Valley Corporation to scratch Leonardsville and Bridgewater off their blueprints, in favor of buying the newly completed seven mile stretch through Brookfield. The Valley Corporation's project will be simplified, for with the erection of a five-mile piece of easily built road, which will follow closely the Beaver Creek bed, and link Brookfield with Sweet's Corners, the Valley Corporation will gain their *only* connection with The Chenango River Valley this side of Sidney, and *your* village will become the focal point of this main route!" It sounded great!

"Now all you people need," said he, "is to raise a bond issue in the amount of, let's say, $100,000.00, which should finish your road, and later on, we persuade the Valley Association to buy it; your share holders will then have all their investment back, with maybe a little to boot."

To those villagers interested in the progress and advancement of their community, and who had feared for its future as they watched station after station bypassing them, his words were music to their ears, so like the Pied Piper of Hamlin, he played most of them into his scheme.

Hank, having so long dreamed of the railway, but having no

means at his command to put the idea into being, was enthralled at the idea, and his enthusiasm bubbled over onto Adelbert Babcock, Peleg Stanbro, Will Stanbro, Mert Brown and many others. A stock company was formed, called the Brookfield Railway Co., with Hank at the head of it. Some $25,000.00 worth of bonds were sold, at $50.00 a share, and the money paid to the contractor, exactly as called for. Columns appeared in the "Courier," reporting the progress in the work and the sale of bonds.

The manual labor was carried on by a band of Italian immigrants, who could speak but little English; while local farmers furnished teams for drawing the dump wagons necessary for moving the fill. Six of the seven miles were completed, as far as the building of the road bed was concerned. This included two great trestles which spanned the hillsides. One trestle, the largest of all, remained to be erected, but this trestle alone was to cover a major portion of that last mile.

Suddenly the unexpected happened; the Italians stopped working, though no one knew quite why. Someone investigated, and discovered that the contractor, who had engaged them, had vacated the territory, with all available funds, and left the workers penniless for some weeks. The fall season, with its frosty mornings was upon them. Hungry, ill-clothed, cold and angry they descended upon the village, where, they deduced, their rightful wages lay in wait. Down over West Hill they swarmed, an advancing army—bent on restitution. A Grand Army veteran, recognizing the band, and the potential danger to innocent citizens, sounded the alarm. "To arms!" he cried. "Grab muskets, men, and prepare to fight!" And the veterans of the War between the States, long out of practice, dashed from every nook and cranny, to defend their own; while women ordered children off the streets, and sought refuge behind the sturdiest walls.

The angry rabble drew closer, and those in position to observe were appalled by the appearance of the laborers. Surely these emaciated, shabby remnants of humanity could not be about to wage warfare! Even the hearts of the hardened were moved, as in broken English and sign language, they told their pitiful story. 'Twas then that the kind hearted citizens appeared, one after another, to donate food, clothing, blankets and such as they had to give, unto some of the least of God's children. Lastly a collection was taken, enough to assure the men food and passage back to their homes. A few, realizing that their donors also had suffered a loss, and were digging deep within their pockets to do their Christian duty, decided that a town such as this they should like to call home, and they stayed, finding employment on various farms within the township.

The crisis over, the stockholders quickly set about assessing their damages. For a fortunate few, the loss was trifling; for others, such as Peleg Stanbro, well-to-do farmer and commissioner of highways, Will Stanbro, Adelbert Babcock, and many heavy investors, it was a crushing blow; but to Hank it was defeat. Defeat in the town which had become his life, the town for which his most cherished dream had been the completion of that railroad.

Hadn't they already planned the celebration to be on that final day when the first passenger car should roll on the steel into the station? Hadn't he, in his fondest dreams, heard the whistle of the engine as she puffed around the last hilltop? Was it all to end like this? Some of the townsfolk, even those who had been his lifelong friends, regarded him now with suspicion. He reasoned with himself that this was only natural, after all, hadn't they been hurt; hurt where it hurts the most? And what of himself, in his earnest endeavor to push this project through at all costs; hadn't he invested nearly every cent of his life savings in the cause? And what of his old age, facing him now? He had been proud, toting in that cherry parlor set, cushioned in red velvet last year—a surprise for Francie's Christmas.—And the marble topped dresser set from the year before—How he wished his Mother could have seen them—Her words of warning had echoed in his mind down through the years —"You will have a hard time there just to make out a livin. Some day your health will be gone and your constitution broke down, and you won't have nothin,'" but he had proven her wrong. And what of Francie, who had just turned fifty this year? Had he been fair to her? Should he have asked her to share with him this obsession to the extent that she would now have to share with him a penniless old age? He squatted, numbly, on the threshold of the woodshed door, a hound on either side. "Man's best friend, how true," he reflected bitterly. "Come on, boys, we're going hunting." He lifted his gun down from the rack, and without a word to Francie, headed for the hills.

He returned at dusk, to face her. "Hank," she cried, recognizing the familiar thump in the woodshed, and flinging aside the kitchen door, "Oh, I'm so glad you're back! I've been out of my mind—!" She left the thought unfinished, and threw herself into his penitent arms.

"Oh, honey—Francie—you're not angry with me?"

"To be truthful—yes—for worrying me so. But I understand why."

"You can *understand?* Surely you can't understand why I threw all our savings out the window, especially when I made such a fuss over Frank and the paper. I was a fool, Francie. A foolproof investment, that's what I said the railroad was. And I turned out to be the fool!"

"*We* threw our savings out the window," she replied tenderly, reaching up to stroke the thinning, close cut gray locks, "and you weren't the only one who thought it was fool proof. Besides, I think through this loss, we've gained something; I don't mean financial, of course; but perhaps found, or rediscovered is a better word —something I wasn't sure we still had, after all these years. I love you, Hank, I love you for what you are—kind, sincere, unselfish, impulsive perhaps, at times, but I love you for every one of these traits, far, far more than the day I married you. The townsfolk will rally round eventually, just give them a little time, 'till the shock wears off.—Frank says he will try to revive interest in the project throughout the winter, by means of the "Courier," she added. "He's hopeful that with the major portion of the roadbed done, we can get financial aid from some outside source."

"I sure hope we can, honey," Hank replied, "but at the moment things never looked darker for our town. Oh, hang the town, honey, I've still got you; and I love you, more than ever, too, but I'm starving! Had no luck hunting, no luck all day.—Anything at all around here to eat?"

Chapter Twenty-one

In 1887, Laurence, first born of three sons, arrived at Frank and Luetta's new thirty-acre farm, just below the village. By coincidence, this was the very place which Frank's great-great-grandparents, Asa and Thede Frink had claimed from the wilderness nearly one-hundred years before; and included the flat west of Papa's, upon which Uncle Hosea's teasles had so prolifically grown. Beaver Creek flowed the entire length of the farm, and for fisherman Frank, the place was a natural choice.

Henry & Frances (Hank & Francie) Spooner

Now Father Time, seemingly idle for a spell, reached out to overtake our family. Sate's husband, George Woodworth, following the death of his idolized Minnie Myrtle, had become a hopeless alcoholic. Throughout the years Sate had borne her burdens quietly, losing neither her faith nor bright outlook. But at last George, broken in health and spirit, shook off the habit of years and embraced the faith which was hers. Their happiness was short lived, for in 1894, at fifty-seven, George left this world. Mama, a frail and withered eighty, soon followed him. Ed Woodworth, Sate's only living child, married the young teacher-boarder whom Sate had taken in following George's demise. And Francie was invaded by a persistent cough which we fervently hoped to be nothing more than the aftermath of a die-hard cold.

At an outing attended by several village families in 1890, an idea had been born; and the men folks acted immediately upon it, by purchasing a lot and constructing thereon the first cabin at Gorton Lake. The "Club Cottage," as it was known, precipitated a sudden rise in lake land values, and was in almost constant usage by its corporate owners.

Mama spent her last days at Francie's, and after she left us, Hank's concern was for that hacking cough which clung to his wife. Hopeful that the altitude might benefit her, he moved his family, which included eleven year old Frances, to the club-cottage for the summer. Apparently their stay retarded the progress of her malady for a spell, but when the cough lingered throughout the winter, Dr. Parr was forced to submit a diagnosis of consumption, and prescribed some harmless little pink pills, to be taken several times a day, purely for their psychiatric value. Consumption was a dread disease, common especially to women, for which there was no certain cure. Early the following May they returned to the lake cottage; Frances remaining with her father, Frank, in order that she might attend the village school.

The intervening years had wrought many changes in my own family. The children had passed to adulthood; Noah and Tamer to their heavenly reward. George Albert had married, and proprieted an engraving studio where he drew and sold illustrations for magazines and newspapers. Fanny's education as a music teacher had been completed, though she still resided with us. As for myself, discouraged with the many years of want; I was re-engaged in my former profession of distinctive millinery, and found a fertile field for customers among those who came to Mr. Knapp for portraits.

Hank Spooner & hound, oil painting by Frank M. Spooner

Brookfield Courier Office, West Main Street, in 1891

During this period Mr. Knapp was avidly engaged with his series of historical paintings; "Salt Boiling," "Surveying For Seneca Turnpike," "First Hotel and Stagecoach," "Arsenal at Onondaga Valley," "Visit of Lafayette," and "Founding of Pioneers' Day," ° as well as the writing of a history of Onondaga County and his own personal memoirs. The historical depictions, though masterfully reproduced with great detail, from recollections, writings, and such likenesses as could be procured of the pioneer period, beginning with 1788; were found to be lacking in buyer appeal, thus we relied solely upon the portraits and my small business for our livelihood. Despite the fact that among his patrons there had been such prominent personalities as General George McClellan, Major General Henry W. Slocum, Major General E. V. Sumner, and his paintings included one of Chief Justice John Marshall, hung in Independence Hall, as well as one of the first Ovarian section; the business was, at best, an uncertain venture, seasonal to some degree, and dependent upon the economics of the times, as well as a satisfied subject. Many a time Mr. Knapp poured his whole heart and soul into a sitting, only to have the subject complain that he did not care for his image at all, and refuse to accept it. As is the case with many artists, he found the majority of his patrons preferred the flattering likeness to one perhaps more true and lifelike.

From the time of foreclosure on our home until 1895, we transferred our household goods seven times, often living in our studio; and it was then that the thrifty, sometimes frugal measures I early learned from Mama stood me in good stead; for I had acquired the art of saving from the times of plenty, in order to tide us over during the times of lean.

It was during one of those lean times, in the summer of 1895, that we made our annual visit to the home town. Since the Brookfield Railway was never revived; we journeyed to Utica, and Bridgewater, from which we traveled on the Unadilla Valley R. R., which had just opened its entire route for passenger travel that year. Hank, notified of our planned arrival, met us in Leonardsville alone. "You will find that Francie has gone downhill a great deal since you saw her last year at Chloe's funeral," he told us. "Doc says it's only a matter of time."

"Does—does she know?" I groped for words, stunned by news of the inevitable.

° This series presently on display at Everson Museum, Syracuse.

"First Hotel & Stagecoach—1803"

The first stagecoach for passengers and mail stopping at Comfort Tyler's tavern, at the corner of Seneca and Salina Streets, town of Onondaga.

Oil by George Kasson Knapp, presently in Everson Museum, Syracuse

He sighed heavily. "I don't believe Doc has told her in so many words, but in her heart I think she knows, though she tries to put up a brave front. I took her up to the lake as soon as I dared; it helped quite a bit last year. I worry about the dampness, though; for Doc says if she takes cold now, it will be the end."

We boarded downtown with Sate, and took Hank's rig daily to the lake. Mr. Knapp was happiest amongst Mother Nature, and looked forward to these sojourns at the tiny body of water. Here he gave Frank his first instructions in oil; for Frank was also talented along those lines. On one of those days, while a lesson was in progress, I had a never-to-be-forgotten discussion with Francie. It was difficult to carry on a conversation with her, for the coughing spasms racked her body continually. I felt she could not last much longer.

"Dosh," she greeted me one morning, struggling to smother a seizure, "are you leaving tomorrow?"

I nodded, ruefully, for something in her tone indicated what the context of our conversation was to be.

"Dosh—you know—I'm not going to be here much longer."

I glanced up sharply, held her gaze briefly, then averted mine. There was no use; Francie was too intelligent to conceal the obvious from her.

We had seated ourselves on the porch in front of the tiny dwelling, where the forenoon sun glinted warmly between the overhanging branches and bathed the rippled water with golden cords. She scanned the spectacle; her son and my husband, standing at the shore, before their easels; and continued. "I'm not sure if Hank knows—but I think he suspects. I worry about him, and Frances. It's almost as if she were my daughter, instead of grandchild. I've tried to do—my best—to be a mother to her."

"We all have tried to do our best for Frances," I interrupted, hoping to spare her this ordeal. "Sate has given her piano lessons. She tells me she is very apt, and has a lovely voice as well."

"That she does." Francie smiled for the first time that day, a sad and wistful smile. "Dosh, I want that she should go to Normal School—you know she hopes to become a music teacher? I know that you understand about these things, because of Fanny.—Will you try to help her, for me?"

"All I can," I promised solemnly, "though I don't think you need have any cause for concern. Frank dotes upon that child of his, and I have no reason to doubt but that he will bestow upon her, every advantage it is within his power to give."

Frances Spooner, daughter of Frank, and Eudocia Hills Knapp, her great-aunt, about 1900

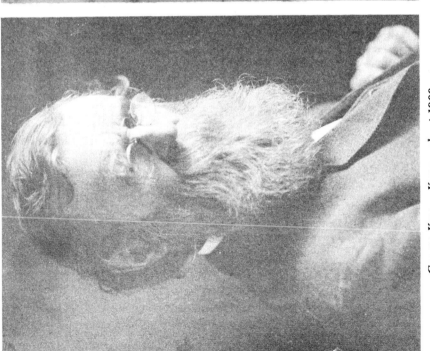

George Kasson Knapp, about 1900

"Of course." She seemed relieved. A spasm of hacking shook her body. She grappled for breath, then plunged into the thought which really bothered her. "One last thing, Dosh. Hank is still a young man—too young to be alone for the rest of his life. If—if he should—*remarry*," she whispered the word, "please—don't hold it against him, for I want him to be happy—and he needs someone."

"Francie, Francie, I choked, grasping her chilly hand in mine, vainly endeavoring to check the determined flow of my tears, "Tell me, so that I too, may know, where do you find the strength to accept these things?"

"It's like this, Dosh." The words came clearly, between seizures. "I believe in the Almighty, and I know that soon He is going to release me from my sufferings, and take me home, to join Mama —and Papa. And when the coughing and the pain get most too hard to bear, I fix my eyes upon that hill." She paused, lost in thought, as she fastened her gaze to the western lake shore and the hill beyond. She raised her chin determinedly, and her features, angular from loss of weight, were still regular and pretty, her searching eyes still deeply blue. "And then I repeat," she continued resolutely, "the words of the 121st Psalm, 'I will lift up mine eyes unto the hills, from whence cometh my help. My help cometh from the Lord, which made heaven and earth.' "

I left her that day with many mixed emotions, and when I next saw my beloved sister, we laid her to rest beneath the young spruce trees, on the lot which Hank had purchased, at her request, right-alongside Papa's.

Chapter Twenty-two

Trips back home were much less frequent after that, for with Papa, Mama, and Francie gone, the place just wasn't the same. We did keep in close touch with Lute. Cazenovia had become a part of her, although, she declared, "there will never be any place quite like home," to which I agreed.

George's visits to her Cazenovia home had tapered off gradually, and during the past several years he had not put in a single appearance. "At first," Lute confided, "I was 'most beside myself,

Frank M. & Luetta Spooner, in 1893

when he didn't return, for so long. But then I learned to lean upon the Lord, instead of George, and I commenced to attend St. Peter's Church here, in earnest. I discovered a need for teachers; and I volunteered my services. I studied right along with my pupils, and now I have reason to suppose I gained a great deal more than they. They needed workers in that little church desperately, but can you imagine! I needed that work far more than it needed me! The years of suffering, because I was barren, and alone; because of George, my ever roaming "where-is-he," have been all but forgotten in the light of my new-found happiness. I have a love, now, that will never fail me! Now, I too, know what Grandpa Clarke meant when he asked us to look up Romans 8:28; that no matter what might happen in our lives, we must look upon it as if it had happened for some purpose; and that some day we would discover that purpose. You remember that day, don't you, Dosh?"

"Oh, yes. I remember alright," I returned, but I'm still searching for the purpose behind some of the events of mine!"

"But you're happy! Aren't you?" queried Lute, shocked surprise registering on her face, while her keen eyes scanned mine. "Surely you *must* be, after all these years! You've raised two children as your own, you have a faithful husband; what more could you ask for?"

"On the surface it looks good," I admitted, "but as far as the children were concerned, George Albert was pretty well raised when I came into the picture, and don't forget Grandma and Grandpa were there to dote upon them both, though I doubt if I could be much more fond of Fanny if she were my own. Times have been hard, but I can weather that. It's just that—well, maybe I'm asking for too much, in wishing for a bit of romance, a bit of love. After all, I was not really in love with Mr. Knapp when I married him, and, then too, he was nearly forty-one. Let me quote you something I jotted in my autograph book the other day. I opened my bag, drawing forth the flowered book inscribed by friends over the years, and laden with quotations I had copied from time to time. I thumbed the pages. "Here it is: 'After forty men have married their habits, wives are only an item on the list, and not the most important.' "And here's another one: 'I wonder if you've the least idea what most women's lives are like. They come into the world with the finest ideals, the most tremendous energies, with a desire for self-sacrifice, that a man can't even begin to understand. Then they discover slowly that none of those things, those ideals,

Frances, daughter of Dennie & Frank Spooner. Laurence, Malcolm, and Jean, sons of Luetta & Frank Spooner, about 1896. Daughter Margaret was born later.

North side Main St., Brookfield, about 1900. Charlie Brown store 2nd from left.

those energies, those sacrifices, are wanted. The world just doesn't need them! They might just as well never have been born."

"And you—you really believe this way, too?" cried Lute, completely disillusioned. "Dosh, you've never showed—even a bit of this—to the world!"

"I guess we all cover a lot of hurts, Lute, though perhaps I'm just greedy," I admitted, "to want to be needed, to expect something like that which I shared with Ed, and which was snatched away from me so soon."

"Dosh, you shared more in those two years with Ed, than I did in half a lifetime with George! And—I hate to remind you, I'm sure you're aware of this, too, but you should have put that to the back of your mind years ago!"

"There are a few things in life, Lute, one can never forget—even if one wanted to." I stated, in a tone which closed the subject.

» » » » » « « « « « «

Only seven months after Francie's death, Sate wrote that Hank had remarried, a beautiful young widow, Sarah Berry Fitch, whose husband, Devillo Fitch, had been our cousin, and had worked for a time in the harness shop with Hank. Devillo was never a well person; and Sarah had been widowed for some eight years. I reflected that without doubt, Hank had been extremely lonely; as Frances had been staying with her father and Luetta, since her grandmother's death. Everyone spoke of Sarah as a lovely person, and recalling Francie's words, I felt that could Francie know, she would be happy for them. Hank was village postmaster then; and I further concluded that the railroad issue and subsequent loss of money had been all but forgotten; for he apparently was again held in high regard by the townsfolk.

In 1897 Frank was offered an excellent opportunity on an Afton publication. Feeling that the larger school in that town would be of particular benefit to Frances in her studies, they moved, meanwhile renting the home farm. Five years were subsequently spent in that village, during which time Frances not only finished high school, but graduated from Oneonta State Normal as a qualified teacher of music, thus fulfilling both her grandmother's and her own wishes. This accomplished, Frank returned to the quiet farm, firmly believing it the best place on earth to rear his three sons and baby daughter.

Sate had also married again, Court Burch, a widower from

near Five Corners. Life's blows apparently were destined to fall heavily upon her, for by 1904 she was again widowed.

Meanwhile Lute accepted an excellent offer on her millinery shop in Cazenovia, decreeing it wise to yield to her nearly seventy years, even though it meant relinquishing a part of her life, in the leaving of St. Peter's parish. But back in Brookfield village, was a recently organized St. Timothy's Episcopal Church, which was struggling for survival. And this tiny church became perhaps even more dear to her than St. Peter's, since the village in Beaver Creek Valley was her heart's first love. Here she and Sate purchased the house ° which sat, kitty-corner, from the Seventh and First Day Baptist Church, where Sate presided over the organ for the Sabbath services. It was a lovely old house, and somewhat reminiscent of Papa's, boastful of three large fireplaces and brick oven, which throughout the years, had not been disturbed. Now I, too, would have reason to visit more often, with two of my sisters "back home."

Our great-niece Frances, perhaps inheriting our love of travel, left about this time, in company with a lady teacher friend, for a tour of the United States. But upon arrival in Seattle, they were so impressed with its majesties, that they decided to remain, and acquired positions there. Here a strange coincidence took place, she met, and married, one Clarence Collins, a handsome fellow whose people had originated from the township of Brookfield, near the Tuttle homestead.

As for myself, I was fortunate, during those years, to enjoy good health; and passed my spare time in the pursuit of art and literature; a set of hand painted china, resplendent with roses and butterflies, becoming one of my fondest projects.

In December of 1905 came an outbreak of typhoid fever and within a short time, in fact on Christmas Eve, George Albert expired; at forty-one, a victim of that dread scourge. Christmas Eve— the date which I had always associated with Ed—our wedding and our subsequent tragedy. The premature death of his namesake was a blow from which Mr. Knapp never fully recovered; for in his son he had envisioned the continuation of his own career, as an artist.

I had a strange premonition it would not be long before I, too, should join the ranks of widowhood. Though we often had seen matters in a different light; I so seldom having felt appreciated, and that my most earnest efforts were for naught; still there remained a

° Present home of Gerald Rogers.

bond between us, that only time can cement into an indestructible edifice.

The hand of death came to claim several others in our family within the short span of a couple of years. In 1906 Hiram Beebe passed away, and was interred in Brookfield, leaving Amelia to live with her children, in Candor.

Hank, ever so strong, healthy and proud of his manly vigor, had been slowly declining in the past few months, the result of a heart condition, and though with an almost superhuman effort, he strained to continue at his usual affairs; on a cold January day he simply faded away, to lie beside his beloved Francie.

As I pored over the obituary and tributes in the "Courier" describing his accomplishments, the many positions he had held about the township, and the regard in which he was held; I wondered what the town would have been without him, for it seemed there was little in which he had not had a hand. Surely I mused, remembering Hannah, and the lengthy letters she had written urging him, over and over to come westward; he would have fulfilled her fondest dreams, despite the fact that he chose to remain in this little eastern town; for after all, the truest measure of a man's success is in the esteem attributed to him by his associates.

» »» » » « « « « « «

Fanny was along in years when she married, a photographer, another George—George Palmer. It was a standing family joke that we could not escape the George's and the Fannie's. They continued to reside with us at 1206 Bellevue Avenue.

Mr. Knapp had many friends scattered about the country, but among his closest was one Dr. George Comfort, director of the Syracuse Museum of Fine Arts, with whom he had helped to establish the College of Fine Arts up on the hill; and who was just one month older than Mr. Knapp. During the spring of 1910 Mr. Knapp completed a portrait of Dr. Comfort, and they had become, perhaps, more close than ever. In the early part of May Dr. Comfort left his earthly domain, and Mr. Knapp was saddened to his very soul.

In the afternoon, following Dr. Comfort's funeral, Mr. Knapp superintended the hanging of his recently completed portrait of Dr. Comfort, in the Art Museum of the Carnegie Library building.

And at dinner that same evening, I noted that Mr. Knapp was still very much affected, so much so that he ate scarcely no supper.

I attempted to persuade him to rest for the evening, but apparently he could not do so, for he decided to pay a call on another of his old associates, Mr. George Fryer. Fanny was then a member of a vocal quartet, which was holding its weekly meeting down the street; and Mr. Knapp accompanied her there, stating that he would call for her on his return.

I awaited their arrival, and rather late, a call came for George Palmer, Fanny's husband. It was Fanny, calling for him to come after her, since her father had not returned. It was unlike Mr. Knapp to be so tardy, and an unannounced chill slid down my backbone. I felt I should accompany George, but he convinced me to wait at home, in case Mr. Knapp should arrive before us.

I was endeavoring to settle my thoughts upon a book when the door opened, and a hesitant footstep, which I recognized as belonging to George, started down the hall. I bolted to my feet, and rushed into the anteway. One look—and I knew my fears had not been exaggerated. "Mr. Knapp"—I breathed.

George moved his head almost imperceptibly, as I groped for the hallstand. I insisted he allow me to accompany him, back to the home where Fanny awaited us, beside the still form of her father. In broken phrases, she blurted out the sequence of events. "Just after I left the phone—to call George—Father came in—Mrs. Fox asked him if he would like to sit down and wait, until we finished rehearsing the hymn, "One Sweetly Solemn Thought." He sat in the rocker, and we continued with the verse: "Be near me when my feet, Are slipping o'er the brink; For I may be nearer home today, Perhaps, than now I think." Suddenly—I heard the sound of—deep breathing. I thought that Father must be thinking again of Dr. Comfort, and was sobbing. I turned to him—and realized he was nearly gone—and then George came—"

So there it was. Out in the open. I had lived in fear of that moment. Perhaps it was because of the manner in which Ed had left me; that I had always felt there would come another day, another circumstance, to nearly equal that first one. I had never fully recovered from those visits to Madame X's, for I still believed with Hawthorne, that the spirits are very close to us at times; but that we have not the vision required to pierce the curtain which separates our worlds. Well, our duties were clear, and together we three, George, Fanny and I went about the arrangements, which included his burial at Oakwood cemetery.

Once again I must make my solitary existence, and the cold,

icy hand of fear gripped me. True—the children were in the house, but they had a right to their own lives. I should have to face whatever future might remain for me alone. ALONE. . . . Well, Sate had done it twice, Amelia, once, and Lute had faced her's almost entirely alone. Where was my courage, where was my fortitude?

It was the middle of May, and the hills would be beautiful now. *My* hills. I would go home, for an extended visit, with my sisters. Amelia was in town again, for she alternated her time between Brookfield and Candor, where her son, Willie Lyman, published the "Candor Courier," which Frank had helped him establish. While in town, Amelia stayed at such homes as had sewing to be accomplished, and occasionally put up with her sisters. Yes, I too, might live in the communal house for the widowed Hills sisters if I liked; but I knew full well that it would never work. There would be just too many old ladies, each with her own opinion, and somehow I felt I was not quite ready to join the ranks of retirement; for in my heart I longed to see the wonders of our nation; of which I yet had only second-hand knowledge.

Chapter Twenty - three

I noticed on this visit back home, the first during which I had had time to make a true appraisal, the rather extensive changes which the township had undergone. Our great-nephew Laurence carried us on a tour of the countryside one sun-shiney Sunday. Where were the cheese factories, which had numbered thirty in the latter nineteenth century? Pitifully few remained. Gone were most of the manufacturing plants; and the saw mills with their rows upon rows of giant matchsticks, waiting to be slivered, by the whining saw blade, into workable lumber.

"Nothing to worry about, the trend of the times," my sisters complacently assured me. "We're not alone; the same thing has happened in all the villages; the industries have simply picked up and moved to the cities."

"But where are all the fields of hop-poles?" I inquired, referring to the tall cedar poles which had dotted many a hillside and level field as well.

"Bottom went out of hops," Laurence informed me, "between

the blue mold and the fact that they can raise them much cheaper on the West Coast. Why, they tell us they don't even have to set poles to grow them out there!"

Scarcely a sheep was to be seen in the entire township. "The sheep?" I queried again, and the answer was the same, "They're raising them cheaper, and in greater numbers, out in the West these days."

"Well, at least we still have our dairies," I sighed, as we passed several grazing herds.

"Yes, but they are running into problems, too," replied Laurence. "With no railroad in town, some of the farmers are hauling their milk to a station, which in some instances, may be as much as seven miles distant. They have a choice, of course," he added wryly. "They can take it to the cheese factories when they are in operation, and if, during the winter months, the factory chooses to shut its doors, for lack of milk, it's the farmer who has to suffer. Either he can make butter from his milk, or cart it to the nearest railroad. But I expect you know cheese factories from way back. They'll give good measure when they need the milk, and when they're flush, they give whatever measure they choose. Either way it's rough, and getting rougher. If only they could have finished the railroad—"

"Well, your Grandfather certainly tried," I interrupted, "and if he had been a millionaire, he would have invested it all in the project, for the sake of his town!"

We were passing through the southwest, near the old Tuttle place, the Quaker and Giles districts now, and I inquired after some of those families I had known in that vicinity. Palmers, I was told, had sold out; seven miles to Poolville being just too far to haul milk, especially on an unbroken road, in the dead of winter, with a team and set of bobs.

Those who sold generally reinvested in land in a more accessible region. I noticed Laurence mentioned several unfamiliar family names, Lithuanians, and Polish, he said, largely come up from the coal fields of Pennsylvania. Hardy and hard working souls that they were, they had been able to purchase some of the farms which the more well-to-do farmers had left.

Had it not been the dry season of the year, most of the horse and buggy trails we were following would have been impassable for the car; and I felt certain as we bobbed around, between, and over the ruts, that with the motor age upon us, the changes had only just begun.

» » » » » » « « « « « «

I passed the summer months in the village, with Sate, Lute and Amelia; and when I announced my intention to return to Syracuse in August, they persuaded me to stay just a bit longer, in order to take in the fair. Although it had been reorganized as the Madison County Fair Society, it was still largely a local event, and first cousin to an old-home day; for nearly all former township residents, living within a reasonable distance, attended. The Chesebro organ, with its dancing figures, the balloon ascensions, and the proverbial fat man, had all contributed to its success.

No doubt we four old ladies presented quite a picture at the entrance gate. Both Sate and Amelia had gained as many pounds as years. Lute was frail, and tottered a bit, as Mama had done; while I, with effort, had managed to remain my original five-foot three, one-hundred pounds.

We were not disappointed in the old-home element, for many of our once youthful acquaintances were present. We wandered past the merry-go-round, the homemade taffy stand, and toured the exhibits of baked goods. Outside the flower exhibition was, of all things, a gypsy tent! I poked Amelia, inquiring as to whether she remembered that long ago day, that had made such an impression on me. "Well," I mused, "the fortune teller foretold bad news to lie often in wait for me; but she also said I would travel and find happiness, too. She was absolutely correct on the first part of her prediction, but as for the last, except for brief periods of my life, I guess she really slipped up!"

Amelia was chatting with Lute during my reverie. An old lady, strangely familiar, approached me, searching my face intently. I returned the scrutinizing gaze. The face was wrinkled and the shoulders stooped, but the eyes, though deeper set and circled, and the smile were the same; and in the instant that I recognized Mae Hickox, she uttered my name, "Dosh!" and then, "Is it really Amelia?"

It was a jubilant encounter, celebrated by a trip to the lemonade stand! Mae had never married; neither, she confided, had Fordyce. She had spent her entire life, after her Father's death, in Sauquoit, and was attending the fair with her cousin, Irving Morgan. Fordy, she related, had become a clerk in a Utica store after his Father's decease, and from there he had worked his way through the west; clerking, amongst other places, in Omaha, and Denver, being presently employed in San Francisco. She was sorry, indeed, to learn of my misfortune in the loss of two husbands, but dwelled mainly on our chance meeting. "You just wait until I write Fordy!" she exclaimed. "Won't he be some surprised when he hears that I ran into you, and your sisters at the fair; and outside the gypsy tent, at that!"

» » » » » « « « « « «

I returned to Syracuse with misgivings. To leave my hills, now at their most glorious, wrenched my heart. But I could not wear out my welcome with the girls; so return I must. Return to what? An empty home. Not empty really, for, to be sure, George and Fanny were there, about their business as usual; but after the first glad amenities had been uttered, the lonely ache descended. I had not remained long enough following Mr. Knapp's leavetaking to know the emptiness, to hear the lonely echoes in the dwelling where his voice had long resounded.

I placed my sign back in the window. A new headdress for someone, surely that would ease my pain. But no one ventured in; so I commenced a creation for Amelia's granddaughter, Susan Beebe. A bird of paradise, atop an original of my imagination. No matter if it did not fit a young girl. That bird in flight seemed as my only hope. Mr. Knapp had made his flight, amongst the heavenly beings, I had no doubt of that; the very hymn that Fanny and her quartette were singing during his last moments was my proof. But as for myself, I could never be certain of such an end—I longed for it, but could receive no assurance that it would ever become mine.

The days in November grew dark and drear, as my loneliness heightened. I recalled the interminably dark ones following Ed's disappearance. Oh, please, don't let that long, dark season happen again! Someone mentioned Christmas, apparently endeavoring to lift my spirits; but the very mention of its approach only heightened old griefs, until their burden seemed to be accumulating at compound interest. All the Christmases I had ever known paraded, in procession, through my memory. The delightful ones with Grandma and Grandpa Clarke, Papa, Mama, and the girls, my wedding night, Christmas eve of 1868, the Christmas Eve version of Ed in the Santa sleigh, the thirty-five successive ones as a part of the Knapp family, and the tragic one, five years ago, when George Albert had been taken.

Why, indeed, was I still here? Grandpa Clarke had believed there was a reason for everything, and so had Grandma. I thought of Mama. Perhaps *her* reason for living had been the propagation of the human race; and her sister, Lucy Clarke Carpenter, the missionary to Shanghai. . . . Her reason for existence must have been the furtherance of God's kingdom, since she was childless. And I—Oh, yes, I had reared two children, but they were not my own, and never had it been more apparent than when we laid Mr. Knapp to rest, and Fanny had changed—almost overnight. True, it was good of her to put a roof over my head, but it was not without double benefits, for since her brother's premature death, and that of her father, she seemed only to be awaiting her own call, and spent a goodly share of her time in bed, while the burden of the house work fell on me. Not that I really minded—it was good to keep busy.

As I mulled all this over in my mind, I penned the following appropriate verses on the hand painted cards I intended to send:

"Oh, Christmas, Merry Christmas, is it really come again?
    With its memories and greetings, with its joy and with its
        pain.
There's a minor in the carol, and a shadow in the light,
    And a spray of cypress twining, with the holly wreath tonight.
And the hush is never broken, by laughter light and low,
    As we listen, in the starlight, to the bells across the snow.

Oh, Christmas, Merry Christmas, 'Tis not so very long,
    Since other voices blended with the carol and the song.
If we could but see the radiance, and the crown on each dear
        brow,
    There would be no sighs to smother, no sudden tear to flow,
As we listen, in the starlight, to the bells across the snow."

How true those verses were! No Mr. Knapp to play the piano, no George Albert to accompany him with his swooning, sobbing violin, while Fanny and I chorused out in harmony. I dabbed at my eyes, and proceeded, determinedly, to complete the remainder of my greetings.

But before I could finish my task, I received an early card, postmarked San Francisco, California. It had been addressed to Brookfield, where by the kindness of my sisters, it was forwarded to me. I knew immediately from whence it came. Fordy—I knew of no one else in that far off city. Eagerly I slit the envelope.

"Dear Doshie," it read, (I hadn't heard that name since Uncle Hosea passed away!) "I hope this card will find you in as good spirits as can be expected. You certainly have had a bad time of it. Mae wrote me about your meeting outside the gypsy tent. Chance does strange things! I only wish I might have been there, but doubt that I will ever see the old town again. I have never returned since that day you turned me down. I decided it best to travel and forget. (I could say much concerning this last statement, but perhaps it is better left unsaid.)

This is great country, wonderful climate; the place is growing like mad. Wish you could see it, it bids fair as a rival to our old hills!

Mae said you were looking real good, despite everything. Would like to hear from you. Wishing you as nice a Christmas as possible and hoping the New Year will bring you unexpected happiness. Sincerely, Fordy.

I promptly drew up an extra card, especially for Fordy. Somehow his communication had spiced up my day; and I accordingly did not pen "Bells Across the Snow" on his greeting, but rather, designed a simple illustration, with an enclosure; in which I discussed old times, as follows:

"Dear Fordy, It was wonderful to hear from you, after all these years. I find myself wondering if I would still recognize you. Tell me, do you still have your freckles?

So much water has gone over the dam. Mama, Papa, and Uncle Hosea are gone, of course; so are Francie, Hank, George Woodworth, George White, and Hiram Beebe, whom Amelia married. (I guess you never knew Hi.) So we are all widows, and the girls have a communal home for the Hills sisters in Brookfield! At least that's what I call it! They have generously offered me a share in it; but for the present, I am continuing to make my home with my stepdaughter, in Syracuse, where I can still "hang my shingle" for millinery.

My widowhood has been something of a shock, though I had felt it coming for some time. Mr. Knapp was down the block, picking up his daughter, when it happened. I went back to Brookfield soon after the funeral, therefore I am still adjusting to changes here. The holidays, for many reasons, have always been a bad time for me, but I am sure, once they are over, I shall be almost as good as new.

I am pleased that you have found a climate and occupation which agrees with you; I should very much like to see the West and the Pacific coast.

I have a great-niece in Seattle, Washington; Francie and Hank's granddaughter, Frances. She recently married; a fellow she met out there. His ancestors, name of Collins, were from the township of Brookfield, near the De Lancy-Moscow district. Remember when we climbed the ledges, played King on the mountain, and could see way off toward the Moscow district?

Do write again. It is good to hear from old friends. Our ranks are thinning daily.   As ever, Doshie"

On January 2nd the postman delivered a letter for me, bearing the San Francisco stamp. "Dear Doshie," it read; "Yours received, and must say I was happy for the prompt reply. My Christmas was thereby made more merry than any I have had since I was a young lad. I found the enclosed clipping in the "Honolulu Times" the other day. It struck me that this bit of poetry expresses almost exactly the sentiments I hold for you; therefore I am taking the liberty of sending it on; praying that you will not think me too forward." Curious, I opened and began to read the fine print on the enclosure.

"Some day I think you will be glad to know,
That I have ever kept you in my heart.
And that my love for you has deeper grown,
In all the time that we have lived apart.

Some day, when you have slipped away from care,
And idly fall to dreaming of the past,
And sadly think of all your life has missed—
Will you remember my true heart at last?

Or will it come to pass, some dreary night,
After a day that has been hard to bear,
When you were weary, heartsick and forlorn,
And there is none to comfort or to care;

That you will close your tired eyes and dream
Of tender kisses falling soft and light,
Of restful touches smoothing back your hair,
And sweet words spoken for your heart's delight.

Perhaps, then you'll remember, and be glad
That I so long have kept you in my heart,

And that your soul's true home will yet be there,
Although we wander, silently, apart."

My eyes swam with sudden tears. Someone *cared!* Someone *still* cared, about *me!* All these long years, he had cared, when I had married the first time, and even when I had married the second. Anyone who cared that much, must surely care a great deal. I read the verses again, pondering and considering each word, especially the last two lines. "And that your soul's true home will yet be there, Although we wander, silently, apart." I folded the precious parchment carefully, tucked it into my apron pocket, and tripped downstairs, with a radiance I could not conceal.

Sleep that night was nearly an impossibility; for I tossed until the early morning hours, mulling over the practicality of embarking on a tour of the west, during which I would visit Frances in Seattle, and just possibly, drop down to San Francisco on my return trip. My sisters would call me a fool, an unmitigated old fool, if they knew of my real reason for going; Fanny would think me ungrateful to her Father's memory. Whom, I finally scolded myself most severely, do I have to please, if not myself, at nearly sixty-seven?— And as for money—well, my emergency fund, from the millinery sales, was still intact, waiting for a lean time—or one last fling. Then it was settled. I would post some letters to announce my plans in the morning, and I straightway fell into the deepest slumber I had experienced in several months.

As suspected, my disclosure was not without opposition, from those who felt I was being hasty, extravagant, foolish, and just plain inconsiderate; but I held my ground, and refused to be dissuaded. By the first of February I had completed my ensemble, and my keepsakes had been stored at Fanny's until my return; an indefinite date, subject to my approval of that distant clime.

I departed early on a zero morn, and for one brief moment, a vague twinge of old fears slid over my being. I squared my shoulders more firmly, and climbed, resolutely; with little aid from the conductor, the alpine steps leading to the sleeper.

Mile upon mile the scenery varied little, for the brilliant winter sheet had been snugly laid, tucked and smoothed, from coast to coast, except close by the cities, where activity, with little regard for the bed maker, had sprawled her grimy fingers.

Scenes I had hoped, but never dared expect to see, thrilled my being as we drew near the towering Rockies, and doubtful it is there were any more young at heart than I, a sixty-seven year old youngster, on that entire passenger train.

Approaching my destination, Seattle, I was enthralled by its magnificence; situated as it was, on seven hills, amidst the Cascade and Olympic Mountain Ranges. Their two most prominent peaks; Mount Baker at the north, and to the south, snow capped Mount Ranier, rising nearly three miles above sea level and boasting of twenty-six glaciers; stood sentry duty.

The city was yet an infant, less than sixty years of age, but it had mushroomed during the Alaskan gold rush; and its port had remained our nation's chief link with that Northerly peninsula.

Though I had revelled in every moment of the journey, Frances voice rang out as chimes unto my gladdened ears, while I was yet descending the stairs. She grasped my arm, guiding me expertly through the clamoring crowd; while on the opposite side, I was immediately relieved of my baggage by a tall, handsome fellow whom I deduced to be her husband. Once through the throng, we paused, for introductions; while he gasped, "If I didn't know better, I would say she was your Mother, you two bear such a strong resemblance!" We smiled, for we had often heard this comment.

Frances had a lovely home, everything, in fact, her grandmother could have wished for her. She was still teaching; so I felt quite at home, as I performed several of the household functions, which enabled us to tour many of the area attractions during my sojourn. It was a two-months stay—with reluctant goodbyes—but it was April, and the beginning of all things.

Thus, not without a certain amount of sadness, but with an almost unexplicable anticipation I boarded the train at Seattle for the second lap of my ramblings, bound for San Francisco. All misgivings vanished as the caravan of cars wound their way southward, dwarfed by the never ending succession of Cascade, Coastal and Sierra Nevada Mountain Ranges, on our left, and the blue, sprawling Pacific ever at our right.

But eventually we neared the object of my journey; and suddenly, my pulse quickened, with a mixture of misgivings and fear. So many years had elapsed since I had seen Fordy! Would I know him? Would he recognize me? What if he should miss me, in the crowd? What was I really doing here, anyway? Oh, if only I could see home now, how welcome it would be! Well, my sisters would have been correct in calling me an unmitigated old fool, for that was *exactly* what I was, a fool, an old fool! "Well, no fool like an old fool," I thought miserably. No way in the world to turn back now. We would soon be unloading at the station, I could feel the train slowing down to a crawl, and shrieking its final whistles. It's comparative safety would no longer be mine. And even if there wasn't any slip-up, even if Fordy was there, as agreed upon—He would be all smiles—Maybe he had made plans for our future— That *was* what the poem had intimated—Was I about to hurt him, deeply, again? Well, he would also be a fool if he should think that we could take up where we had left off fifty years ago. Surely no man in his sane mind could be capable of such a fantasy!

"San Francisco!" the conductor boomed, then repeated, "San Francisco! All off for San Francisco!"

I struggled to my feet; I had been sitting too long, and my joints were stiff. I picked my way gingerly down the aisle; and with the conductor's aid, to the platform below. I moved back a bit; away from the wheezing monster, to take stock of the situation. I saw no one resembling Fordy. As I pondered my ridiculous predicament, and wondered, apprehensively, what my next move should be; an erect, well-dressed gentleman approached me timidly.

"You are expecting someone, Madame?" he ventured, tipping his hat, while searching my face; and in that instant doubt and fear gave way to recognition for both of us; as we saw in each other the same personages who had played king and queen eternities ago. Age had not changed us that much, except for hair coloring, and somehow I knew, even long before he asked it, what my answer would surely be.

Linking my arm in his, he escorted me to a table in the lunch room, and ordered coffee, with a sandwich. Oh, the comfort, the security, the wonder of it all! Years dropped away as if they had never been, and we were together, picking teasels, playing in the creek, climbing up the ledges, and I heard Fordy repeating, "Please don't punish her, Mrs. Hills, she hurts enough as it is!"

"Doshie," Fordy was standing very close, interrupting my reverie, as we left the table, I've something—important—to tell you. Remember—that you didn't like—my drinking? Well, I gave that up, back about forty years ago, and now I'd like to ask you just once more—There's nothing in life I ever wanted to do more than to take care of *you*—Will you let me, *now*, Doshie?"

"Fordy—dear, *dear* Fordy," I replied, "I came all this way to hear you ask it, and to hope against hope that you would."

"My darling, I've waited a lifetime!," he breathed, and oblivious to the surge of humanity about us, he gathered me in his arms; and his arms were, to me, as secure as the cradle of Mama's.

We applied for a license and were married that very evening; spending our wedding night in a picture magazine hotel overlooking San Francisco Bay and the Golden Gate. I had considered Seattle the most impressive city I ever laid eyes on, but San Francisco bid fair as its rival; nestled among lofty hills which, from their heights, provided a panoramic view of its entirety, and the waters which all but surrounded it.

Busy San Francisco, with its Nob Hill, home of millionaires, Chinatown, cable cars ascending and descending continually from its rises, and pea-soup fogs sweeping in from the bay and the Pacific beyond, to shroud the city. San Francisco, with its legend of romance and lawlessness at the time of the great gold rush, its extreme disaster when the San Andreas fault settled, creating almost total destruction in the resultant conflagration. Fordy told me of his own narrow escape; in which he salvaged nothing but his mantle clock. San Francisco, with a snap and a sparkle in the air, where the inhabitants possessed the recipe for getting the most out of life. Surely this was the place for me, where I should be rejuvenated, and I penned accordingly in my flowered book, "I am receiving helpful forces, I am open to all good influence. Stream of power for body and soul are pouring in. All is well."

Life with Fordy was more than I could have hoped for at any age, let alone nearly seventy. He was cheerful, patient, ever faithful, and we were happier than I had imagined possible. On his off days we visited Baker's Beach, Golden Gate Park, and were privileged to attend the San Francisco Symphony during one of its first concerts. Until 1913, our home was a cozy apartment there; during which time we saw the ashes of the city rise into a restoration acclaimed, the world over, as a major triumph.

But fall came, and a grumbling arthritis, agitated by the dampness of the ocean breezes, set more deeply into my limbs, forcing us to seek out the other side of the bay, in Oakland. This, too, was a port city, but was attached to the mainland; rendering it more quiet than the former.

My condition improved slightly here, and that summer we thrilled to a vacation, by rail, to one of the most magnificent parks in the nation, the famed Yosemite. Here were the lofty giant sequoias, their size unfathomable, until seen with one's own eyes. Yosemite Valley, with its sheer walls, cliffs, and pinnacles, towering as

184

much as forty-eight hundred feet above the valley floor; and the falls with an overall drop of nearly twenty-five hundred feet, defied description. We bubbled over each breath taking wonder, like a couple of school children. Occasionally dignity would demand precedence; and we would, until the next spectacle hove into view, act our ages.

"But on the other hand," argued Fordy, "we have many years to make up for, and since we are strangers to everyone about us, what's the harm in acting like a couple of kids if we want to?" He gave me a little squeeze, and recited one of his favorite sayings, "The ways, they are many and wide, and seldom are two ways the same, side by side. May we stand at the same little door when all's done; the ways—they are many—the end—it is one."

Fordy had come in contact with a powerful evangelist a number of years earlier, and had been converted to the ranks of believers. Although we did not attend services regularly, his faith was unswerving, and not the least of his consternation was the fact that I did *not* share his unquestioning belief. He was given to a rather persistent and frequent discussion of the subject, which tended the more to sway me in the opposite direction; despite the fact I realized his concern was borne out of his constant love for me.

Chapter Twenty-four

Once the initial shock of my re-marriage had subsided, my sisters and even Fanny sent their best wishes; however, the girls allowed that I was running true to my usual unpredictable form! Sate also related that Lute, though of sound mind, was becoming increasingly feeble, and daily longed for the death which would release her from her sufferings.

She told, as well, of the big news of the village, which intimated that Brookfield might yet have a chance to compete with the rest of the world. For the last forty-five or more years the streets in the hamlet had been illuminated by gas lights; big lanterns suspended by wires from two high poles stationed at opposite sides of the street; and placed at strategic distances. The lanterns were hung on a sort of iron cog which enabled them, each evening, to be individually lowered, filled, lighted, and raised once again. The gas lights served their purpose with excellence; but left something to be desired in the manner of maintenance. As far as lighting in the homes was concerned, most were lit by kerosene lamps; smelly, smoky, and generally quite a trouble, nevertheless, an immense improvement over the tallow tapers which served the purpose when I was a girl.

Now it seemed that Mrs. Harriet Babcock Gardner, beautiful daughter of Adelbert Babcock, who had twice married into great wealth; had decided to do something for the town in which she had spent her girlhood. Mrs. Gardner had offered the townspeople their choice of either piping water for the village from Gorton Lake, or, a power plant to provide electricity for the same. By this time most cities had their own water supplies and power of a sort, but few country towns had been electrified.

At a communal supper and meeting in the G. A. R. Hall, the matter was debated. Allowing that the water would be nice to have, the majority felt, since most citizens had drinking water handy in their yard pumps, plus cellar cisterns for wash water; that the power plant would be the best selection. It was pointed out that the New York State power line was expected to come through, 'ere the lapse of many years. Those still living, who could recall the ill-fated railroad, advised that they had best grasp the power opportunity while it presented itself; as perhaps they would once again be bypassed.

Well, the upshot was that on January 22, 1914, the village board, composed of Frank Spooner, President, Emory Morgan, Bert Rollins, Emmet Dennison, and Henry Dyball, trustees, unanimously resolved to grant to the Brookfield Electric Light and Power Company (of which Adelbert Babcock, Harriet's father, was President), the exclusive right to establish within the village a power plant, with which to provide power for public and private use, and to erect poles, wires, lamps, etc.; with the stipulation that if the company should fail to furnish power for a period in excess of three months, the franchise would become void.

The new-born power company was ill-fated from the start, for exactly four weeks from the contract date with the village, its president, seventy-three year old Adelbert Babcock, lay dead.

Nevertheless, construction was begun in the spring, and the power plant, consisting of a turbine run by water power, a number of batteries, plus a rheostat to reduce the flow of current to the batteries during high water level, when the turbine inadvertantly put out too much voltage; was installed in a converted blacksmith shop, just above the Main Street bridge. A supplementary gasoline engine, used as an auxiliary power source, to boost the turbine output in low water times, was located in the center of the village.

At Mrs. Gardner's request, the first building in town to boast of wiring for light bulbs was the store owned by Charlie Brown, cousin to Mrs. Gardner, and a life-long friend of Frank's. Great was the celebration as residents followed one another in the conversion, some of them so ecstatic as to be tempted to toss out their old, faithful, kerosene lamps. But certain of the older, more far-sighted inhabitants, foreseeing possible difficulties, prevailed upon the younger to "hang onto the lamps". And it proved wise that they did so; for indeed the venture seemed plagued.

In the spring of the year, when the current came surging downstream, the rheostat must be observed and regulated continually, to prevent the overcharge from burning up the batteries. In the summer, as the water level lowered, the gas engine was brought into action, and the batteries drawn upon at times of greatest load. For this reason the power plant required almost constant attention, and shifts were placed, around the clock, during certain periods of the year. When power was ample a saw mill alongside the plant was in operation, with the mill workers observing and regulating the rheostat. In this manner the system held together for some time, with a fair amount of satisfaction, but with a great investment in man hours.

At last the day arrived when the delicate balance between output, usage, battery capacity, and so on, came to a halt. The batteries, sometimes over and sometimes undercharged, because of the uncontrollable water variation, had been depleted, and the flickering power ceased. Down from the top shelves came the standby kerosene lamps, and other out-dated appliances. Criticism of the sharpest nature was heard on every hand; and well they might criticize, for each had invested a considerable amount of elusive capital in the wiring of his home. Where was the new power company? And the supposedly responsible citizens, who had formed it?

A hasty meeting between power company and village board was called, but none could conceive of a solution to restore the power. Harriet Gardner's gift had not included maintenance.

Frank trudged home from the meeting, heavy hearted. The responsibility rode on the light company, nevertheless, he was president of the village. But how could he work out such a riddle? During a sleepless night he hit upon the answer. Arising early in the morning, he strode immediately to Charlie Brown's store; where he found its owner just uncovering the shelves, preparatory to the morning's trade. "Charlie," said Frank, coming directly to the point, "how do you think the power plant would work down on my farm?"

Charlie placed the folded cover cloth upon a shelf; squinted at him through the morning sun, and counter-questioned, "Why should it work any better down there than it does up-town? There's no more water in the creek down there."

"No," reasoned Frank, "but our problem is the water *level*. We've enough water, but it's got to be channeled into a narrow stream with some force behind it; force and depth enough to keep that turbine rotating, and some manner of controlling both, to keep the output steady. Now you know my place; on the west side of the creek is that high bank. Suppose we cut back into that bank, a strip about eight feet wide, and toss the excess dirt over next to the creek, then we would create a new bank for the creek; but at the same time we would have scooped out a ditch, or sluiceway, into which the water could flow as we desire."

"Could be." said Charlie, scratching his head thoughtfully, "You'd have to dam up the creek at the head of the ditch, though."

"Right," said Frank, "but that would be the simple part of the operation. I say, we dam it up, and at the west bank we start our sluice, just where the water spills over the dam. Right here," he was sketching on a piece of Charlie's brown wrapping paper, "we put the sluice gate, and another at the entrance to a small flume, where the water enters the turbine, so that we can raise and lower these gates at will, to control our water flow."

"You'd still have to have a pretty good fall," debated Charlie.

"I'm not certain as to what that would be," agreed Frank, "but from the way the water moves down there, I'm pretty sure it's enough. I'm going to call on some of the light company members now, and see what they think."

"As I see it, there's just one small item," said Charlie. "I understand Harriet's donation has run out. What are you planning to use for funds? This won't be any small investment; a lot of man-hours in that ditch. How long does it need to be?"

"I figure at least a thousand feet," answered Frank, ignoring Charlie's upraised eyebrows and low whistle. "Let me talk with the boys on the board, see what they say, and maybe we can figure something out on the financing. See you later!"

A second emergency meeting was called, whereupon Frank laid out his proposition. All thought it the ideal solution, *if* there were moneys available. Someone suggested the company, already incorporated, might sell bonds.

"Not a chance," spoke up Bert Rollins. "You think these folks are about to invest money in a power plant that has failed once?"

"Failed through no fault of its own, simply because it wasn't properly installed," defended Frank.

"Try to tell them that," returned Bert. "Some of these folks don't realize that the mechanical age is here to stay, all they can think of is how much money they lost on some of the other village enterprises!" The meeting disbanded at length, all agreeing the proposal was desirable; if only another public minded citizen of means might come forth with an offering comparable to Mrs. Gardner's.

Frank nibbled at supper that evening; then, informing Luetta that he was going down in the pasture to look around; he tramped up and down the edge of the creek bed, following the pebbled walk the receding waters had paved. He trailed the cowpath up the side-hill above the stream, and down to where he imagined they should locate the building to house the turbine, to retrace his steps to a spot just below his private bridge, where he believed the dam should be constructed; and the entrance to the sluiceway established.

Charlie Brown found him there. "Letta told me you were down here, but I figured you'd be, anyhow. Where's the fish pole?" he laughed, attempting to dissolve Frank's serious expression.

"Now here's what I was telling you about," said Frank, oblivious to Charlie's effort at humor; and with Charlie at his side, they paced the entire route once more.

"Looks good to me!" remarked Charlie. "Just one trouble, like I said this morning, where's the green stuff coming from?"

"*I'm* going to do it," replied Frank, shortly.

"What do you mean—*you're* going to do it?"

"I'm going to see that it gets done."

"With *what?*" demanded Charlie. "You don't have that kind of money!"

"Maybe not," returned Frank, "but I'll get it."

"But why *you?*" persisted Charlie. "You're fifty-five years old now, and your old age is just around the corner. *You* can't afford to sink your money into this thing—Harriet was different. She's got so much, they'll never miss it! You know—I wonder—if Harriet knew the mess we are in, maybe she'd help us out again."

"Well, I'll never ask her," returned Frank. "Just because she got the first divorce ever heard of in these parts, some of our self-righteous ladies have high-hatted her already. I figure that's Harriet's business—none of ours; and we should be mighty grateful that she thought of us all. Nope, it's up to us to carry the ball. You know as well as I do that since Adelbert went that Power Company has fallen to pieces. They got along as long as the money held out. Now —no money—no leader; these fellows don't know which way to turn. In the meantime our people are suffering for it. They wired their places in good faith. Now, as president of the village, this is something I have to do, if it takes every cent I have! Who can we get to help dig the ditch, Charlie?"

"By gum, there's no use arguing with you when you get your mind set," sighed Charlie, "you always were a stubborn one!"

"There's one more thing, Charlie," said Frank, "we've had our little secrets over the years—Let's keep where the money came from just between ourselves, alright?"

"Frank, it you ain't the damndest," muttered Charlie, "but if you say so—"

The sluice was dug, the creek dammed, building to house the outfit completed, and the turbine installed. New batteries were purchased to replace the old, new wires and poles strung, to span the longer distance. As the bills piled in, Frank and Charlie both knew the unforseen cost to Frank. His life savings were consumed, and even this was not enough. A mortgage was placed upon his farm to finish the project, and on that final day, when the work was accomplished, the gates were opened. Like a giant turned loose, the water rushed down the sluiceway, spilled into the flume, boiled up, around, and over the turbine; and the great finned piece of steel began to slowly rotate, creak and groan, the clanking gears meshed into the turbine revolved, the heavy shafts moved up and down in an ear-splitting but joyful din, and a small steady stream of power was generated to flow across the lines, to restore not only electricity for the villagers, but their faith in humanity as well.

Chapter Twenty - five

Before Sate could relate the entire power company episode, in periodic installments, a night letter, announcing Lute's death, arrived. Sate followed it closely by a more personal communication.

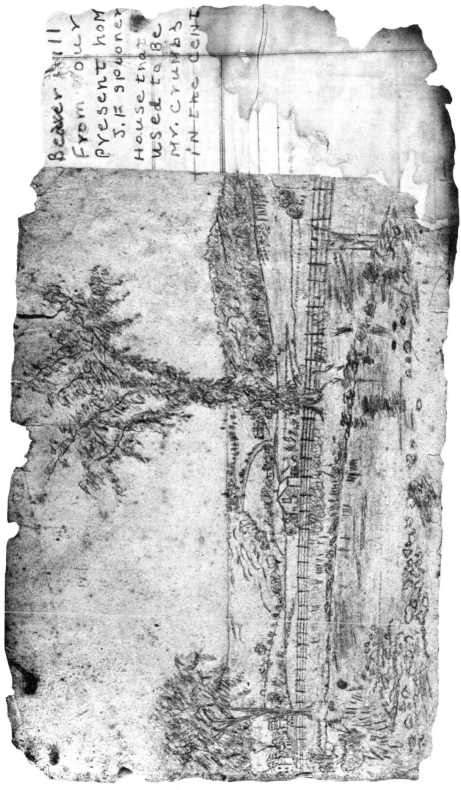

Beaver MILL
From MOLLY
present home
J. F. Spooner
House that
used to Be
Mr. Crubbs
iN the cent

Sketch of Beaver Creek and Beaver Hill, by Frank Spooner, as seen from near site of power plant.

Brookfield, N.Y.
Sept. 17, 1915

Dear sister Dosh and Fordy,

I imagine the telegram about Lute was not too much of a shock. We had expected it at any time, and Lute herself was anxious to go. So sad though it was, it was beautiful. You know she had been partially paralyzed since her stroke last week. Although she couldn't speak she was fully conscious. Just before her death (Meal and I were with her), she motioned toward pencil and paper. We gave it to her, and she scrawled on it, "Romans 8:18."

Meal opened Lute's Bible, found the passage and began to read: "For I reckon that the sufferings of this present time are not worthy to be compared with the glory which shall be revealed in us,", and before she could finish, Lute was gone. But the most beautiful part of it all was that just then the sun crept 'round the shade and lit upon Lute's smiling face. There was no doubt but what she'd gone to know that glory.————"

Although it was now too late to visit the sister I had not seen in four long years, my heart ached to return to the old town, and the members of my family still abiding there. Fordy generously suggested this, but I could not accept the sacrifice. Travel was out of the question for oldsters, in our position; for our savings were trifling. Meanwhile, the stiffening in my joints, which had improved for a time, was growing more extensive. Consequently, we relocated, in San Diego, another port city, but some four-hundred miles to the south. In this ancient Spanish city, the oldest in California, the ocean breezes still blew, but they were soft and warm.

Our nation was at war again in 1918; a World War this time, and again there was a shortage of able-bodied men. Thus it was that Fordy, now well past seventy, but adept in his line, easily secured a position in a San Diego quality men's shop.

Fordy had never looked his years. His jaunty step, erect carriage, and thick white hair, had made him an object of admiration, by men and women alike. He was the personification of a gentleman from the old west; he knew the legend of its rising—for he had been there, during its composition. He lived for tomorrow, and the excitement of the newest chapter, when the page was turned. He left for work at precisely eight A. M.; and I'd watch him stride briskly down the street. By the corner mailbox, he'd always turn, and wave—and I would settle down, to await his return.

Time never hung heavy on my hands. A piece of china, or a sketch to paint, an article of fancywork, even a custom made bonnet now and then, occupied my waking hours. I had done my dishes and tidied the apartment that spring morning of 1919; and was vigorously shaking the duster out of the window, when my attention was suddenly drawn to a figure down the street. He was dressed exactly as Fordy always did. I strained my eyes—yes— white hair, and all. But the step was slow, uncertain; and the shoulders stooped.

I turned aside, put up the duster, and drew my embroidery hoops and floss from the dresser drawer. Did I hear footsteps in the hall? I listened, someone was *turning a key* in my door! I slammed the bedroom door, and jammed my body against it.

"Doshie?" a familiar voice called.

"Fordy!" I hurried to the kitchen. "You're ill!"

He was slumped in a chair beside the table, his head in his hands.

"Fordy! What's wrong!" I felt of his forehead, no fever. "Coffee, dear? There's a cup left in the percolator."

"Thanks," he said, barely audibly.

"Then it *was* you I saw coming down the street! Please, Fordy, tell me what it is—or do I know?"

"I guess it was a short morning," he began. "The manager called me in, shortly after 9:00.

"Good morning! Mr. Hickox. And how are you this lovely spring day?"

Obviously he was hedging, so I replied, "Fine, sir! And just what is on your mind this morning?"

"Haaaruumph!" he cleared his throat noisily, and began, "Mr. Hickox, just how long have you been in our employ?"

"Since last year, sir."

"Yes, yes, you came during the War, and we never troubled to look at your card—at your *age*. Mr. Hickox, do you know exactly how old you *are*?"

I replied that I guessed I should, but for his information I had just turned seventy-four.

"Seventy-*four!* You certainly don't show it!" he remarked, enviously, for he is getting along. "Now, Mr. Hickox, you have been doing a *fine* job, with our firm—and understand we have *no* complaints about your work. None *whatsoever!* But—you are aware of this, I'm sure—California today is geared to the *young* man— our clientele is of *young blood*—blood that California *needs* to spurt ahead—as ahead she *will!"*

"Now we have young men coming in here *daily*—begging for work—*veterans,* you understand—and at *your* age—well, quite frankly, Mr. Hickox, I'm afraid you're predisposed to an *accident*— for which you'd hold our firm *liable.* You understand, I'm sure—"

"You're trying to say, sir, that I'm through," I interrupted.

"Not *through!* We'll furnish you with a two weeks notice, and a *grand* letter of recommendation, Mr. Hickox."

"Thanks, but I'll get along," I replied, choking, and rushed, unceremoniously, from his office. It started to sink in when I reached the street, and noticed the milk wagons still making their rounds. I should be working, but I was on vacation! Vacation—without pay!"

"I trudged toward home, and passed a bar. Doshie, in forty years I've never stepped inside one! I turned back, placed my hand on the door, and turned away again. It must have been God that kept me from it——God! Oh, God! What are we going to do?" he sobbed, uncontrollably.

I leaned forward, placed my arms about his convulsing shoulders, and rested my face beside his. "Fordy," I said distinctly, "there is no place like home—and that is exactly where we are going."

"But Doshie, Doshie, don't you *understand?* I can't retire! Our savings are next to nothing, and we may live—Lord only knows how many years!"

"I know, my dear, but I also know that somehow we must be among friends; and that back in the country where you and I were raised, we must have a *few* left!"

"That's it!" he exclaimed, nearly upsetting his chair as he jumped to his feet. "Mr. Hunter! You know, he was one of my best friends, as a young fellow! He owns a store now, in Utica, on Franklin Square! I *know* I can get a job with him! And you'll be close to Sate! You're right! We *are* going back home, home where things are peaceful, and people are still human; home to our hills, at last, Doshie, and to what families we have left."

Strange that the losing of a job, and farewells to that delightful clime, should fill our aging minds with joyous anticipation; but as we packed our meager belongings our souls overflowed, with the bounding happiness that only homesick hearts can know.

The long train ride back east should have been even more pleasurable than my original one, to the west, since it was summer; but gazing mile after endless mile at the mountains, prairies, rivers, and cities I realized my desire for travel had at last been fulfilled. I yearned for nothing further now than to spend these last days in the companionship of my faithful Fordy, our families, and my beloved central New York; and as the conductor cried out in succession the familiar places: "Rochester, Syracuse, Canastota, and Rome", my heart beat in an ever increasing tempo, to the clack of the wheels upon the steel——"You're going home—You're going home—You're going home—You're going home———"

_Fordy was right, and he was also in luck, for A. S. and T. Hunter's, in Utica, had an immediate opening, to which they assigned him. We located an apartment on West Street, where Ford's debonair California manner soon won him distinction.

Following Lute's death, Amelia had returned to Candor, while Sate had given up her home in Brookfield, to live with her son, Ed Woodworth, in Utica.

The Ed Woodworths carried Sate and us back to the home town for the annual Decoration Day services and community dinner at the G. A. R. Hall. Searle Post, as the Grand Army Veterans called themselves, had organized in 1884. Six years later they had dedicated their hall, of Gothic type architecture, and the pride of the community. It stood west of the Courier office on Main Street, where it had become the focal point of village life, since the burning, about 1895, of the old Ganny Clarke opera house.

We visited the cemetery after dinner, and then called next door, on Frank and Letta. He had progressed, during our absence, to township supervisor, and due to his increased duties, had sold the "Courier" to Lynn Worden, who carried on the weekly under its original name. Frank was secretary, as well, of the Madison County Fair. The fair society had established new grounds, prior to the turn of the century, just under Beaver Hill, north of the village. Due to its picturesque location, and the fact that it possessed one of the best half-mile tracks in central New York; its officers had persuaded the County Agricultural Society, in 1899, to take up residence therein; and since that date, several permanent buildings had been erected on the site.

As far as family was concerned, Frank and Luetta were alone, with the exception of Jean, who had remained at home, to help with the farm.

We visited on the front porch, and Frank pointed with pride to the hillside south-east of the gully and ledges we had climbed as children. "Set out our first plantation of lumber, a couple of years ago, red pine," he revealed. Jean ° put about a thousand pine on his, too. He bought the old Gates place, you know. Look close in that field to the right of the ledges. You can *just* barely make them out. They looked like shocks of buckwheat setting up there all winter.——Guess he plans on setting out some cedar this year."

"But why all this reforestation, on cleared land?" I puzzled.

"Cleared land! Huh! Do you know, some of that side hill is so steep you can't put a wagon on it?——Should never have been cleared in the first place.—Don't know what the old-timers were thinking of.—Of course, compared to what they had down in Stonington, and some of the other rock-bound New England shores, I suppose it looked great. But trees today are a good investment; the average man doesn't realize that we are cutting off a great deal of our natural resources, at quite an alarming rate. These trees will check erosion, help conserve water, and prevent those accursed thorn-apples from getting a further hold on the land as well as beautify the country. A few of Jean's *are* set on the old Gate's meadow," he confessed, "but that piece of ground had run out; it's hard to get up there with the manure, and harder yet to get back down here with the crops. We tip over about one load in four! Back when David Gates owned it, his barn was nearby, and the old road ran alongside that meadow, so he could work that chunk of land without any trouble."

"*That* road's not traveled now?" I queried, astonished.

"Can't, it just a cow path, full of brush, bogs, and mud-holes."

"But why are they letting our old roads go like this?" I cried.

"Township can't keep them up," Frank answered. "We're trying to keep our villages alive, and with scarcely no industries left, it's more than difficult. Our funds are limited, no means of travel to this village except by car or horse, as you well know, so we have poured most of our tax-money into the improvement of our main roads, between villages; with the hope that, if we cannot induce new industry to move in, we can at least prevent those which remain from moving out. We are the largest township, and have more miles of roadway, than any other in Madison county. *I* know

° Father of Donna Spooner Tanney, the author of this book; and whose home is constructed with lumber from these pines.

we should not abandon all these roads; I fear the day will come when we will suffer greatly from it. Already those who can possibly swing it, are moving from our most remote farming areas, to relocate in more accessible regions. The handwriting is on the wall, and we are helpless to stem the tide of the inevitable."

» » » » » « « « « « «

"It's dying," I stated matter of factly, as Fordy and I, back in our apartment, laid sleeplessly in bed that night.

"What's dying?" he demanded, bolting upright.

"The *town*—our town, is dying—*dying*, just as surely as the rest of us."

"For heaven's sakes, Doshie, you're just being melodramatic!"

"No—no—it's true—you can't *see* it? The handwriting *is* on the wall, and there is nothing any of us can do to prevent it."

"Oh, come on, dear, go to sleep," he soothed, tucking his arm securely about me. "If there is nothing any of us can do, there's no point in our losing sleep over it. Let's just remember it as it was in it's hey- dey, all neatly painted, bustling, and happy; with teasels, hops, and kids like us growing all over the place!"

Chapter Twenty - six

It was 1922. Fanny and her photographer husband, George Palmer, were still on Bellevue Avenue, in Syracuse. Her health had not improved with the passing of time, and neither had Fordy's. They persuaded us to move to Syracuse with them, since they knew of a little shop where Fordy, now seventy-seven, could work piecemeal. The arrangement appeared advantageous to both parties; since we would be assured of a home, and the Palmers of a housekeeper, for Fanny was often confined to bed.

It was good to be back in the city which had been home for thirty-six years; and Fordy's part-time work enabled us to assert a degree of independence, as well as indulge ourselves in the little necessities of life.

Early in December I addressed my customary stack of season's greetings. There were many preparations to be accomplished; since

I had also issued invitations to a few of our old neighbors, for a pre-holiday gathering. The house would be trimmed in old-time decor, and the refreshment table with favorite goodies of yester-year. My mind pre-occupied with preparations, I hurried along to the corner mailbox with my stack of cards. Suddenly my feet slipped from beneath me, and down I went; striking heavily on my side. Instantaneous pain and fear gripped me, as I attempted to rise from the frosty slate on which I sprawled.

I had by now commanded the attention of two of my neighbors, who transported me into the nearest house, then called Fordy, and the Doctor. They arrived in minutes; the Doctor stating he feared my hip had been fractured. His diagnosis was correct; the joint was set, and after a visit at the hospital, I returned to Bellevue Avenue, just two days prior to Christmas.

It was then that the familiar lines "Oh, Christmas, Merry Christmas, Is it really come again? With its memories and greetings, with its joy and with its pain" flashed through my mind. I had penned those verses in this very household; but that day they were more than appropriate, for the pain of Christmas was literal.

The place was in a turmoil, as Fanny dragged about, attending to a few daily chores. Between his job, assumption of extra household duties, and my care, poor Fordy was worn ragged.

At last the heavy cast was removed. Then began the weary performance of trying to stand, and move, upon that joint. With advancing years my arthritis had worsened, and now, after weeks in bed, it seemed that none of my limbs wished to cooperate in the slightest. The doctor suggested a wheel chair; and the big, clumsy contraption became standard decor. By spring, I had learned to help myself in and out of it, and had resumed several of my tasks, though never again did I walk.

That spring, as soon as the highways were bare, Ed and Ann Woodworth brought Sate over, for a Sunday visit. Dear sister Sate —eighty-two years old then, but just as jolly, and not a little fatter than sixty years before. She hung her cane up on the hall tree, and hobbled over to greet me affectionately. Tears welled around the corners of my eyes, and I struggled to speak.

"Well, Dosh," she spoke brusquely, as she seated herself in the rocker beside my monstrosity, "I see you've got yourself into another predicament. So at least you can get around without a cane!" She chuckled, and I smiled wryly, in spite of myself. "You know," she continued, looking me squarely in the eye, "You're still a very fortunate woman. Now I *know* you've been sitting here feeling sorry for yourself most all winter, but don't. I say DON'T. You've got something here," she glanced significantly at Fordy, "Most women your age would give their eye teeth, (if they still had them,)" she chuckled again, "to have; a patient, kind, and loving husband. So you just quit all that nonsense and blubbering right now, 'cause I came over here to cheer you up, and not to watch you soil all your hankies! Here, take mine, it's bigger!" she ordered. "Now, how's about me drumming out a few tunes for you on the piano? These old fingers don't move about the keyboard quite like they used to, but they'll limber up in a minute. What would you like to hear?" We named off several favorites. As she obliged, the gnarled fingers relaxed, and the notes rang out, clear and steady. One after another the songs rolled out; until at last she turned the stool, her face flushed, and spoke. "I've got just one more number before I'm through, and it wouldn't be fitting if I didn't play a hymn for Sunday. She whirled around and broke into the strains of "Onward, Christian Soldiers." I swear to this day that the old piano *rocked* as she pounded out the chords, chords that swelled and echoed through every corner of that house; chords so indelibly impressed upon my being, that whensoever after I reminisced of sister Sate, I could still see her hands, moving steadily, surely, up and down the eighty-eight, beating out the martial rhythm of that ageless hymn.

I never heard Sate play again, for eighteen months later, just eleven days short of her eighty-fourth birthday, she went to join her George and Minnie Myrtle.

» » » » » » « « « « « «

Our family ties were pretty well severed then, since Amelia dwelled so far away. We saw her only a couple of times following Sate's funeral. In 1923, we moved with the Palmers, to the nearby town of Oneida.

Our home town news still came to us by way of the "Courier." In 1925, an article appearing therein revealed that three men, William Norman, of the Madison County Farm Bureau, Jack Charlton, Principal of Brookfield School, and Sherrill Palmer, native Brookfieldan, had formed a company, called Brookfield Forest Products, Inc., for the purpose of reforesting some of the abandoned land in southwest Brookfield Township. Brookfield Forest Products proceeded to establish a plantation of thirty-thousand trees, on the farm where Mr. Palmer was raised, and which had lain, idle, for twenty years.

Concerned over the large acreage similarly vacated within this vicinity; Mssrs. Norman and Charlton secured an appointment with Henry Morganthau, Jr., then chairman of Governor Franklin Roosevelt's Agricultural Advisory Committee, and persuaded him to discuss with Governor Roosevelt the possibility of New York State buying up this unused land, for the purpose of reforestation. Their idea was sold, and the State commenced to purchase land about 1927, for $2.50 an acre, later raising the price to $4.00 per acre, where it remained for some time.

1925 was to be a year of changes for our town. That October one of our "Couriers" did not arrive on schedule. The "Utica Observer-Dispatch", October 22nd. issue, carried the reason, and story of the conflagration in our home town. During the weekly showing of movies in the Local Grange Hall, (formerly G. A. R. Hall;) a spark from a short circuit ignited both film and movie projector. Fanned by a raging wind, the beautiful building, pride of the community, with its gothic architecture and stained glass windows; was soon disintegrated. But the destruction by no means ended there. When, in spite of the combined efforts of the Unadilla Forks, Leonardsville, Bridgewater, and Brookfield Fire Companies, the situation had been declared hopeless for the salvation of the Hall; and the blaze had consumed the shoe store adjacent on the west; efforts were concentrated on the printing office to the east, a large two-story building, bearing across the roof top of its entire frontage in four-foot letters "HOME OF THE BROOKFIELD COURIER." Frightened residents, fearing the ravagement of the entire village, emptied nearby homes of furniture. Alas, all labors seemed in vain, for within three hours not only were those three buildings demolished, but also Ray Sampson's barn, east of the printing office. Here the holocaust was finally arrested. Losses were estimated at $16,-000.00 in currency, to say nothing of the loss to Brookfield's citizens; as they viewed, by light of the new-born day, the charred and smoking ruins of their Main Street. The desolation of approaching winter, its leafless trees, and brittle frost-tipped grasses, the chill North wind whipping through the village, distributing both a curtain of thick gray smoke and the melancholy toll of the school bell, cut to the core of those inhabitants with foresight; for they recognized that morning, in their familiar bell, a death knoll, tolling for the beginning of the end.

None of the buildings were ever replaced; the Grange bargained for the old Keith Hotel on the corner, and the Wordens, owners of "The Courier," purchased new equipment and the large building on Main Street, which had formerly housed the undertaking parlor of Roy Chesebro.

» » » » » « « « « « «

I found each day, after my confinement to the chair, to be little different than its predecessor. We fell into a monotonous routine, broken only by the appearance of callers and unusual news or reading material. Most of my spare time was consumed by the latter, and when anything commanded my especial interest, I copied it into the flowered book.

Accordingly, since anything relating to the phychic captured my attention, I placed this clipping inside its cover.

"George Ade says Mother Shipton would have been put in a padded cell, if she had predicted all that has come to pass in the first quarter of the Twentieth Century. Back in the days of witches, Mother Shipton did a good business in prophecies. She made kings happy? by predicting the dates of their executions. The most famous poem credited to Mother Shipton created a great stir in 1881, when everyone put on his Sunday manners, in expectation of the end of the world. As a matter of fact it has since been discovered that this prophecy, which is printed below, was written by a Charles Hindley about 1862. The so-called Mother Shipton's prophecy—

"Carriages without horses shall go, and accidents fill the world with woe.
Around the earth thoughts shall fly, In the twinkling of an eye.
The world upside down shall be, And gold be found at the root of a tree.
Through hills men shall ride, And no horse be at his side.
Under water men shall walk, Shall ride, shall sleep, shall talk.
In the air men shall be seen, In white, in black, in green.
Iron in the water shall float, As easily as a wooden boat.
Gold shall be found and shown, In a land that's not known.

201

Fire and water shall wonders do, England shall at last admit a foe.

The world to an end shall come, In eighteen hundred and eightyone."

I pondered considerably on this prophecy. It had failed to materialize in 1881, to be sure, for this was the latter nineteen-twenties. Could it be, I mused, that Charles Hindley was exactly one century premature in his predicted date for the destruction of the world? Of only one thing I was certain, I should never know the answer, one way or the other.

In twenty-eight there were more changes. Little sister Amelia left to join our family in the great beyond. Fordy, at eighty-three, could no longer cope with even the part-time work. Medicine and an occasional doctors visit melted our savings away at an alarming rate. Fanny, ill and irritated by two oldsters continually under foot, took matters into her own hands and penned the following note to Frank:

"Dear Frank and Luetta;

I sincerely hope this finds you both well. Things are not going so well here in Oneida. You may not know that Fordyce has been unable to work for the past month or so. Of course he does help Mama putter about the house, but to put it plainly I find it very annoying to have them both continually under foot; in fact I have reached the point where my nerves simply cannot take it any longer. Neither are we in a position, financially, to keep them, as George's photography business has fallen off of late.

Unless you have some other suggestion, I can see no alternative but to take them to Eaton, to the poor-house. However, since you and Ed Woodworth are the only close blood relatives left, I felt we should contact you before making definite plans. I have mentioned none of this to them. Hoping to hear from you soon. Fanny Knapp Palmer"

Seldom one to anger, Frank's wrath rose to the surface upon receipt of that letter. "Apparently," he stormed, "Dosh isn't able to do much of the housework now, after Fanny has used her all these years. Dosh always spoiled her, every blamed member of that family pampered Fanny, and gave in to her every whim! A farmer does better by an old horse than that!" He fell silent a few moments, while childhood scenes raced through his mind. "Let—it would kill Aunt Dosh to send her to the poorhouse! All she has left now is her pride—and must we destroy that just because she has outlived a normal lifetime? I know we don't have much to share—but we do have extra room. Can we bring them here, Let? Can we—bring Dosh—home?"

And Luetta, sixty-five years old herself, and well aware of the sacrifice involved, but unselfish as they come, answered in the affirmative.

The succeeding weekend we were transported, bag and baggage, to the large front bedroom in Frank's house, which overlooked our Beaver Creek, the meadow where Uncle Hosea had cultivated his teasels, and the little Cape Cod cottage I had known as home.

Chapter Twenty-seven

It had been a red-letter day for us. Not only were our fondest memories wrapped up in the visible landscape, but Frank and Luetta were kind, and spared no effort to welcome us. We were confined to the house, of course, for Frank had no car, and getting both of us into and out of one, was almost a day's undertaking.

The large east room overflowed with our belongings. The high-headboarded bed, a Round Oak stove, my cumbersome chair, the commode, and a washstand, laden with pills of every description, dominated the room; while in the odd corners we stored our few keepsakes; a chest containing photos, letters, diaries, reading and magnifying glasses, the worn valises housing our best clothes, and remnants of jewelry, a couple of Mr. Knapp's paintings on the walls, and Fordy's treasured mantle clock he'd saved from the San-Francisco fire.

Together we watched the coming and going of the four seasons from the two huge windows. First of all came fall, old Beaver Hill putting on a perfectly splendid show of brilliant autumn plumage, while the native hemlock, pine and cedar plantations contributed subdued accents to its heights.

Winter followed swiftly, to clothe the slopes in majestic white, and lace the wind-stripped branches with its frosty feathers, irridescent as rarest jewels in the frigid sunlight.

At last came spring, with its melting snows, abandoning their season's habitat, revealing only muddy drabness; the trees, starkly silhouetted against the hillside, exposing the ledges in all their barren nakedness, and the roaring creek, bursting its seams to race across the meadow, bearing upon its torrents the season's harvest of driftwood.

Suddenly, Oh, magnificent morning! The sidehill pastures had overnight taken on a brilliant chartreuse, as though the Master Painter had restored them, with a brush dipped into His palette at the end of the rainbow, whilst we were sleeping, all unaware. And the trees, not to be outdone, adorned themselves in rapid succession, each with its very own shade and shape of becoming spring bonnet. The apple and pin-cherries, oh, fortunate maidens, adorned themselves twice, firstly in fragrant garlands of pink and white, in preparation for the forthcoming wedding of spring to summer; and once the marriage had been consummated, appropriately changed that headdress to a solid green, more befitting their new matronly status.

Lastly came summer, with its sweet smelling clover, timothy and orchard grasses, as they lay curing, preparatory to drawing into the hayloft; and the long, hot days, during which we were content to seek out the coolness of the house, and to receive the occasional breeze which wafted across the flats, bearing upon it the exuberant voices of the townschildren, swimming beneath the bridge, even as we had done so many years before.

Fordy wheeled my chair out onto the front porch, during those precious days; where from the North end I could more clearly view the Cape Cod cottage. It had become a weathered red; and the owner's name was Burdick, instead of Hills, but it was still home.

And on one never-to-be-forgotten day, they carefully lifted my chair down the back steps—and into the drive. Fordy guided me down the incline, across the echoing wooden bridge, and the dusty lane, to Academy Street, where he turned to the right, and pushed me slowly toward the faded homestead. We stopped near the front lawn, where the horse chestnut had stood, and rested, for precious moments; then turned and made our way homeward. Fordy was exhausted, but satisfied, for this was his greatest gesture of love.

I cannot say that Fordy was as content as I during our stay at Frank's, for, despite the fact that he enjoyed being on home territory, his pride, of utmost importance to the masculine sex, suffered more than I could probably imagine. His fondest dream had been to be my husband, and as such, to bestow upon me all the love, honor, and favors possible for a man to grant his wife. His chosen duty was to labor unceasingly for my welfare, and in his position he felt he could no longer fully perform that responsibility. He wore himself ragged in quest of opportunities to assist Luetta, and strove to wait upon me constantly.

Our savings had been depleted; while we were in Oneida, but there yet remained a few stocks which Fordy had purchased, prior to our marriage, as insurance against the time he might need them, for his last sickness, or burial. These we had carefully stowed away, in a metal box; that we might have proper funeral rites.

But in late October of twenty-nine came the great Wall Street crash, the overnight depletion of many a fortune; and not one soul in these great United States escaped the wrath of that ravenous monster. Worthless, along with Frank's, were our precious stocks, hoarded zealously against those terminal days, and with this loss, the last vestige of Fordy's pride was stripped from him, and his indominitable spirit shattered.

On November fifth, as we combined our efforts in the daily chore of raising me from the bed into the chair, he collapsed, and struggled, vainly, to rise. I reached to help him, steadying myself with one hand on the bedstead, but to no avail; and I called for help. Frank and Luetta managed to roll him up and onto the bed, and me into the chair.

Heartsick, I waited for Frank to fetch Doctor Brown; while the knowing premonition clawed once more at my being. Stroke of paralysis, Doctor pronounced it, as I had known it was.

Fordy was semi-conscious but unable to talk. He smiled, a sad little one-sided smile, and his eyes told me how he had battled, how very long he had tried, to be the last to go; so I would not be left alone. But in that moment we both knew the truth; as I took his helpless hand in mine, and laid my cheek beside his, once more. For now I was the caretaker and the comforter, and as I smoothed his aching brow, I whispered, "Thank God, Fordy, I thank God for *you* and all the happy years we've had together, every precious moment of them."

He heard, and smiled once more, to lapse then into unconsciousness, and three days later, at just daybreak; he left me.

I sat alone with him for a few brief moments, while the first faint rays of dawn streaked the eastern sky. Well, the dreaded day had at last arrived, and I was alone, so utterly, undescribably alone. I was the last leaf on the tree; no one left but me. I stared blankly through the window, seeing nothing. Abruptly my attention focused on the hill, my beloved Beaver, its ledges clearly visible in the bleak November landscape. *It* was still there; it always had been, and it always would be.

From across the years I heard Francie's voice, reciting distinctly, the words of the 121st Psalm, "I will lift up mine eyes unto the hills, from whence cometh my help. My help cometh from the Lord, which made heaven and earth."

Surely God, if He ever had been, still *was*, and instantly, I was on my kness, yes, in spite of the hip, and even though the pain was excruciating, there could be no other way to come to Him. This God, in whom I had once believed; God, who had answered my prayers with the long-ago vision of Ed; and whom I had repudiated ever since with lip-service only, must still be there. Suddenly the words came tumbling from my lips—"Have mercy upon me, O God, according to thy lovingkindness; according unto the multitude of thy tender mercies blot out my transgressions. Wash me thoroughly from mine iniquity, and cleanse me from my sin.——Cast me not away from thy presence; and take not Thy holy spirit from me.—— The sacrifices of God are a broken spirit: a broken and a contrite heart, O God, Thou wilt not despise;" and as the words flowed from my lips, the tears flowed from my eyes, tears I had long ago ceased to shed; only now they were the tears of happiness, because now I *knew* that the same God who had belonged to Grandpa and Grandma, to Francie, Lute, Fordy and all the rest; was *mine,* and that through Fordy's loss had come a gain so great that it defied all terms of measurement.

A hasty family consultation followed, during which Ed Woodworth offered two graves on sister Sate's lot. I accepted, gratefully, and Fordy was entombed next door; but imprisoned, as I was, in that wheel chair, I could not even visit his grave.

» » » » » » « « « « « «

The entire country, as well as a great deal of the world, was now enveloped in dark despair; the result of the Wall Street collapse. Frank had invested, along with million of others, in a few stocks, which were now worthless. Under resultant discussion came the Ayres flats, which lay north of the village, in the area known as Stillwater. On Ayres flats was the site of an abandoned brickyard, formerly owned by Uncle Hosea Clarke and his sons, Norman and

Lafayette. Back in 1875 when the village was growing like mad it had been operating full blast. But after a while a vein of marl appeared in that pure blue clay. As far as the brick business was concerned the discovery of that marl spelled only failure; for even one small chunk of marl contained in a brick could cause it to burst under the tremendous heat of the kiln.

Hank and Frank Spooner, Samuel Main, the wagon maker, and my old friend, Sherman Daboll, town lawyer, then purchased the area, contemplating the founding of a small fortune in the marl business. Though other towns and sections of the country could lay claim to fame and fortune through the discovery of gold, silver, copper, oil, or even coal; the closest our good folks ever came to riches amongst these shale rock hills and valleys was with the discovery of those marl beds.

Marl is a pure carbonate of lime occasionally found at the bottom of old lake beds, and usually topped with a thick layer of peat or muck. In process of manufacture the marl was pressed into bricks, which were then burned in a kiln to obtain the lime content. The lime so produced was remarkably white, and was used in the manufacture of Portland cement, mortar, etc.

Shortly after purchase of the marl beds, heavy machinery was invented, capable of crushing limestone, thereby developing nearly the same end product, but without the cumbersome burning process, necessary to the marl deposits. A negligible amount of the marl was then put up and sold as silver-polish, while some was spread directly onto nearby fields, to sweeten the soil. But in general, the investment never paid off; and Frank, now sole owner, fifty years older, and hard pressed for money, sold this acreage to the State; henceforth opening a new area of State acquired property in the Northern section of the township.

» » » » » » « « « « « «

Christmas of 1929 was the most desolate holiday I had ever experienced. If ever I had supposed life tiresome; I had no knowledge of its possible depth of melancholy. The winter was more frigid than ever, and my windows frosted so thickly it was impossible to see beyond them. Despite the soapstones kept heated for me on the faithful Round Oak, I froze, night after night, alone in the chilly bed. Nothing at all to look forward to—but another birthday, and spring, (that magic word); when the marrow in these old bones might take some comfort.

Each day seemed identical to its predecessor—I thought of the past, I prayed that I might be released to join my loved ones, and for warmer weather; but the monotony of the new dawning was broken only by the change in the daily cross word puzzle. I had become quite expert at crosses, I quipped; crossing the puzzles, crossing each day off the calendar before retiring, and crossing my fingers—when there was nothing better to do.

I longed to converse with others; but during the winter we were isolated, back in that lane; and I sensed Luetta and Frank grew tired of the "I remember whens". And then they'd look at me sometimes, when I'd endeavor to inquire brightly concerning their affairs, a look which plainly stated: "You just asked me that; but I'll humor you, and answer patiently, again."

At last my crosses had covered the calendar up to March fifth. My eighty-fifth birthday! Should I celebrate the attainment of that milestone? Or weep, for my miserable self? For what reason had my number not been called?

And a long-ago day came back to me then, as I recalled old Grandpa Clarke rocking on his sunlit porch, admonishing Lute and Francie that, "No matter what happens, look on it like it happened for a purpose, and some day you'll discover that it did."

Well, the purpose of these long years *had* been revealed, for it had taken eighty-four of them for me to really know my Lord, to feel His presence; to pray with more than formal ritual, meaningless because of its repetition.

While I was thus reminiscing, my thoughts turned to a bit of poetry done by my second cousin, many years ago. It was somewhere amongst the souvenirs. I rummaged through the assortment in the box, then emerged, triumphantly, with my treasure.

Roxie Randall, an own cousin to Mama, was its composer. She was the daughter of Robert, a pioneer Brookfieldan, who had lived about a mile south of Clarkville, at one of the highest points on Beaver Hill. Surely she *should* have had a good outlook on life, I joshed privately, straining my dry English humor. Roxie was a maiden lady, who had attained the age of ninety, but this poem she'd written on *her* eighty-fifth birthday. It was made to order: "

MY NATAL DAY

I hail once more my natal day, still in my tenement of clay.
With many favors blest—and He who placed this structure here,
Can prop it up another year, if He should think it best.

Long has it stood through snow and rains, and braved life's fearful
    hurricanes.
While many a stronger, fell—The reason why we cannot see,
But what to him seems mystery, the Builder knows full well.

But now 'tis weather-worn and old, the summer's heat and winter's
    cold
Pierce through the walls and roof. 'Tis like a garment so worn out
To mend there is no whereabout, so gone is warp and woof.

The tottering pillars are so weak, the poor old thirsty hinges creak,
The windows, too, are dim. Those slight discomforts we'll let pass,
For looking darkly through a glass, we catch a hopeful gleam.

Nature and reason tell us all, this shattered frame 'ere long must
    fall;
Where, when or how is all unknown. We'll leave that to the Archi-
    tect,
And trust His wisdom to direct the taking of it down.

And when you see it prostrate lie, let not a teardrop dim the eye,
The tenant is not here. But just beyond time's little space,
She finds some quiet resting place, no more to date her year.

And though she walks with you no more, the world will move, just
    as before.
'Tis best it should be so. Let each his house in order set
That he may leave without regret, when—called to go."

Oh, never before had I truly appreciated those beautiful lines.
I read, and re-read them, while their soothing phrases surged
through my soul, as a transfusion of fresh blood through tired veins.
    Not many days later I awoke with a pounding headache. Auto-
matically I reached for a glass of water on the washstand, intending
to swallow a couple of aspirins. That is to say, my brain directed
the message, though my arm refused to cooperate. I tried again,
with the same frightening result. Awkwardly shifting my body, I
extended the other arm and clutched the pills. I poked them
through the corner of my mouth; and spilled the liquid down my
nightdress. Exhausted, I sank back against the covers, and waited.

My mouth was numbed, my side and leg as well. "This is it," I remember thinking, "and it's *my* number that's up now."

I do not recall much after that, except that everything turned hazy. Myriads of fuzzy shapes, without identities, kept coming and going, as days turned into nights, and nights into endless eternities. Someone washing my body, and having no idea, nor caring, who it was. Someone forcing unwanted food between my teeth. Pills, drinks, and bed-pans, and *so* tired of lying in bed. Just so—so tired of living. Or was I living? I didn't know, but if I wasn't, then this must be Hell. Oh, God, my God, take me—deliver me from this mad house of confusion, wherever I may be!

And then one daylight I awoke. The fog and haze had lifted, but where was I? Who were these strangers? Where was my east room, with its two great windows, in which I had drifted off to sleep? I studied the bed in which I was lying. Not my bed—hospital bed. Yes, there was a white-gowned woman hurrying down a long corridor, and an old lady in a bed just like mine.

The old lady spoke. "Why, Mrs. Hickox, at last you're awake! We thought you never would—"

"What day—what day is this?" I mumbled, desperately trying to pull my mind together.

"Calendar right there on the wall!" she returned proudly. "It's Tuesday, and two days from tonight is *Christmas* Eve!"

"Christmas Eve?—Oh—no—it can't be—It was coming spring—"

"You've been here a little longer than you think, dearie."

"But this—hospital—" My speech was unfamiliar, slurred, and difficult. "Can't stay—costs—money—haven't any." I struggled to rise, searching vainly for my familiar chair, my blanket and some clothes.

"Now, now, dearie, you just calm yourself. Nobody has to pay in here," she soothed.

"Nobody pays—why *not?*" I was afraid of her answer.

"Please, Mrs. Hickox, don't get so excited, or I'll have to call the nurse. Nobody has to pay here, because this is the *county* home, supported by the taxpayers, for the poor who have no other place to go. So you have no need to worry about your bill at all! Now aren't you *happy?*"

She went on chatting, but I wasn't listening. I had closed my eyes, in mortification. My God, this was the poorhouse! The end of the road—a downhill skid to the poor-house! Where was Frank? Why had he done this terrible thing to me? The POORHOUSE!

210

Oh, why could I not have died with Fordy? Oh, Fordy, dear, dear Fordy, come and take me with you, wherever you are! Deliver me from the shame of it all! I hid my face in the pillow to absorb the tears coursing down my cheeks, and soon I began to dream, whether or not I was asleep, I cannot tell; but we were in the gorge once more, tousle-haired, freckle faced Fordy and I, climbing, slipping, groping up its mossy inclines.

So hard to climb, so difficult to catch my breath—I was panting, quite exhausted. I lunged at a young hemlock and pulled myself over the brink by it. A dense green mossy patch lay just ahead, and I threw myself gratefully into its coolness, gasping one great puff of air, then expelling it. How comfortable and soft it was—I felt weightless—I was drifting—drifting high on a beautiful cloud—never had I experienced such a feeling—It was then that I spied them—one, two, three, no; clumps and *clumps* of them! The spring beauties *had* blossomed again! "Fordy! Fordy!" I giggled aloud. "See! Over here! *I've* found the first spring beauties!"

» » » » » « « « « « «

Poor Aunt Dosh! If only she could have realized the anguish my Grandfather Spooner had suffered when forced to place his beloved Aunt in the Madison County Home. Forced because he himself had vacated his farm, and moved to his daughters; forced for lack of money, because of Luetta's advancing age, and Dosh's senility, to send his revered Aunt to that institution, to exist for her terminal days. Only because of the condition of her mind, had he agreed to it at all. On December 22nd, he received the telegram: "Eudocia Hickox died-7:30 A. M. Regained consciousness few minutes. Sending body Chesebro's."

Our dog met Grandpa on the far side of the bridge, as we children raced to the front windows to see whom he was announcing. Grandpa's gait was shuffling, uncertain. He made his way onto the side porch, moving slowly through the door, as though a great weight were upon him. He dropped heavily into a kitchen chair; then spoke, wearily, "Well, Aunt Dosh is gone—died this morning. All these months she's known nothing, and this morning she regained consciousness, just before she died. Why did it have to happen? She was always such a proud woman—must have killed her when she found out where she was." He propped his elbows on the table, laid his head in his hands, and continued, "Services will have to be the day before Christmas. Strange, isn't it! I'll never forget her wedding to Edwin Tuttle; I was nine then, and they put on quite a splurge—'Twas Christmas Eve, a long, long, time ago. Expect there's one grave left, on Sate's lot, for her—" As if talking to himself, he muttered, "Might as well begin on the obituary, 'twill be a long one!"

And as Roxie Randall's verse had said, "And though she walks with you no more, the world will move just as before, 'tis best it should be so," the little village bustled on about its holiday preparations, and scarcely noticed the passing of one of its eldest daughters.

But in October of 1933, when Grandpa also bid farewell to this earthly clime, what was probably the last press mention of the Hills family was composed for the home-town weekly by his life-long friend, Lute P. Burdick:

FRANK SPOONER'S GRANDPARENTS
Just below the hometown, In a house painted red,
There lived Uncle Jimmy and Aunt Chloe, 'tis said.
Uncle Jimmy shod horses, from morning 'til night,
He could hoop a barrel, and make it real tight.

Two red and white cows, in the pasture content,
To add to his income their services lent.
Jimmy's corn field was clean—Do you ask how I know?
'Cause I rode the old mare an hour or so—

To drag out the tares, from the fast growing grain,
A custom long common, since Abel and Cain.
Jimmy's sons were all daughters—Why was that do you 'spose?
Some fault in the planning? Only ONE ever knows.

Henry L. Spooner in search for a wife
Called on Uncle Jimmy for a partner for life.
"Why yes," answers Jimmy, who never spoke wrong,
If others should want one, just bring them along."

Just a minute, please—Now this was really so. If you don't believe me, ask Aunt Sarah Berry Fitch Spooner, as she never tells lies, if the rest of us do.
Here we go again:

So Henry chose Frances to crown all his joys,
And produced, consequently, the best of the boys.
George Woodworth caught Sarah the very first whack
She was closer between joints and had a broad back.

So in time Jimmy's daughters, left home everyone,
To live all their days with somebody's son.
If we could unto Jimmy and Chloe, and Frances and Hank,
We'd express admiration for the noble boy, Frank."

1912. "Miss Dora Burdick, Mrs. Lute (Ella) Burdick, Lute P. Burdick & Raymond Burdick. St. Timothy's Episcopal Church, Main St., Brookfield, in the background."

Epilogue

It is 1973 now—Approximately one hundred and eighty years since the colonizing of our town. The State has continued to repurchase land since the twenties, reforesting much of it in the thirties, with the aid of the C. C. C.

During the great depression some of the less secure farmers lost their holdings; and roads, except for those most traveled, were neglected, due to lack of funds. With the advent of the forties, and subsequent employment at its highest level due to the total war in which our nation was engaged, a large percentage of farmers who had been hanging on "by the skin of their teeth", obtained work in the cities, at hitherto unheard of wages. Soon, many had chosen to vacate their homes permanently. The buildings and land on their idle places depreciated rapidly, and resultant sale of such acreage to the State became commonplace.

New York State continued to redeem land in the southwest corner of the township, until today there is a nearly complete block of reforestation there, encompassing over eight-thousand acres, in the area of the fire tower; and including the original plantation of the Brookfield Forest Products, Inc. In addition to this block there are approximately seventeen-hundred and fifty acres located in the north-east and north-central portions of the township, comprising a total of nearly ten-thousand State owned acres.

During the nineteen-sixties, State authorities entered the township, demanding that the owners of those places situated on the banks of the upper Beaver Creek Valley and the section known as Stillwater, sell their holdings to the State; for the purpose of a lake to be constructed, which should serve a triple purpose, that of recreation, water conservation, and wildlife refuge. Consequently, nearly all these farms, still in production, as well as homes within the area, were purchased; and the buildings leveled.

Now the State, having decided against the lake, has reforested these so recently productive acres. This portion of State acquired property totals about nineteen-hundred and twenty-five acres, and

It's tall timber now! View of The Lone Rock Homestead sleigh traveling through the first reforestation in Brookfield Township. Planted by Jean Spooner, father of Donna Tanney, in 1918.

Jean F. Spooner, son of Frank, as he looked when he purchased his first holdings, the "Gates Forty".

Annual E. S. H. A. parade (1972) through Brookfield village. Charles & Donna Tanney & son Dan (far right), escorting trail ride officials at the Madison Co. Fairgrounds.

is tax-exempt, since it was purchased under the twenty-year recreational plan.

It is ironic that this same State, which once encouraged settlers to locate in this area, is again the owner of nearly thirty percent of the township; and it is even more ironic, that today, between the State-owned acres and wide-spread land speculation by outside investors, a young man, desirous of owning a farm, cannot find available land at prices in line with his expected income. State owned acres today, declare the officials, belong to the State and heirs of the State, *forever.*

New York State has determined Brookfield's terrain to be best suited as a resort area, and has accordingly constructed one-hundred winding miles of horse trails throughout its reforestation. Three times throughout the summer season, Brookfield hosts the Empire State Horseman's Association. Then, when winter's storms grace the hillsides with a plenteous snowfall, the trails spring to life once more, with myriads of buzzing snowmobiles.

In 1929 the several district schools about the township began to centralize, until finally only Brookfield, Leonardsville, and North Brookfield remained. During the sixties North Brookfield closed its doors, in a merger with Waterville. Leonardsville combined with

Covered Wagons in Brookfield territory, vintage 1973. The Lone Rock Homestead Caravan on tour.

West Winfield and Bridgewater in the lately established Mount Markham district, leaving Brookfield Central the only independent school in the township. This school, along with the township highway department, is the mainstay of the village, and even now is threatened to be consumed in a further merger of schools in this area; in accordance with the programmed blueprints of certain State executives.

Little survives of the once thriving township. Largest in Madison County, and at one time one of the most productive; it is now well-nigh covered by a network of abandoned roads and wooded expanse.

In the village of Brookfield, the only continuing industry from the past is "The Brookfield Courier," now in its ninety-seventh year. Gone are the doctors, lawyers, bankers, jewelers, the cheese and furniture factories, lumber and grist mills, the druggist, milliner, clothier, and cobbler; there existing among other private enterprise; but one store, three garages, a hotel, one printing establishment, and several building contractors.

Yet the burying grounds about the township, nestled between the eternal hills remain; to verify the existence of those who struggled to claim for themselves, and those who should come after, this territory from the fearsome wilds.

William b. 1629 (original immigrant)

Joshua Pratt

Bathsheba

Hannah Pratt

William Spooner, 2nd.

William Spooner

Alice Blackwell

Benjamen Spooner

Samuel Toby

Joanna Toby

Alicia Toby

Joseph Hills — baptized in England, 1602

buried in England, John Clarke 1559

John Clarke

Thomas Clarke — landed in Boston, 1637

Rose Clark

Joseph Hills, 2nd

Samuel Hills

David Wheeler

Joshua Spooner — Elected deputy to R.I. colonial legislature in 1760

Benjamen Spooner, 2nd. — Corporal in the Revolution. Resided Springfield, Vt.

Freelove Westcott

William Langsford

Maria Langsford

Mary Jackson

Thomas Scofield

Joshua Spooner, 2nd. b. 1793 — Resided in Loganville, Wis.

Luther Scofield b. 1804

Henry L. Spooner b. 1835

Hannah Scofield

Capt. ... in Scotland

... of the Colonial Assembly, R.I.